A Special Issue of
The European Journal of Cognitive Psychology

The Contribution of Cognitive Psychology to the Study of Individual Cognitive Differences and Intelligence

Edited by

Cesare Cornoldi
University of Padova, Italy

T0347468

 Routledge
Taylor & Francis Group
LONDON AND NEW YORK

First published 2006 by Psychology Press Ltd

Published 2018 by Routledge
2 Park Square, Milton Park, Abingdon, Oxon OX14 4RN
52 Vanderbilt Avenue, New York, NY 10017

First issued in paperback 2018

Routledge is an imprint of the Taylor & Francis Group, an informa business

British Library Cataloguing in Publication Data
A catalogue record for this book is available from the British Library

This book is also a special issue of the *European Journal of Cognitive Psychology* and forms Issue 1 of Volume 18 (2006).

Cover by Anú Design, Tara, Co. Meath, Ireland
Typeset by DP Photosetting, Aylesbury, Buckinghamshire, UK

ISBN 13: 978-1-138-87765-8 (pbk)
ISBN 13: 978-1-84169-802-1 (hbk)
ISSN 0954-1446

Contents

The contribution of cognitive psychology to the study of human intelligence
Cesare Cornoldi   1

Why are reasoning ability and working memory capacity related to mental
speed? An investigation of stimulus–response compatibility in choice
reaction time tasks
Oliver Wilhelm and Klaus Oberauer   18

Do working memory and susceptibility to interference predict individual
differences in fluid intelligence?
Erika Borella, Barbara Carretti, and Irene C. Mammarella   51

Intellectual functioning of deaf adults and children: Answers and questions
Marc Marschark   70

Individual differences in the ability to avoid distracting sounds
Emily M. Elliott, Katie M. Barrilleaux, and Nelson Cowan   90

Relationships between working memory and intelligence from a
developmental perspective: Convergent evidence from a neo-Piagetian
and a psychometric approach
Anik de Ribaupierre and Thierry Lecerf   109

Intelligence and executive functioning in adult age: Effects of sibship
size and birth order
Sara Holmgren, Bo Molander, and Lars-Göran Nilsson   138

Subject index   159

EUROPEAN JOURNAL OF COGNITIVE PSYCHOLOGY
2006, 18 (1), 1–17

The contribution of cognitive psychology to the study of human intelligence

Cesare Cornoldi

Department of Psicologia Generale, University of Padova, Italy

Cognitive Psychology (CP) in the last 50 years has shown impressive development, producing a large body of data mainly concerned with specific elements of the complex cognitive architecture of the mind. The focus on single processes, in large part necessarily narrow and detailed, has not prevented the development of general concepts, paradigms, and models that can be useful to all areas of psychology. In fact, since the mind's operations typically studied by CP, such as memory, attention, language, reasoning, and so on, are the basis for every psychological activity and behaviour, their scientific analysis can be used by other associated areas of study, for example Social Psychology, Clinical Psychology, Applied Psychology, Educational Psychology, Developmental Psychology, etc. Indeed, we are observing in these areas an increasing interest in concepts emerging from CP.

The potential contribution of CP to the study of human intelligence is particularly representative and interesting. In fact, the consideration of individual differences in cognitive abilities and, in particular, in intelligence is one of the main topics that should be covered by CP. But this has not been the case for many years. Despite its obvious importance, the concept of intelligence has been suspiciously considered by many researchers and in particular by researchers working in the cognitive area. An implicit consideration has been that the concept "intelligence" is ill-defined and lacks an association with a well-supported research tradition. The misleading and circular definition of "intelligence", as the dimension measured by intelligence tests, was considered representative of the theoretical poverty of the field. For this reason the study of intelligence was mainly left to psychologists working in the psychometric tradition and to a certain extent the field of developmental psychology. However there are now signs that the time has come for CP to make a more substantial contribution to the study of individual differences in intelligence and other related cognitive abilities.

Correspondence should be addressed to Cesare Cornoldi, Dipartimento di Psicologia Generale, Via Venezia 13, 35131 Padova, Italy. Email: cesare.cornoldi@unipd.it

© 2006 Taylor & Francis
DOI:10.1080/09541440500215889

THE USE OF THE CONCEPT "INTELLIGENCE"

One of the reasons for the immediate interest of lay people in the concept "intelligence" and the simultaneous reluctance of researchers to study this concept is the fact that intelligence has been defined in numerous ways and the term has been used in a variety of different and partially contradictory contexts.

First, the term "intelligence" has been used according to two main orientations, a general one and a differential one. The general orientation focuses on what different individuals have in common and relates specifically to humans, for example in the expression "Humans have the gift of intelligence". The Latin origin of the term from the verb "intelligere" (to understand) reflects the general idea that intelligence is what allows us to understand reality, rather than simply being passively exposed to sensory data. Obviously the "comprehension" process can be at the highest levels where comprehension is difficult and requires complex reasoning and problem solving, but can also be referred to more ordinary activities. Similarly, intelligence has been defined as the capability of efficiently/adaptively solving a problematic situation working from a mental representation of the problem. Since the latter representation can also be very basic, it is not surprising that intelligence has been considered a characteristic not only of mature human minds, but also of infants, animals, and even machines, as is explicitly assumed in expressions such as "animal intelligence", "artificial intelligence", and so on.

In practice, the general definition of intelligence may refer to all the different aspects of cognitive functioning, like perception, attention, language, memory, reasoning, and so on. This very broad notion of intelligence does not seem particularly fruitful, as it simply considers the overall range of mind activities. Following this view, the study of intelligence implies a consideration of the overall architecture of mind which can then be better specified by studying the specific underlying functions concerning perception, attention, memory, etc.

The differential approach, on the contrary, emphasises the specificity of the concept "intelligence" and investigates its relationship to other concepts. The focus of research following this view is what makes an individual different from another and what the interactions between the different cognitive functions may be. In the differential approach to intelligence the typical focus is quantitative, exemplified in the expression "to have poor or superior intelligence". However, qualitative differences also can be considered, especially when intelligence is seen not as a single measurable quantity, but as a complex system involving the interaction between different functions.

Actually, if intelligence were just the sum of the differences in the various cognitive functions, like memory, reasoning, and so on, there would be no good reason for studying intelligence *per se*, since the respective fields of memory, reasoning, etc. would offer the relevant information to explain individual differences. In fact, these fields may offer information on individual differences in particular areas, competences and abilities (see Cooper, 1999), but they cannot study what is in common, connects, or underlies these specific difference, which is what the study of intelligence has the ambition to do. In order to reach this goal the study of intelligence may use a series of different approaches, starting from the consideration of intellectual differences within an homogeneous population. Even if the approach uses a series of sophisticated procedures and convergent external indexes, it meets the above mentioned problem. In order to study the characteristics of individuals of a single population manifesting different levels of intelligence, there is no external criterion defining the "high level intelligence" vs. the "low level intelligence" individuals. Typically the research refers to well-established psychometric tools, such as the Raven Matrices (Raven, 1938) and the Wechsler batteries (see, e.g., Wechsler, 1971), which longstanding tradition has confirmed as central to the study of intelligence. To a certain extent the validation of these tools comes from external criteria, like the correlation with variables assumed to be related to intelligence, for example school achievement, life adaptation, high intellectual achievements, and so on. However, more robust external criteria are found in the comparison between different populations. For example it is well known that, more than 100 years ago, in a series of pioneering studies on intelligence and mental retardation, Binet and Simon (see 1916/1973) derived their measures from the assumption that intelligence is what differentiates the cognitive functioning of younger and older children. This assumption was so strong that the most widely used quantitative description of a child's intelligence was the discrepancy between the age at which children typically show the cognitive competencies possessed by that particular child and his actual age (Intelligence Quotient = Mental Age / Chronological Age). The approach of contrasting different groups was then extended to consider clinical conditions (mental retardation, mental deterioration on the elderly, dementia), where lower levels of intelligence were immediately apparent. Finally Comparative Psychology, with the underlying assumption that philogenesis mirrors ontogenesis, suggested that intelligence could also be studied by comparing humans and nonhumans. It is obvious that a powerful theory of intelligence should be able to describe what is common to these different comparisons and what is specific to each one.

PSYCHOMETRIC APPROACHES TO THE STUDY OF HUMAN INTELLIGENCE

The most longstanding approach to the study of human intelligence is psychometric and refers back to the traditional view of intelligence as an adaptive ability. This view was in some way influenced by Darwin's idea that adaptation skills are essential for living beings since only those with high adaptive skills will survive the natural selection process. Hence it was no coincidence that only a few years after Darwin's most important work on the origins of the species

(Darwin, 1859/1964) one of his relatives, Galton, published the first systematic contribution to the study of human intelligence entitled "Hereditary genius" (1869/1892). This work presented the statistical and genetic assumptions that affected the subsequent research tradition in the field of intelligence.

Galton mainly focused on individual differences in simple tasks where speed was critical, thus anticipating one of the most influential modern approaches in the study of intelligence. In this respect, two other pioneers of the psychometric tradition, Binet and Simon (see 1916/1973) were offering another, not necessarily opposed, view of what is critical in the measurement of intelligence. Their approach, in fact, mainly focused on the presentation of complex tasks and measured high level abilities, like reasoning and comprehension.

However, psychometric approaches to the study of intelligence did not only differ in the choice of tasks assumed to be crucial for the measurement of intelligence. One of the most important debates concerned whether intelligence is substantially unitary or is made up of a series of different abilities. It is interesting to note that even the statistical treatment of the same data, roughly starting from the computation of correlations between a series of different measures of intelligence, could lead to the two opposite conclusions (and this problem seems to be present also in the contemporary treatment of differential data). In fact, Spearman (1927) concluded that a single general factor (the "g" factor) was able to explain the real intellectual differences between people, whereas Thurstone (1938; Thurstone & Thurstone, 1941) argued in favour of a series of substantially independent primary abilities. This debate (one or more intelligences?), although substantially dismissed, may be a critical issue also for CP.

COGNITIVE PSYCHOLOGY AND PSYCHOMETRIC THEORIES OF INTELLIGENCE

What do cognitive studies suggest as regards the different theories of intelligence? Evidence is against a completely unitary view of intelligence. The large number of dissociations documented by experimental and neuropsychological studies show a mind that has to be fractionated. Low level processes, like sensory discrimination, rapid naming, etc., can be described as independent modules largely automatic, out of the control of central processes (Fodor, 1983) and transfer effects (de Beni, Cornoldi, Larsson, Magnussen, Ronnberg, in press). People who are very good in a particular ability are not necessarily good in other basic abilities (de Beni et al., in press). This evidence could be considered in favour of the popular view that there are different forms of intelligence. For example the multiple intelligence theory (Gardner, 1993) assumed that there are different and independent forms of intelligence substantially defined on the basis of the domain involved: numbers vs. language vs. logical concepts vs. music vs. space vs. motor representations.

However research has very often documented that a complete separation of functions is easier for low level processes than for high level processes. The same type of description and differentiation given for basic skills does not apply to high level processes, like reasoning, cognitive control, etc. These abilities are not based only on automatic processes, they can be at least partially transferred and involve a series of interconnected operations. In this respect it is hard to demonstrate that domain specific forms of intelligence all have the same cognitive status and that they also share the same status with more domain free skills concerning reasoning, problem solving, and general knowledge. People can still be very efficient in a large range of situations, even if they are poor in musical or kinaesthetic intelligence, but this is not true, at least not to the same extent, if they are poor in logical or verbal intelligence.

With reference to the studies of human intelligence, one could simplify the issue by asserting that only high level processes define intelligence, whereas the other ones offer a simple support to intelligent operations but are neither critical to intelligence nor can they be easily differentiated between people. However this simple conclusion would underestimate the importance of the extraordinary manifestations of intelligence associated with specific forms of intelligence, for example in the areas of music, art, or calculation, etc. Furthermore, there is substantial evidence showing that basic automatised computations, like immediate memory or speedy processing (Hunt, 1987; Kail & Salthouse, 1994), can explain an important portion of the variance in human intelligence as measured by traditional tests.

In other words, it seems that neither unitary, nor multiple models of intelligence are in complete accordance with the evidence emerging from studies in CP. Following results from this field it seems that both basic independent processes and high level interconnected processes contribute to the expression of intelligence. This view fits well with another traditional view of intelligence—the hierarchical one—according to which there are more general abilities that are shared by different types of tasks and more specific abilities associated with specific types of task. One of the most popular and recent psychometric views of hierarchical intelligence is the strata theory proposed by Carroll (1993). Carroll analysed a pool of data, collected by different researchers, involving 130,000 individuals, and concluded that the best factorial solution was based on a hierarchical organisation involving three different strata. The basic stratum concerns a very large number of different specific abilities, which—speaking in terms of modern CP—could be identified in specific dissociable components of the mind. The other two strata involve more general abilities, eight in the case of the second one and a single factor (of the g-factor type) in the third one.

Another successful theory based on psychometric data and offering a hierarchical view of intelligence was elaborated by Horn and Cattell (1966) and stated the existence of two main factors: general fluid intelligence (Gf) and general crystallised intelligence (Gc). Although the two factors seem apparently to have the same degree of importance in a hierarchical representation of intelligence, the Gf component seems more central since the authors suggested, in their "investment" theory, that the Gf component allows for the development of the Gc. In fact, Gf refers to the mind's ability to make a series of operations (like classifications, seriations, analogical reasoning) without the need to refer to preexisting knowledge. On the contrary, Gc refers to the mind's operations which strongly rely on knowledge, i.e., on cultural background and on stimulus familiarity, which in turn have been developed through the critical contribution of Gf. (Examples of contexts and tasks measuring Gc can be found in the areas of numerical, mechanical, and lexical abilities.) The two-factor theory offers a series of interesting elements of attraction. In particular it seems able to explain age variations in intelligence, because both factors develop with age but very soon the Gf starts a slow decline (although the issue is still under debate, see Espinosa et al., 2002; McArdle, Ferrer Caja, Hamagami, & Woodcock, 2002), whereas the Gc remains high until old age, explaining why elderly people may meet difficulties with unfamiliar material, and yet be highly competent in verbal tasks and in the manipulation of well-known material.

HIERARCHICAL THEORIES OF INTELLIGENCE

Psychometric approaches may offer important methods and inputs for the study of human intelligence. However, they are in some way theory-opaque because they define their constructs on the basis of tasks and statistical indexes. This may not be a problem in applied fields but can create difficulties when the constructs must be inserted within a description of psychological functioning. Furthermore, in certain practical contexts, psychometric indexes may not be entirely adequate, for example in the case of an individual who is particularly poor in a specific intellectual component and needs a rehabilitation programme. How can the component be rehabilitated and a specific programme devised if its nature and characteristics and its relationship with other cognitive functions are unknown?

In particular hierarchical theories based on psychometric evidence pose one serious problem: It is not clear to which psychological processes the highest stratum or components correspond. Cognitive Psychology has isolated powerful cognitive mechanisms that appear to be critical predictors of high level intelligence and underlie different cognitive tasks. Reference to these mechanisms could help in the specification of the most central components of human intelligence. In this context, some classical cognitive studies have been able to show the relationship between intelligence and efficiency in certain basic computations. In a pioneering study, Hunt (1978) showed that the efficiency in basic computations, like short-term memory span and the speed in simple comparisons, predicted individuals' IQ.

Along the same line of reasoning, Kail and Salthouse, both separately and together (e.g., Kail & Salthouse, 1994; Salthouse, 1996), proposed that basic speed of processing could underlie a series of different cognitive tasks: Smarter people are faster; the development of intelligence in children is associated with the development of speed and elderly people lose speed. In this respect, there is evidence that even the speed in very simple tasks, for example in the inspection of simple patterns or lines for giving identity judgements, is highly correlated with intelligence. Grudnik and Kranzler (2001), in a meta-analysis on 4000 cases, found a correlation of .50 between IQ and inspection time. They also found that this correlation was not affected by the age of the individuals or by the nature of the to-be-inspected stimuli. If we consider intelligence according to the traditional view, i.e., the ability to solve problems and/or to perform complex reasoning tasks, the association of intelligence with speed in doing trivial comparisons can seem bizarre and unconvincing.

It may be worth mentioning once more that this view goes back to the origins of the study of intelligence and to Galton's work (1869/1892) that indeed relied on speed measures. These were subsequently eliminated in favour of other cognitive tasks involving higher functions, which appeared more appropriate than the simpler speed measures (see also de Ribaupierre & Lecerf, 2006 this issue). However supporters of the speed of processing view argue that the importance of this capacity is that it offers the possibility of treating a larger amount of information in a limited period of time. For example it has been suggested (Verguts, de Boeck, & Maris, 1999) that the success in a critical reasoning task such as the Raven matrices (which represents the task with the best g-factor load) can depend on the speed with which the individual generates the appropriate rules. However, this relationship has not been sufficiently demonstrated. It is counterintuitive to consider speed of processing as a critical factor even when other problem-solving tasks are considered where the rapidity and/or simultaneous generation of different rules is not crucial and no time constraints are set. In fact, the correlation between inspection time and IQ could be overestimated to the extent to which IQ is actually being measured only with time constrained tasks.

More recently, it has often been stressed that the best cognitive description of intelligence should be looked for in association with the prefrontal "executive" functions of the brain (see Kane & Engle, 2002, for a discussion). Although articulation, definition, and specification of measures of executive processes are still under debate, their use appears critical for understanding intellectual differences and in particular age-related intellectual decline (for a critical analysis, Salthouse, Atkinson, & Berish, 2003). Working memory too is sometimes considered as a good example of executive processes and appears to represent a powerful measure of them (e.g., Holmgren, Molander, & Nilsson, 2006 this issue).

The classical triarchical theory of intelligence proposed by Sternberg (1985) also distinguished between controlled central processes and basic computations, within a general description of intellectual functioning involving experience and context. Executive functions have been mentioned widely and have sometimes revealed themselves to be good predictors of intellectual functioning (e.g.,

Holmgren et al., 2006 this issue). In an effort to offer a description of "executive functions", cognitive psychologists proposed different lists of operations not, however, necessarily related. Amongst them: planning, control, inhibition of irrelevant information and/or of impulsive responses, shifting from a task to another, simultaneous control of two different operations. These are but some examples, many more descriptions and classifications have been reported. For example, T. Shallice (personal communication, 2005) distinguished three main executive functions—the generation of strategies, setting intentions, and monitoring—and was able to show their relationships with different parts of the brain.

Executive processes are numerous; they are partly heterogeneous but not necessarily highly correlated with one another and this can create the impression that the core of intelligence is just the sum of a series of controlled functions, rather than something more specific. Furthermore the relationship between executive functions and intelligence can be questioned on the basis of a series of elements. First, the correlations between measures of the ability of performing executive processes and IQ are far from perfect. Second, patients with lesions associated with executive processes can still have a high IQ. Third, there is the case of at least one population (individuals with ADHD syndrome) where a problem in the executive processes is not associated with low IQ (see, e.g., Cornoldi, Barbieri, Gaiani, & Zocchi, 1999).

However, as we will see later, CP has also mentioned more specific mechanisms and/or principles related to the domain of executive processes. For example, it has been suggested that working memory could be a critical component and could be also defined as the amount of available attentional resources (Engle, Kane, & Tuholski, 1999; Kane & Engle, 2002). According to Wilhelm and Oberauer (2006 this issue), an attentional description of working memory could be critical in intellectual functioning and could explain the role of processing speed. In fact, controlled attention is also needed for fast reactions to stimuli, in particular in the presence of a distraction. Reduced control might lead to increased conflict between several response alternatives in choice tasks, and thereby to occasionally prolonged response times or errors. Another associated explanation of the link between working memory and speed of processing could be related to the fact that every response time task requires that the subject maintains some critical information (when to react, how to react, etc.) highly activated, at the same time reducing activation of the irrelevant information (disturbing thoughts, memory of the preceding responses, etc.).

THEORIES OF INTELLIGENCE AND NEUROSCIENCE

Cognitive Neuroscience has recently offered a series of contributions useful for developing a concept of intelligence. In general, it is logical to relate intelligence and its development to the characteristics of the central nervous system. Given that its main characteristics concern neurons, dendrites, synapses, and myelinisation of the axons, one could look to one or all of these to find the neurological correlates of intelligence. However, the numbers of neurons or dendrites are not good candidates since they do not seem to reflect intellectual development and/or functioning. On the contrary the myelinisation process does seem to parallel intellectual development and, in particular, the number of synaptic connections seems to describe a main feature of intelligence, i.e., the organisation of experience.

The myelinisation view could offer a neurological correlate to the hypothesis that speed is a crucial factor of human intelligence, because a completely myelinised fibre increases the speed of transmission of the neural impulse. However, neurological evidence of this relationship seems weak. Reed and Jensen (1992) found a positive, but modest, correlation between speed of neural conduction and measures of intelligence, but other research came to the conclusion that it is not true that the most intelligent brains are also the fastest.

The number of synaptic connections seems to offer a rough but better approximation of the characteristics of human intelligence. Support for this view also comes from artificial intelligence simulations showing that an increase in the number of connections improves the system's power. The view is a rather rough guide because it looks only at the quantity and not the quality of the connections, yet it appears reasonable to the extent that an increased number of connections facilitates the retrieval of information useful for establishing associations and performing a series of different operations. This view can also be brought back to the traditional assumption, proposed in the past centuries by the Italian physician Malacarne and then later by Binet and by neurological studies (Vernon & Mori, 1992), according to which the size of the brain is a measure of the quantity of accumulated experience and, more or less directly, the quantity of intelligence. The traditional approach to the issue was based on the measurement of the size of the cranium, which actually is also used as an index of the foetus' brain maturation and a predictor of later cognitive development (Frisk, Amsel, & Whyte, 2002).

However, a quantitative view of intelligence can create the confounding assumption that the optimal operations of the mind are related to the highest level of system activation. This assumption contrasts with evidence showing exactly the opposite result, i.e., that highly intelligent operations in highly intelligent individuals are related to a modest and focused degree of activation. According to the "neural efficiency hypothesis", intelligence is related to a reduced brain activation. For example, Haier and collaborators (see Haier, 2003), using the PET (positron emission tomography) scanning technique, analysed the rate of accumulation of glucose in a time period of 32 minutes in individuals engaged in the Raven matrices. The results showed a series of negative correlations between the degrees of activation of different areas of the brain and the scores obtained with the Raven matrices.

Haier (2003) described less smart people (i.e., with lower Raven's scores) as individuals mentally struggling in order to meet the task's requirements, with a high intensity of work, but reduced success: Intelligence should be related to a greater use of specific resources and a lower use of general aspecific resources. Haier and collaborators also found that mentally retarded individuals have a smaller brain but a greater level of brain activation (with a correlation of −.60 between degree of activation and IQ). It is interesting to observe that a similar differential pattern of activation can be found in more intelligent individuals when they are involved and they are not involved in important intellectual activities. In fact, Haier, White, and Alkire (2003) found that individuals with high Raven's scores also present a lesser but more specific degree of activation (involving specific posterior brain areas) when they are relaxed and watch videos. This evidence is consistent with the observation that children have a higher activation than adults and are less competent in complex intelligent operations but better in simple associative learning.

Assuming a relationship between the degree of brain activation and the degree of physiological/motivational activation, the general pattern of results could be also interpreted within the traditional framework offered by the Yerkes and Dodson's (1908) law showing that the optimal degree of activation decreases in correspondence with increases in task difficulty. In fact, Yerkes and Dodson found that, for simple associative tasks, a high degree of activation (produced by the risk of a high punishment) produced the best learning curve, but for problem-solving tasks the best activation was very far from being the highest one.

The results supporting the "neural efficiency hypothesis" cannot be univocally interpreted because they also seem to be related to personality characteristics (they seem mainly valid for introverted people; Rindermann & Neubauer, 2001) and task anxiety. Feelings of poor self-efficacy and other disturbing psychological events could be the real cause of a greater activation in less intelligent individuals. However the data patterns produced within the context of the "neural efficiency hypothesis" suggest that a simple quantitative view of neural activity does not offer the best description of intelligence. This does not exclude that, *ceteris paribus*, increases in brain activation are related to an increasingly effective mental effort, since, for example, highly competent individuals present a greater activation in correspondence with increases in the difficulty of a working memory task (Haier, 2003).

Concerning the localisation of the most intelligent operations, prefrontal lobes seem to have a central role (Duncan, 2005). For example, Obonsawin et al. (2002) found a strong relationship between scores in a series of executive tasks (with the exception of a classification task) typically associated with prefrontal functioning and the *g* factor measures with the WAIS test. However, consistent with the "neural efficiency hypothesis", the most intelligent individuals do not necessarily use the prefrontal areas to a greater extent, because—when it is not necessary—they can rely on lower level semiautomatic processes or other more specific brain areas, as may happen if the task request concerns specific mind operations. For example, using a spatial task, van Rooy, Stough, Pipingas, Hocking, and Silberstein (2001) found a high involvement of parietal and occipital lobes in smart people. A curious, although less stringent support to the latter results comes from the postmortem study of Albert Einstein's brain, whose major anatomical difference with respect to typical brains concerned the characteristics of the parietal lobes (this observation is reported by Gardner, Kornhaber, & Wake, 1996).

The "neural efficiency hypothesis" is apparently against the working memory and cognitive resources views of intelligence because it suggests that operations requiring a high degree of intelligence do not need greater resources. However, a most efficient working memory does not necessarily mean a greater amount of activated cognitive resources, because the greater activation could concern other brain structures or a more permanent involvement, rather than a specific use of the available resources. Furthermore, some working memory approaches have suggested that a better use of working memory is associated with better control, which reduces the quantity of involved resources by reducing the number of to-be-processed information. For example May, Hasher, and Kane (1999) found that working memory performance is enhanced in correspondence with a reduction of proactive interference due to the preceding information, and de Beni, Palladino, Pazzaglia, and Cornoldi (1998) showed that people with a high working memory performance are better in reducing the influence of irrelevant information.

More recently, Borella, Carretti, and Mammarella (2006 this issue) and Elliott, Barrilleaux, and Cowan (2006 this issue) suggested that the ability to control for irrelevant information or distracting information may have a critical role for an increased success in working memory and intelligence tasks. According to this line of reasoning, the degree of control and the degree of activation (of implemented resources) can be dissociable concepts. The hypothesis that the highest levels of working memory control do not necessarily imply the highest levels of activation is compatible with models distinguishing activation and focused attention (see Cowan, 1995; see also Engle et al., 1999). This point was also commented by Baddeley (1990) when he observed that the executive component of working memory has specific limitations that do not overlap with the overall limitations of the cognitive system. Baddeley offered two types of evidence. First, dual task requests are difficult for people having problems in the use of the executive component, although if they are simple. Second, task difficulty and/or complexity does not specifically affect the central executive as it may similarly affect different cognitive components (for a discussion of the dissociation between task complexity and degree of required control, see also Cornoldi & Vecchi, 2003).

WORKING MEMORY AND THE STUDY OF HUMAN INTELLIGENCE

Working memory remains a good candidate for the individuation of the critical variable within a hierarchical cognitive model of intelligence. The view that working memory can explain a substantial part of intelligence and in particular the g factor has been proposed in the last part of the twentieth century and has progressively found increasing support. Recently, de Ribaupierre and Lecerf (2006 this issue) showed how two completely different research traditions, i.e., the neo-Piagetian and the human information one, are converging to the basic assumption that working memory is strongly related to intelligence. From a neo-Piagetian point of view (e.g., Case, 1992) the development itself of intelligence could be attributed to the number of units the child is able to maintain in working memory and this number would increase approximately by one unit every other year. The success in the classical Piagetian tasks would also be a consequence of this capacity.

The reference to the construct of working memory is intuitively appealing as many high level mind operations seem to require the simultaneous consideration of more elements (Primi, 2002). In particular, Verguts and de Boeck (2001) suggest that the relationship between factor "g" and working memory capacity is due to the fact that people with a better working memory are better at storing subresults and solution principles: Consequently, confronted with a complex reasoning task, they are able to deconstruct the problem and not only to proceed step by step, but also to anticipate and store more solution principles. All these examples focus on the actively controlled component(s) of working memory (including functions of elaboration of the maintained information and maintenance *per se*) and only marginally take into consideration simple immediate memory functions.

Within Baddeley's (2000) working memory model the critical functions do not involve the ancillary loop and sketchpad systems, but are related to the central executive and are mainly content free. Within a continuity model (Cornoldi & Vecchi, 2003) the assumption is less radical because not only very central working memory functions, but also other functions involving a decreased degree of control and an increased content specificity may be related, although to correspondingly decreasing degrees, to intelligence. The higher flexibility of the continuity model seems more capable of explaining group differences. Theories of intelligence must be able to cope not only with the outcomes of the differential studies within homogeneous populations with typical development but also with the outcomes deriving from the study of intelligence and cognitive functions in special populations (e.g., Marschark, 2006 this issue).

The Cornoldi and Vecchi (2003) model tried to test the continuity model with different atypical groups. In particular, the model seems productive in the examination of cognitive developmental disabilities (Cornoldi, Carretti, & de Beni, 2001) where it predicts deficits at low control levels (e.g., in phonological memory) in cases of highly specific disabilities, deficits at the intermediate level in the control continuum, or deficits at the highest levels. Deficits in the intermediate level may be content specific and related to language in cases of reading comprehension difficulties (see also de Beni et al., 1998), to the visuospatial content in cases of nonverbal learning disabilities (see also Cornoldi, Rigoni, Venneri, & Vecchi, 2000), or to all the types of content in the case of ADHD individuals (Cornoldi, Marzocchi, et al., 2001). On the contrary, in the case of mental retardation, working memory deficits are expected to increase in correspondence with increases in the control continuum. Lanfranchi, Cornoldi, and Vianello (2004) tested a group of individuals with Down's syndrome, whose low level of intelligence was assumed by definition (and also confirmed by intelligence testing). This allowed the researchers to avoid the confounding circularity between working memory measures and intelligence tests which also rely on working memory. Lanfranchi et al. found that Down's individuals presented a linear increase of the deficit in correspondence with increases in the degree of control required by the working memory tasks, suggesting that their intellectual deficit is related to a working memory deficit and especially to its more controlled functions. They also found that, according to a hypothesised distinction between different contents (the "horizontal continuum"), verbal deficits were dissociable (as they were more severe) from visuospatial deficits, but this happened (according to the reciprocal interaction between the continua) primarily in low control tasks.

In conclusion, working memory seems to be a particularly good candidate for giving a cognitive description of the central mechanisms associated with the most important components in a hierarchical model of intelligence. However, many issues are still open. Given the complexity of intellectual functions, it is improbable that a single cognitive construct can explain the whole variance associated with such a general and broad concept as intelligence. A cautious attitude against excessive generalisations also comes from evidence showing that the correlation between working memory and central components of intelligence is far from perfect (Ackerman, Beier, & Boyle, 2002, 2005). However, the analysis and the conclusions of Ackerman et al. (2005) have been criticised on many grounds. For example, Oberauer, Schulze, Wilhem, and Suess (2005), reanalysing the same set of data, concluded that the typical correlation between working memory and fluid intelligence is higher than indicated in the original paper (around .70 rather than below .50). Also with reference to methodological issues, de Ribaupierre and Lecerf (2006 this issue) commented that correlations between working memory and fluid intelligence can be underscored if calculated in homogeneous populations, where domain specific competencies can become more determinant. In their study they also found that working memory is more strongly correlated with Piagetian intelligence tasks than with the Raven matrices task traditionally used in American studies examining fluid intelligence. (It must be noticed that, in this study, a combination of measures of working memory, on one side, and of speed, on the other side, was able to explain a consistently larger portion of variance than one of them taken separately.)

In any case, the relationship between working memory and the other main cognitive candidates must be better understood. In particular attentional resources, speed of processing and executive functions should be considered. Speed of processing represents the most intriguing case. For example, in the study of the relationship between working memory and speed of processing sometimes the first seems to explain the second (e.g., Wilhelm & Oberauer, 2006 this issue), but the opposite relationship cannot be excluded. The cases of attention and executive processes seem more consistent with a working memory view since they have been identified more frequently. However, it is not clear if attention can be identified with the active component of working memory (Engle, 2002), or if the latter also includes other active manipulation operations that do not necessarily imply a greater attentional request in respect to low level short-term memory processes. Furthermore it is not clear which is the relationship between working memory and other executive processes and why working memory, deeply rooted in the individual's neurological structure, can be more sensitive to sociocultural influences (Holmgren et al., 2006 this issue) than a cognitive function like vocabulary which is typically associated with the individual's cultural experience.

THE PRESENT ISSUE

The present special issue of the *European Journal of Cognitive Psychology* originated from a symposium I organised at the biannual conference of the European Society for Cognitive Psychology (ESCOP) held in Granada, Spain, in September 2003. Many of the authors here made a presentation at the symposium and the others develop points that were under discussion during the symposium. At that time I was the President of ESCOP and I felt the responsibility to show the scientific community why Cognitive Psychology is not only a specialised and highly sophisticated area of Psychology, but also offers a potential contribution to the analysis of the main psychological concepts. At that time many elements were showing how cognitive psychologists had started their elaborations of intelligence. In recent years these elements have increased their importance and visibility and I am sure that fewer psychologists could question the possibility that the study of intelligence can take advantage of the analyses of Cognitive Psychology. In particular the examination of the relationship between working memory and intelligence has become one of the most popular topics in the field. This topic is particularly well represented in this issue, but I am happy that other topics are also represented, like the role of language (in the Marschark paper) and the social influences (in the Holmgren et al. paper), in order to offer a larger range of methods and problems illustrating the contribution of Cognitive Psychology to the study of individual differences and intelligence.

REFERENCES

Ackerman, P. L., Beier, M. E., & Boyle, M. O. (2002). Individual differences in working memory within a nomological network of cognitive and perceptual speed abilities. *Journal of Experimental Psychology: General, 131*, 567–589.

Ackerman, P. L., Beier, M. E., & Boyle, M. O. (2005). Working memory and intelligence: The same or different constructs? *Psychological Bulletin, 131*, 30–60.

Baddeley, A. (1990). *Human memory.* Hove, UK: Psychology Press.

Baddeley, A. (2000). *Short-term and working memory.* In E. Tulving & F. I. M. Craik (Eds.), *The Oxford handbook of memory* (pp. 77–92). London: Oxford University Press.

Binet, A., & Simon, T. (1973). *The development of intelligence in children (The Binet-Simon Scale)* (Elizabeth S. Kite, Trans.). New York: Arno Press. (Original work published 1916.)

Borella, E., Carretti, B., & Mammarella, I. C. (2006). Do working memory and susceptibility to interference predict individual differences in fluid intelligence? *European Journal of Cognitive Psychology, 18*(1), 51–69.

Carroll, J. (1993). *Human cognitive abilities: A survey of factor-analytic studies.* New York: Cambridge University Press.

Case, R. (1992). *The mind's staircase.* Hillsdale, NJ: Lawrence Erlbaum Associates, Inc.

Cooper, C. (1999). *Intelligence and abilities.* London: Routledge.

Cornoldi, C., Barbieri, A., Gaiani, C., & Zocchi, S. (1999). Strategic memory deficits in attention deficit disorder with hyperactivity participants: The role of executive processes. *Developmental Neuropsychology, 15*, 53–71.

Cornoldi, C., Carretti, B., & de Beni, R. (2001). How the pattern of deficits in groups of learning-disabled individuals help to understand the organization of working memory. *Issues in Education, 7*, 71–78.

Cornoldi, C., Marzocchi, G. M., Belotti, M., Caroli, M.G., de Meo, T., & Braga, C. (2001). Working memory interference control deficit in children referred by teachers for ADHD symptoms. *Child Neuropsychology, 7*, 230–240.

Cornoldi, C., Rigoni, F., Venneri, A., & Vecchi, T. (2000). Passive and active processes in visuospatial memory: Double dissociation in developmental learning disabilities. *Brain and Cognition, 43*, 17–20.

Cornoldi, C., & Vecchi, T. (2003). *Visuo-spatial working memory and individual differences.* Hove, UK: Psychology Press.

Cowan, N. (1995). *Attention and memory: An integrated framework.* New York: Oxford University Press.

Darwin, C. (1964). *On the origin of the species.* Cambridge, MA: Harvard University Press. (Original work published 1859.)

De Beni, R., Cornoldi, C., Larsson, M., Magnussen, S., & Ronnberg, J. (in press). The study of expertise. In T. Helstrup & S. Magnussen (Eds.), *Everyday memory.* Hove, UK: Psychology Press.

De Beni, R., Palladino, P., Pazzaglia, F., & Cornoldi, C. (1998). Increases in intrusion errors and working memory deficit of poor comprehenders. *Quarterly Journal of Experimental Psychology, 51A*, 305–320.

De Ribaupierre, A., & Lecerf, T. (2006). Relationships between working memory and intelligence from a developmental perspective: Convergent evidence from a neo-Piagetian and a psychometric approach. *European Journal of Cognitive Psychology, 18*(1), 109–137.

Duncan, J. (2005). Frontal lobe function and general intelligence: Why it matters. *Cortex, 41*, 215–217.

Elliott, E. M., Barrilleaux, K. M., & Cowan, N. (2006). Individual differences in the ability to avoid distracting sounds. *European Journal of Cognitive Psychology, 18*(1), 90–108.

Engle, R. W. (2002). Working memory capacity as executive attention. *Current Directions in Psychological Science, 11*, 19–23.

Engle, R. W., Kane, M. J., & Tuholski, S. W. (1999). Individual differences in working memory capacity and what they tell us about controlled attention, general fluid intelligence, and functions of the prefrontal cortex. In A. Miyake & P. Shah (Eds.), *Models of working memory: Mechanisms of active maintenance and executive control* (pp. 102–134). Cambridge, UK: Cambridge University Press.

Espinosa, M., Garcia, L. F., Escorial S., Rebollo I., Colom, R., & Abad, F. J. (2002). Age dedifferentiation hypothesis: Evidence from WAIS III. *Intelligence, 30*, 395–408.

Fodor, J. A. (1983). *The modularity of mind.* Cambridge, MA: MIT Press.

Frisk, V., Amsel, R., & Whyte, H. (2002). The importance of head growth patterns in predicting the cognitive abilities and literacy skills of small-for-gestational-age children. *Developmental Neuropsychology, 22*, 565–593.

Galton, F. (1892). *Hereditary genius: An inquiry into its laws and consequences* (2nd ed.). London: Watts & Co. (Original work published 1869)

Gardner, H. (1993). *Frames of mind: The theory of multiple intelligences.* New York: Basic Books.

Gardner, H., Kornhaber, M. L., & Wake, W. K. (1996). *Intelligence: Multiple perspectives.* Fort Worth, TX: Harcourt Brace.

Grudnik, J. L, Kranzler, J. H. (2001). Meta-analysis of the relationship between intelligence and inspection time. *Intelligence, 29*, 523–535.

Haier, R. J. (2003). Brain imaging studies of intelligence: Individual differences and neurobiology. In R. Sternberg, J. Lautrey, & T. I. Lubart (Eds.), *Models of intelligence* (pp. 185–193). Washington, DC: American Psychological Association.

Haier, R. J., White, N. S., & Alkire, M. T. (2003). Individual differences in general intelligence correlate with brain function during nonreasoning tasks. *Intelligence, 31*, 429–441.

Holmgren, S., Molander, B., & Nilsson, L.-G. (2006). Intelligence and executive functioning in adult age: Effects of sibship size and birth order. *European Journal of Cognitive Psychology, 18*(1), 138–158.

Horn, J., & Cattell, R. B. (1966). Refinement and test of the theory of fluid and crystallized general intelligences. *Journal of Educational Psychology, 57*, 253–270.

Hunt, E. (1978). Mechanics of verbal ability. *Psychological Review, 85*, 109–130.

Hunt, E. (1987). Science, technology, and intelligence. In R. R. Ronning, J. A. Glover, J. C. Conoley, & J. C. Witt (Eds.), *The influence of cognitive psychology on testing* (pp. 11–40). Hillsdale, NJ: Lawrence Erlbaum Associates, Inc.

Kail, R., & Salthouse, T. A. (1994). Processing speed as a mental capacity. *Acta Psychologica, 86*, 199–225.

Kane, M. J., & Engle, R. W. (2002). The role of prefrontal cortex in working-memory capacity, executive attention, and general fluid intelligence: An individual-differences perspective. *Psychonomic Bulletin and Review, 9*, 637–671.

Lanfranchi, S., Cornoldi, C., & Vianello, R. (2004). Verbal and visuospatial working memory deficits in children with Down syndrome. *American Journal of Mental Retardation, 6*, 456–466.

Marschark, M. (2006). Intellectual functioning of deaf adults and children: Answers and questions. *European Journal of Cognitive Psychology, 18*(1), 70–89.

May, C. P., Hasher, L., & Kane, M. J. (1999). The role of interference in memory span. *Memory and Cognition, 27*, 759–767.

McArdle, J. J., Ferrer Caja, E., Hamagami, F., & Woodcock, R. W. (2002). Comparative longitudinal structural analyses of the growth and decline of multiple intellectual abilities over the life span. *Developmental Psychology, 38*, 115–142.

Oberauer, K., Schulze, R., Wilhelm, O., & Suess, H. M. (2005). Working memory and intelligence—their correlation and their relation: Comment on Ackerman, Beier, and Boyle (2005). *Psychological Bulletin, 131*(1), 61–65.

Obonsawin, M. C., Crawford, J. R., Page, J., Chalmers, P., Cochrane, R., & Low, G. (2002). Performance on tests of frontal lobe function reflect general intellectual ability. *Neuropsychologia, 40*, 970–977.

Primi, R. (2002). Complexity of geometric inductive reasoning tasks: Contribution to the understanding of fluid intelligence. *Intelligence, 30*, 41–70.

Raven, J. (1938). *Progressive matrices*. London: H. K. Lewis.

Reed, T. E., & Jensen, A. R. (1992). Conduction velocity in a brain nerve pathway of normal adults correlates with intelligence level. *Intelligence, 16*, 259–272.

Rindermann, H., & Neubauer, A. C. (2001). The influence of personality on three aspects of cognitive performance: Processing speed, intelligence and school performance. *Personality and Individual Differences, 30*, 829–842.

Salthouse, T. A. (1996). The processing speed theory of adult age differences in cognition. *Psychological Review, 103*, 403–428.

Salthouse, T. A., Atkinson, T. M., & Berish, D. E. (2003). Executive functioning as a potential mediator of age-related cognitive decline in normal adults. *Journal of Experimental Psychology: General, 132*, 566–594.

Spearman, C. (1927). *The abilities of man*. New York: Macmillan.

Sternberg, R. J. (1985). *Beyond IQ: A triarchic theory of human intelligence*. Cambridge, UK: Cambridge University Press.

Thurstone, L. L. (1938). *Primary mental abilities*. Chicago: University of Chicago Press.

Thurstone, L. L., & Thurstone, T. G. (1941). *Factorial studies of intelligence*. Chicago: University of Chicago Press.

Van Rooy, C., Stough, C., Pipingas, A., Hocking, C., & Silberstein, R. B. (2001). Spatial working memory and intelligence: Biological correlates. *Intelligence, 29*, 275–292.

Verguts, T., & de Boeck, P. (2001). On the correlation between working memory capacity and performance on intelligence tests. *Learning and Individual Differences, 13*, 37–56.

Verguts, T., de Boeck, P., & Maris, E. (1999). Generation speed in Raven's progressive matrices test. *Intelligence, 27*, 329–345.

Vernon, P. A., & Mori, M. (1992). Intelligence, reaction times, and peripheral nerve conduction velocity. *Intelligence, 16*, 273–288.

Wechsler, D. (1971). Intelligence: Definition, theory, and the IQ. In R. Cancro (Ed.), *Intelligence: Genetic and environmental influences*. New York/London: Grune & Stratton.

Wilhelm, O., & Oberauer, K. (2006). Why are reasoning ability and working memory capacity related to mental speed? An investigation of stimulus–response compatibility in choice reaction time tasks. *European Journal of Cognitive Psychology, 18*(1), 18–50.

Yerkes, R. M., & Dodson, J. D. (1908). The relation of strength of stimulus to rapidity of habit formation. *Journal of Comparative and Neurological Psychology, 18*, 459–482.

EUROPEAN JOURNAL OF COGNITIVE PSYCHOLOGY
2006, 18 (1), 18–50

Why are reasoning ability and working memory capacity related to mental speed? An investigation of stimulus–response compatibility in choice reaction time tasks

Oliver Wilhelm

Humboldt University, Berlin, Germany

Klaus Oberauer

University of Potsdam, Germany

A study with 114 young adults investigated the correlations of intelligence factors and working-memory capacity with reaction time (RT) tasks. Within two sets of four-choice RT tasks, stimulus–response compatibility was varied over three levels: compatible, incompatible, and arbitrary mappings. Two satisfactory measurement models for the RTs could be established: A general factor model without constraints on the loadings and a nested model with two correlated factors, distinguishing compatible from arbitrary mappings, with constraints on the loadings. Structural models additionally including factors for working memory and intelligence showed that the nested model with correlated factors is superior in fit. Working-memory capacity and fluid intelligence were correlated strongly with the nested factor for the RT tasks with arbitrary mappings, and less with the general RT factor. The results support the hypothesis that working memory is needed to maintain arbitrary bindings between stimulus representations and response representations, and this could explain the correlation of working-memory capacity with speed in choice RT tasks.

It has been known for a long time that general intelligence ("g") is correlated with measures of speed on relatively simple tasks, such as choice reaction time and even simple reaction time tasks (for reviews see Danthiir, Roberts, Schulze,

Correspondence should be addressed to Oliver Wilhelm, Institut für Psychologie, Humboldt Universität Berlin, D-10099 Berlin, Germany. Email: oliver.wilhelm@rz.hu-berlin.de

This research was in part supported by a TransCoop grant of the Alexander v. Humboldt foundation to the second author. We thank Olga Kunina for programming the tasks, and Olga Kunina, Marina Chernivsky, Franziska Heckel, Lea Joskowicz, and Anne Ruhmland for help with collecting the data. We are grateful to Florian Schmiedek, Nelson Cowan, and anonymous reviewers for valuable advice on a previous version of the manuscript.

DOI:10.1080/09541440500215921

& Wilhelm, 2005a; Jensen, 1993). When intelligence is differentiated according to structural models, the relationship with speeded reaction time (RT) tasks is strongest for psychometric speed factors, but also substantial for factors reflecting reasoning ability (e.g., Neubauer & Bucik, 1996). The correlation between intelligence test scores and variables extracted from individual RT tasks rarely exceeds $r = .30$, but when several tasks are aggregated or combined into a latent factor, the correlation can be much higher (Kyllonen, 1994; Neubauer & Bucik, 1996; Vernon, 1983).

The correlation between intelligence scores and RTs has inspired researchers to speculate about the nature of intelligence. One line of research was directed at measuring the speed of information processing through so-called elementary cognitive tasks, which were assumed to measure the time of individual processing steps (e.g., the slope in the Sternberg memory search paradigm as reflecting the time for a single comparison). Proponents of this approach have been frustrated by the fact that the correlation of RT variables with ability test scores is largely driven by the baseline or residual and not the component isolated through contrasting experimental conditions (Lohman, 1994). Others have argued that speed on relatively simple RT tasks reflects some aspect of general neural efficiency that contributes to the biological basis of intelligence, such as nerve conduction velocity (Vernon & Mori, 1992) or degree of myelination (Jensen, 1998; Miller, 1994). Direct evidence for a link to parameters of neural processing has been difficult to obtain reliably, however (e.g., Wickett & Vernon, 1994). The prospect of using presumably simple, well-understood experimental RT tasks as a window to the basis of intelligence has further been clouded by the finding that the domain of RT performance has a complex, hierarchical structure of its own, with a general factor and several subordinate factors (Kranzler & Jensen, 1991; Roberts & Stankov, 1999).

Mental speed has also received a prominent role as an explanatory construct in developmental research. Speed of processing accounts for substantial amounts of variance in age-related increases of cognitive performance during childhood (Fry & Hale, 1996; Kail & Salthouse, 1994; but see also de Ribaupierre & Lecerf, 2006 this issue, for a theoretical account assigning equal status to working memory and processing speed). Psychometric speed measures account for the larger part of cognitive declines in old age (Salthouse, 1996). The relationship of speed—assessed with psychometric speed tests or RTs in experimental tasks—with intellectual abilities seems to be much larger in age-heterogeneous samples than their correlations in age-homogeneous samples.

When it comes to predicting individual differences in intelligence in young adults, in particular reasoning ability (which is often equated with fluid intelligence), measures of working-memory capacity (WMC) have been more successful than speed variables (Ackerman, Beier, & Boyle, 2002; Conway, Cowan, Bunting, Therriault, & Minkoff, 2002; Kyllonen, 1994; Kyllonen & Christal, 1990; Süß, Oberauer, Wittmann, Wilhelm, & Schulze, 2002, see also Borella,

Carretti, & Mammarella, 2006 this issue). In these studies, with the exception of Conway et al. (2002), the WMC factor was itself strongly related to the factor representing speed. Large correlations between speed variables and WMC have also been obtained with children (Fry & Hale, 1996; Miller & Vernon, 1992) and old adults (Salthouse, 1992). Hence, it seems that there is variance shared by all three constructs: reasoning ability, WMC, and simple speeded tasks (including psychometric speed tasks and RT tasks). It is unclear what this common variance is. We might label it "g", but that simply begs the question.

In what follows, we will first discuss different kinds of explanations for the association between measures of speed and of capacity (i.e., WMC and reasoning ability). Then we introduce our hypothesis about the common denominator of speed, WMC, and reasoning.

EXPLANATIONS FOR THE SPEED–CAPACITY LINK

We distinguish four categories of explanations for the association between speed on simple processing tasks on the one hand, WMC and complex cognitive abilities (i.e., reasoning, fluid intelligence) on the other hand. The first appeals to shared method variance: Like speed tasks, WMC and reasoning tests are usually administered with a time limit, such that fast processing pays off. This explanation probably accounts for part of the common variance tapped by the three categories of measures, but not all. In studies that administered reasoning tests without time limit, a substantial correlation with speed measures was still obtained (Vernon, Nador, & Kantor, 1985; Wilhelm & Schulze, 2002), although reduced relative to speeded administration in one case (Wilhelm & Schulze, 2002).

The second kind of explanation gives mental speed causal priority. Speed is assumed to help performance on working memory and reasoning tasks. One rationale for this approach is the assumption that representations in working memory decay quickly, and therefore fast processing helps to complete a task before necessary information is lost (Jensen, 1998; Salthouse, 1996). The crucial assumption of this explanation, that representations in working memory decay within seconds as a function of time, has been questioned by recent experimental work (Barrouillet, Bernardin, & Camos, 2004; Lewandowsky, Duncan, & Brown, 2004; Saito & Miyake, 2004). The amount of concurrent processing is more critical for forgetting than the mere passage of time. A second rationale is to assume that processing and short-term maintenance of information share a common resource. In RT tasks, this resource could be fully devoted to maximising speed and accuracy on a single process, whereas in working memory and reasoning tasks, it must be shared between proces-sing one representation while keeping available others (e.g., intermediate results). The resource-sharing account, however, has been questioned, because an increase in memory load reduces speed on a concurrent processing task only under specific conditions (Oberauer, 2002; Oberauer, Demmrich, Mayr, & Kliegl, 2001).

The third approach takes working memory as the causal prior. For example, Engle, Kane, and their colleagues argue that working-memory capacity refers not to the capacity of a memory system but to the ability to control attention (Engle, Kane, & Tuholski, 1999; Kane & Engle, 2002; see also Elliott, Barrilleaux, & Cowan, 2006). Controlled attention is also needed for fast reactions to stimuli, in particular in the presence of distraction. Even without external distraction, endogenous fluctuations in the cognitive system might require continuous control to keep the task goal highly activated. Reduced control might lead to increased conflict between several response alternatives in choice tasks, and thereby to occasionally prolonged RTs or to errors. This explanation predicts that the correlation between speed and WMC should be larger in tasks or situations with high distraction or high conflict (Kane & Engle, 2003).

Finally, there is a fourth possibility: Speed on simple tasks and capacity of working memory, as well as reasoning ability, might depend on a common cause that cannot be identified with any of the three constructs involved. No well-elaborated concept on the level of cognitive functions that could take this role is in sight. It is tempting to speculate about features of the neural substrate of cognition that affect both speed of processing and the capacity to maintain and manipulate multiple information elements simultaneously, as it is required for working memory and reasoning tasks. One such factor could be, for example, the degree of myelination (Miller, 1994). Better myelination would on the one hand increase neural conduction speed; on the other hand reduce the likelihood of cross-talk between axons. The former might lead to faster reaction times; the latter might help to maintain multiple representations in working memory without mutual interference. Another common cause at the neural level could be the gain parameter in connectionist networks, which is assumed to depend on the level of dopamine (Cohen & Servan-Schreiber, 1992). A higher gain parameter increases the responsivity of neurons (or units in connectionist networks) to input. It can lead to better WMC (Li & Sikström, 2002), and it is plausible that it also leads to higher processing speed.

BINDING AND STIMULUS–RESPONSE COMPATIBILITY

Our own approach is a case of the third class of hypotheses discussed above. We venture that speed on relatively simple choice RT tasks depends on WMC. In particular, we assume that WMC is important to maintain a robust representation of the mapping between stimuli and responses in choice RT tasks. This leads to the hypothesis that the size of the correlation of choice RTs with WMC and reasoning ability depends on the compatibility of stimulus–response mappings for the choice RT tasks.

We start from the assumption that all tasks that measure WMC, as well as all reasoning tasks, have one feature in common: They require access to *relational representations*. By this we mean representations of a relation between two or more elements. A relational representation is not a chunk that is treated as a single unit, but a structure in which the components are still available independently (Halford, Wilson, & Phillips, 1998). This makes it possible, among other things, to compare the structure of two relational representations while abstracting from the features of the elements. Structure comparison is the hallmark of analogy (Hummel & Holyoak, 1997), which lies at the heart of most inductive reasoning tasks in intelligence tests, such as series completion and matrices. Relational representations are built by temporarily binding elements to places of a cognitive coordinate system (e.g., a mental space or time dimension) or to the roles of a preexisting structural schema. We argue that the main function of working memory is to quickly set up and update temporary bindings in the service of maintenance and flexible manipulation of relational representations. This motivates our hypothesis that the limited capacity of working memory relates to a limit on the number of elements that can be bound into a structure simultaneously while still kept apart (Oberauer, Süß, Wilhelm, & Sander, in press).

When we extend this idea to the representation of task sets, we can expect that high WMC is helpful for maintaining temporary bindings between stimulus categories and response categories, thereby increasing the efficiency on speeded choice tasks. People with low WMC have less robust bindings, and this should result in slower activation of the appropriate response representation by a stimulus, or in occasional losses of the bindings between stimuli and responses in working memory, so that they would have to be reconstructed from representations of the instructions in long-term memory. Temporary stimulus–response (S–R) bindings are particularly important when the mapping of stimuli to responses is arbitrary or incompatible, whereas with a compatible mapping the contribution of working memory should be less necessary. This assumption rests on the model of Kornblum, Hasbroucq, and Osman (1990). According to that model, stimulus representations can be translated into response representations along two paths. The rule-based path is mediated by a representation of the instructed S–R mapping, set up ad hoc in the test situation according to instructions. This path can translate any stimulus into any response. The associative path is mediated by preexisting associations between stimuli and responses that overlap in some or all of their feature dimensions.

For example, if the stimuli have a spatial location, varying on the left–right dimension, and the responses are key hits on the left and on the right, there is overlap in the left–right dimension between stimuli and responses. In that case, a left stimulus would automatically activate a left-key response, and a right stimulus would activate a right-key response. In the case of dimensional overlap, we can distinguish between compatible and noncompatible S–R mappings. A mapping is *compatible* if each stimulus is mapped to the response that corresponds to it on the overlapping dimensions (e.g., respond with a right key press to a stimulus on the right, and with a left key press to a stimulus on the left). A mapping is not compatible if stimuli are mapped to responses with different values on the overlapping dimensions. Reaction times are substantially faster with compatible than with noncompatible S–R mappings (for reviews, see Kornblum et al., 1990; Lien & Proctor, 2002).

When more than two stimuli and their corresponding responses are used, the noncompatible S–R mappings can further be broken down into *incompatible* and *arbitrary* mappings. Incompatible mappings can be derived from compatible mappings by a simple rule. For example, when a row of four stimuli arranged from left to right is mapped to a row of response keys arranged from left to right, an incompatible mapping can be produced by inverting the compatible mapping, so that the leftmost stimulus is mapped onto the rightmost response key, the middle-left stimulus onto the middle-right key, and so on. An arbitrary mapping, in contrast, would be a mapping that is not related by any obvious rule to the compatible mapping. Figure 1 illustrates the taxonomy of tasks relevant for the present work.

We assume that WMC is needed for maintaining bindings between stimulus representations and response representations to establish the rule-based path. When the S–R mapping is not compatible, or when there is no dimensional overlap to begin with, this is the only path that mediates translation of stimuli into responses, and therefore WMC should have a large effect on the speed and accuracy of reactions in tasks with incompatible and with arbitrary mappings, as well as with tasks lacking dimensional overlap. When the S–R mapping is compatible, both paths contribute to the generation of responses. WMC should still affect speed and accuracy of responses, but to a smaller degree than in noncompatible tasks. Therefore, we predict that RTs from tasks with noncompatible bindings should correlate more with WMC than RTs from compatible bindings, at least with only moderate amounts of practice with the RT tasks. Over the course of practice noncompatible S–R mappings can be acquired in the form of associations in long-term memory, which eventually might become as strong as those between compatible S–R combinations. Stimulus–response compatibility effects, however, are quite persistent over practice (Dutta & Proctor, 1992) and, as we will show below, the amount of practice in our study did not come close to eliminate compatibility effects.

To sum up, we expect that the correlation between WMC and speed in choice RT tasks should be higher with incompatible and arbitrary than with compatible S–R mappings. Furthermore, we assume that bindings between elements in working memory are also necessary to build the relational representations underlying reasoning. Therefore, WMC should be highly correlated with reasoning (and fluid intelligence, which is largely coextensive with reasoning), and reasoning also should be related more strongly to choice RT tasks with noncompatible than with compatible mappings. These hypotheses were tested in the present study.

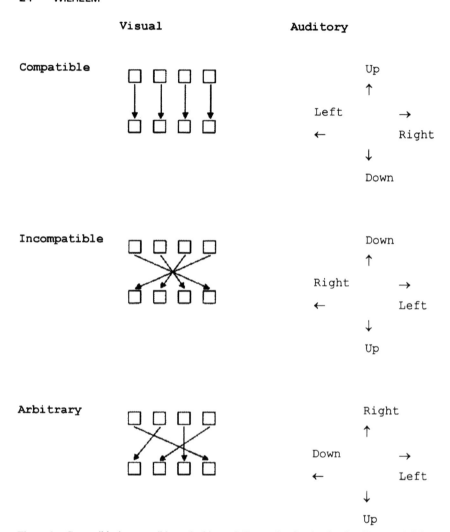

Figure 1. Compatible, incompatible, and arbitrary S–R mapping for visual and auditory modalities.

METHOD

Participants and apparatus

Participants were recruited through newspaper and magazine ads. They were initially recruited for a study on the structure of mental speed (Danthiir, Wilhelm, & Schacht, 2005b). From this first testing session, which took approximately 4 hours, only data on reasoning ability and crystallised intelligence will be presented here. Participants were invited again for a second testing session that took approximately 3.5 hours. One hundred and fourteen participants (80 female, 34 male) were included in the final sample. Thirteen additional participants were excluded for various reasons: Four participants had severe problems with arbitrary S–R mappings, one participant was an outlier in almost all tests administrated, two participants did not meet the age restriction, and six participants were not sufficiently fluent in German to provide unbiased ability estimates, as judged from achievement test data. Mean age of the final sample was 24.9 years ($SD = 4.7$), ranging from 18 to 36 years. Four participants did not indicate their age but seemingly fell into the age range accepted in this study. Ninety-three of the subjects had a high-school degree and 72 of them were currently enrolled as students at a university. Participants received feedback about their results and were paid approximately 5€ per hour as compensation for their participation.

Both testing sessions were run in a group lab with between one and eight participants. All testing sessions were run by trained students. Sessions with more than four participants were run by two students. The time between both testing sessions ranged from 1 week to several months.

All tasks were administered by computer. Tasks were programmed in Inquisit 1.33© and run on IBM compatible Pentium 4 computers with 17-inch monitors. The refresh rate of the monitors was set to 85 Hz and the resolution to 1280 × 1024 pixels.

Materials and procedure

S–R compatibility tasks

A set of four-choice RT tasks was generated according to an experimental design with the factors S–R mapping (compatible, incompatible, and arbitrary mappings), modality (visual vs. auditory tasks), repetition (first vs. second administration), and sequence. Sequence was a between-subjects factor that was randomly assigned to groups of participants within a session. There were six groups, corresponding to the six possible sequences for compatible, incompatible, and arbitrary mappings. For each participant, the same sequence was used in both modalities. Participants completed two series of blocks that were identical apart from the block sequence within each series, which was reversed in the second series. Each series consisted of three blocks of the visual task, followed by three blocks of the auditory task.

Stimuli for the S–R tasks varied on one relevant dimension and one irrelevant dimension. Stimuli for the visual task were squares that appeared at one of four locations in a row (relevant dimension) and had one of four colours (red, blue, yellow, or green, irrelevant dimension). The size of the squares was 120 × 120 pixels. Stimuli for the auditory tasks were location words (''above'', ''below'', ''left'', or ''right''; relevant dimension) recorded from four different speakers (irrelevant dimension) and presented through headphones. The stimuli were equated with regard to onset of word, duration, and volume by editing the sound files. Participants responded by pressing one of four response keys. For the visual task, the response keys on a customised keyboard were arranged in a row, corresponding to the relevant dimension of the visual stimuli; for the auditory task the response keys were arranged in a diamond shape, thereby corresponding to the relevant dimension of the auditory stimuli. The S–R mappings used for both tasks in compatible, incompatible, and arbitrary conditions are illustrated in Figure 1. For the compatible mapping, each stimulus is mapped onto its corresponding response key. Incompatible mappings were the mirror images of corresponding mappings. Arbitrary mappings were generated so that no obvious rule governed the assignment of stimuli to response keys. Incompatible and arbitrary mappings were the same for all participants and remained constant throughout the experiment.

Each condition began with an instruction and practice period that focused on the given S–R mapping. Feedback on accuracy was provided for all practice items but not for the test items. After 16 practice trials testing began. The first trial in each block was a warm-up trial that was discarded in all analysis—as were the practice trials. During the test trials a reminder displaying the current S–R mapping was presented after every 16 trials. Each block consisted of 64 test trials with the same S–R mapping. The stimuli within subblocks of 16 trials were fully balanced across both stimulus dimensions in both modalities. The sequence of these predefined 16 trials was randomised once for each group of 16 consecutive trials and then fixed for all participants in all conditions. Intertrial intervals were randomised for all trials but constant across participants in both modalities. Latencies were recorded from stimulus onset. Stimuli were presented until participants responded in the visual task. No new stimulus was presented until participants responded in the auditory tasks.

Across the six sequences that were varied between subjects there were six measures of compatible, incompatible, and arbitrary S–R mappings in each modality, each based upon 64 trials. Table 1 provides an overview and descriptive statistics of latencies and accuracies of the S–R measures used in this study.

Working memory capacity tasks

Memory updating (MU). In this task (modified from Oberauer, Süß, Schulze, Wilhelm, & Wittmann, 2000) participants saw a 3 × 3 grid on the computer screen. In a subset of the nine cells digits were presented one by one, for 1 s each. Participants had to memorise which digit was presented in which cell. After presentation of 2–7 digits four arrows were displayed, one by one, in four selected cells. Each arrow was presented for 1 s, after which the next arrow followed immediately. An arrow pointing downwards indicated that the participant had to decrease the current value memorised for this cell by one, and an arrow pointing upward instructed participants to increment the current value by

TABLE 1
Descriptive statistics for latencies and accuracies for all S–R mappings

	Latencies				Accuracies			
	M	*SD*	*Skewness*	*Kurtosis*	*M*	*SD*	*Skewness*	*Kurtosis*
Visual compatible 1	500	73	1.08	2.74	0.98	0.02	−1.97	5.45
Visual compatible 2	466	·53	0.41	0.09	0.98	0.03	−2.22	7.08
Visual incompatible 1	794	188	1.53	3.29	0.94	0.09	−2.67	6.65
Visual incompatible 2	668	135	0.95	0.60	0.96	0.05	−2.80	11.79
Visual arbitrary 1	1191	301	0.63	−0.16	0.84	0.18	−1.52	1.66
Visual arbitrary 2	952	223	1.29	2.05	0.93	0.10	−2.89	8.50
Auditory compatible 1	580	82	0.75	0.27	0.98	0.02	−1.85	4.33
Auditory compatible 2	566	82	0.83	−0.03	0.98	0.03	−1.97	3.96
Auditory incompatible 1	839	129	0.69	0.50	0.96	0.04	−1.37	2.32
Auditory incompatible 2	837	149	0.57	−0.13	0.95	0.05	−1.12	0.75
Auditory arbitrary 1	895	168	0.78	0.49	0.94	0.06	−2.06	4.95
Auditory arbitrary 2	853	156	0.84	0.56	0.95	0.04	−2.12	6.66

one. After the last computing instruction was given the recall cue appeared for 2 s. Participants then had to respond to question marks appearing in individual cells by entering the final digit of that cell. In total there were 18 test items (= trials). The score for MU was the mean of the proportion of digits correctly recalled for each item.

Counting span (CS). In this task (Engle et al., 1999; Kane et al., 2004) participants had to remember digits while working on a concurrent counting task. Each trial consisted of a sequence of screens. In each screen 3–9 dark blue circles, 1, 3, 5, 7, or 9 dark blue squares, and 1–5 light green circles were shown on a grey background, approximately balancing the number of the three kinds of figures. The participant was asked to count the number of dark blue circles in each screen. Once participants were finished they were asked to proceed to the next screen immediately by pressing a key on a customised keyboard. After pressing a key the screen was blank for 550 ms, followed by the next set of figures. The last set of figures was followed by a recall cue. Participants then had to recall the totals they counted from the preceding sets by entering the series of digits on the keyboard in correct order. The number of displays ranged from two to six displays per test item. In total there were 15 items. The score for CS was the mean of the proportion of counts recalled correctly in the correct list position for each item.

Rotation span (RS). In this task (Kane et al., 2004; Shah & Miyake, 1996), participants had to recall a sequence of short and long arrows radiating out from the centre while concurrently engaging in a letter-rotation task. Again, each test item consisted of a sequence of screens. The processing part of each screen consisted of a normal or mirror-reversed G, F, or R, rotated at 0, 45, 90, 135, 180, 225, 270, or 315 degrees. Participants were asked to mentally rotate the letter and then to indicate by a key press whether the letter was normal or mirror-reversed. Half of all the letters were mirror-reversed. The response to the letter-rotation task was followed by a 750 ms intertrial interval, after which a short or long arrow pointing into one of eight directions was presented for 1 s. After this, the next letter-rotation task was displayed immediately. At the end of a sequence of letter–arrow pairs the recall cue appeared. Participants then indicated the directions of the arrows in correct order by clicking the corresponding locations with the mouse. There were 12 trials, with list length ranging from two to five arrows. The score for RS was the mean of the proportion of arrows recalled correctly in correct list position for each item.

Reasoning tasks

All reasoning tasks were computerised. The tasks used to assess reasoning were the 18 odd-numbered items from set II of the Advanced Progressive Matrices (APM; Raven, Raven, & Court, 1998), Form B (Part 1) of the Cattell Culture-Fair-Test with 14 items (CFT; Cattell & Weiss, 1971), a traditional number series test with open answer format consisting of 17 items (Wilhelm, 2005), arrow series, from the Omnibus Screening Protocol (Roberts & Stankov, 2001) with eight response alternatives consisting of 15 items, and a verbal propositional reasoning task (18 items) using the propositions ''and'', ''or'', and ''if . . . then'' describing the actions of a hypothetical machine (Wilhelm, 2005). For the number series test the response keys were the number keys on top of the customised keyboard; for the other tasks participants used the mouse to select their chosen response on the screen.

Crystallised-intelligence tasks

Crystallised intelligence was measured by a general knowledge test and a vocabulary test, each presented by computer and administered with five response alternatives. The general knowledge indicators were taken from the IST-2000-R (Amthauer, Brocke, Liepmann, & Beauducel, 1999; Beauducel & Kersting, 2002). Three composites were built by computing sums for three groups of 28 items. Each composite included a mixture of symbolic, verbal, and numeric item content. Apart from that, variables were selected for the composites in an arbitrary way. The composites therefore are not intended to reflect different aspects of knowledge. They were formed only to obtain several independent indicators for a single latent factor of crystallised intelligence. The vocabulary test was taken from Form 1 of the WILDE Intelligence Test (Jäger & Althoff, 1983). For all crystallised tasks the mouse was used to click the chosen response on the screen.

RESULTS

Data treatment

Within each block of 64 trials on the RT task we first determined as outliers those RTs that surpassed an individual's mean by more than 3 standard deviations. These outliers were set to the mean + 3 *SD*. The next step was to eliminate all latencies associated with erroneous responding. The third step was to repeat the first step across equivalent blocks in the two repetitions. Pooling the data from first and second repetition served to set a stricter outlier cutoff on the RTs from the first repetition, which were slower and more variable. Across all conditions and repetitions ($12 \times 64 = 768$ trials) a mean of 12.4 data points per participant (maximum = 20) was defined as outliers through this procedure. After this treatment, the RT data were averaged within each block. This resulted in 12 means for each participant (2 repetitions $\times$ 2 modalities $\times$ 3 S–R mappings).

Some of the participants had exceptionally bad performance scores on some of the tasks, so that we suspect they did not fully understand the instructions. If participants had only one or a few minor problems the values of these variables were set to missing and subsequently imputed by the missing variable procedure in SPSS (2004) relying on an expectation-maximisation (EM) estimation (Dempster, Laird, & Rubin, 1977; Schafer & Graham, 2002).[1] Participants who had pervasive problems on a group of indicators were eliminated from the final data set (see Participants section).

Experimental effects

To assess the effects of the experimental factors on performance in the S–R-compatibility tasks, analyses of covariance (ANCOVAs) with S–R mapping (3) and repetition (2) as within-subject factors and sequence (6) as between-subjects

---

[1] Eliminating entire cases of the data from further analysis has no effect on the validity of conclusions only when the missing data are missing completely at random, i.e., whether or not a data point is available can not be predicted from data values recorded or missing. If the eliminated cases are systematically different from the other cases, statistics may be seriously biased. Additionally, in many cases discarding cases has a negative effect on statistical power of intended comparisons. The basic idea in dealing with the missing data in this study is to consider all possible values of the missing data under the assumption of multivariate normality, weighting each value by its probability, conditional on the other available data. The so-called EM procedure is an iterative algorithm. Starting with parameter estimates for means and covariances, the expectation-step calculates the conditional expectation of the log-likelihood for the complete data given the observed data and the parameter estimates. Starting from this log-likelihood for complete data, the maximisation-step finds the parameter estimates to maximise the log-likelihood for the complete data from the expectation-step. These two steps are iterated until the iterations converge on a specified criterion. The iterative algorithm replaces missing values optimally by taking the information of the observed values into account. Computationally more effortful procedures with multiple imputations can be advantageous in cases with more missing data points.

factor were computed, separately for the visual and the auditory tasks and for latencies and accuracies as dependent variables. The results are summarised in Tables 2 and 3. For experimental purposes the current sample size is very large. Hence, the power to detect small effects is comparatively high. Rather than focusing on statistical significance the results should be evaluated in terms of the magnitude of effects.

For both the visual and the auditory tasks the main effects of S–R mapping were very large. The main effects for sequence were not statistically significant for both modalities. The main effect of repetition was substantial for the visual tasks and significant but much smaller for the auditory tasks. We interpret this result as a learning effect present for the visual tasks but wearing off for the auditory tasks, which were always administered after the visual tasks. There was a significant interaction between sequence and S–R mapping: Participants who began with the arbitrary condition had longer latencies on this condition than participants who began with another condition. This interaction, however, was rather small for the visual task and practically nonexistent for the auditory tasks. The between-subjects variable sequence hence had only a very small impact on the size of the S–R compatibility effect. The interaction of S–R mapping and repetition was substantial for the visual modality and significant but small for the auditory modality. The S–R compatibility effects were reduced substantially (but remained dramatic nevertheless) in the second repetition for the visual

TABLE 2
Overview of experimental effects for latencies

	df_{num}	df_{den}	F	p	par. η^2
Visual tasks					
Seq	5	108	0.34	.889	.015
S–R	2	107	480.33	<.001	.900
Repetition	1	108	325.30	<.001	.751
Seq × S–R	10	216	3.86	<.001	.152
Seq × Repetition	5	108	2.76	.022	.113
S–R × Repetition	2	107	98.18	<.001	.647
Seq × S–R × Repetition	10	216	0.957	.482	.042
Auditory tasks					
Seq	5	108	1.98	.087	.084
S–R	2	107	491.70	<.001	.902
Repetition	1	108	14.25	<.001	.117
Seq × S–R	10	216	1.07	.387	.047
Seq × Repetition	5	108	1.19	.319	.052
S–R × Repetition	2	107	5.00	.008	.085
Seq × S–R × Repetition	10	216	2.54	.007	.105

df_{num} = df numerator, df_{den} = df denominator, par. η^2 = partial Eta square (effect size), Seq = Sequence, S–R = stimulus–response mapping.

TABLE 3
Overview of experimental effects for accuracies

	df_{num}	df_{den}	F	p	par. η^2
Visual tasks					
Seq	5	108	1.17	.329	.051
S–R	2	107	87.28	<.001	.620
Repetition	1	108	35.89	<.001	.249
Seq × S–R	10	216	1.83	.056	.078
Seq × Repetition	5	108	1.14	.342	.050
S–R × Repetition	2	107	33.85	<.001	.388
Seq × S–R × Repetition	10	216	2.01	.034	.085
Auditory tasks					
Seq	5	108	0.73	.601	.033
S–R	2	107	84.66	<.001	.613
Repetition	1	108	3.83	.053	.034
Seq × S–R	10	216	1.21	.284	.053
Seq × Repetition	5	108	2.15	.065	.091
S–R × Repetition	2	107	5.13	.007	.087
Seq × S–R × Repetition	10	216	1.51	.138	.065

df_{num} = df numerator, df_{den} = df denominator, par. η^2 = partial Eta square (effect size), Seq = Sequence, S–R = stimulus–response mapping.

tasks. The interaction of sequence, S–R mapping, and repetition was not significant in the visual modality and very small in the auditory modality.

The small, but significant interaction of the between-subjects factor sequence with S–R mapping introduces an unwanted source of individual differences variance: Participants working in a sequence starting with the arbitrary mapping received larger individual estimates of S–R compatibility effects than participants working in another sequence. This variance is obviously unwanted because it reflects nothing but the random allocation of participants to sequences. Therefore, we regressed all measured variables from the S–R compatibility tasks on a set of dummy codes representing the sequence factor. The residuals were then taken as variables for the following multivariate analyses.

The accuracies were within the normal range for RT data except for the first arbitrary block in the visual modality, in which they were exceptionally low. This result is in line with the above interpretation of subjects being overwhelmed by the first arbitrary mapping but adjusting quickly in the following administrations. The dispersion in this condition is also exceptionally high, indicating that there were several participants doing particularly poorly. These participants were not eliminated because their inclusion did not affect the results reported and because apart from the poor performance in some experimental conditions they contributed valuable data. To compensate for the lack of normality in the data the accuracies were probit-transformed before running analyses (following the procedure detailed in Cohen & Cohen, 1983). This transformation turns probabilities into their corresponding z-scores and thereby allows expressing differences between participants in the familiar metric of the normal distribution. The experimental effects for the accuracies are shown in Table 3. They closely followed the effects observed for the latencies, demonstrating that there was no differential tradeoff between speed and accuracy across conditions.

One important difference between the visual and auditory modality is that the difference between incompatible and arbitrary mappings was much smaller for the auditory tasks. For the visual tasks incompatible mappings were associated with much faster RTs than arbitrary mappings, but this was not the case for the auditory tasks. Therefore it is not clear whether the information processing demands in incompatible trials were comparable across modalities. The processing demands of incompatible trials are unclear also theoretically—participants might treat them like arbitrary mappings, using only the rule-based path to translate stimuli into responses, or else they might treat them like compatible mappings, using the associative path, and then reverse the mapping according to the mirror-image rule. The different results in the two modalities raise the suspicion that participants might have handled the incompatible mappings by different strategies in the two modalities. For this reason we limited our further analyses to the compatible and the arbitrary mappings.

Correlational data

The appropriate methodology to answer the central research questions is confirmatory factor analysis (CFA). With CFA it is possible to test whether theoretically motivated models are capable of explaining the observed covariances. Usually a distinction is made between measurement models and structural models. With a measurement model the primary concern is to find a model that explains the internal structure of a group of indicators. With a structural model the primary concern is to test correlations between latent factors.

Criteria for model assessment

There are many statistics to assess the fit or adequacy of measurement or structural models (Marsh, Balla, & McDonald, 1988). A very fundamental statistic is the χ^2-value associated with each model for a given data set. The χ^2 test is supposed to express how similar the model implied covariance matrix and the observed covariance matrix are. Significant values of χ^2 indicate a deviation of the observed from the implied covariance matrix that is larger than deviations that can be attributed to sampling error. Relying on fewer estimated parameters improves parsimony of a model but usually impairs model fit. Differences in the fit of two models can be compared inferentially with each other in some cases. For example, models can be derived from each other by constraining estimated parameters. This test of the difference of the χ^2 statistics of both models follows a χ^2 distribution with degrees of freedom equal to the difference in degrees of freedom from both models. Significant values of this test indicate that constraining some of the estimated parameters impaired model fit.

Akaike's Information Criterion (AIC) combines the χ^2-value of a model with a penalty for its lack of parsimony, as reflected in the number of free parameters. As with the χ^2 statistic lower values indicate better fit, but no inferential tests and no threshold values are available. The χ^2-test is not optimal, given that its power strongly depends on sample size. Hence, it is desirable to report additional fit indices compensating for these shortcomings. The root mean square error of approximation (RMSEA) is an estimate of the misfit due to model misspecification per degree of freedom. The Comparative Fit Index (CFI) is an incremental fit index that expresses the proportion of improvement in overall fit relative to the independence model (i.e., a model assuming no correlations between the manifest variables).

Taking these fit indicators together allows acceptable assessment of model fit. Strict recommendations for minimal values of these fit indicators are not sensible (Hu & Bentler, 1995, 1999). Nonetheless, some cutoff values have been established as rules of thumb. If the sample size is not very large, the χ^2 statistic should not surpass the conventional level of significance very far. Regardless of sample size the CFI values should be .95 or higher, and RMSEA values should be .06 or smaller.

For the purpose of illustration and to allow reanalysis the correlations between all variables included in the measurement and structural models are provided in Table 4. A complete data set is available upon request.

Measurement models for S–R compatibility data. We tested a general factor model (model 1) as the baseline model, representing the assumption that RTs from tasks with compatible and tasks with arbitrary S–R mappings reflect the same latent factor. Model 2, a so-called nested-factor model, represents our assumption that RTs from arbitrary mappings reflect a specific source of variance in addition to the variance of the general factor. The logic of this model is similar to the logic of additive experimental factors: The general factor explains the common variance among all eight RTs and the nested factor explains the variance that is common to RTs from arbitrary mappings and not shared with RTs from the compatible mappings (Oberauer, Wilhelm, & Schmiedek, 2005b). In our theoretical framework, we interpret the general factor as reflecting general speed in choice RT tasks, and the specific factor as reflecting the ability to uphold arbitrary S–R bindings. Model 3 results when the two factors in Model 2 are allowed to correlate with each other. This captures the assumption that latent variables representing cognitive ability constructs are likely to be positively correlated, in line with the ubiquitous finding of a positive manifold among cognitive tests. The three model architectures considered here are illustrated in Figure 2. An additional feature of all three models is that we

TABLE 4
Correlations for all variables included in the measurement models and structural models

	VC1	2	3	4	5	6	7	8	9	10	11	12	13	14	15	16	17	18	19
2.VC2	.792																		
3.AC1	.556	.574																	
4.AC2	.591	.599	.886																
5.VA1	.400	.420	.386	.396															
6.VA2	.498	.570	.372	.399	.726														
7.AA1	.449	.405	.594	.561	.442	.517													
8.AA2	.475	.485	.538	.563	.397	.521	.777												
9.CS	-.182	-.308	-.260	-.196	-.167	-.414	-.407	-.255											
10.MU	-.205	-.292	-.351	-.341	-.358	-.443	-.468	-.393	.467										
11.RO	-.300	-.402	-.324	-.371	-.353	-.540	-.446	-.424	.572	.549									
12.Raven	-.202	-.265	-.251	-.187	-.163	-.260	-.223	-.115	.430	.384	.435								
13.CFT30	-.059	-.061	-.116	-.015	-.148	-.191	-.122	-.094	.181	.197	.094	.183							
14.Propo	-.268	-.250	-.221	-.223	-.189	-.233	-.133	-.150	.190	.380	.374	.324	.153						
15.Num Ser	-.215	-.218	-.252	-.212	-.220	-.388	-.300	-.186	.470	.440	.373	.503	.236	.342					
16.Arr Ser	-.245	-.128	-.225	-.185	-.207	-.258	-.253	-.228	.323	.365	.383	.402	.238	.336	.432				
17.Know1	-.209	-.206	-.294	-.288	-.272	-.305	-.270	-.288	.253	.290	.248	.385	.140	.269	.354	.299			
18.Know2	-.300	-.296	-.355	-.350	-.211	-.314	-.330	-.362	.356	.392	.281	.425	.250	.357	.469	.448	.670		
19.Know3	-.220	-.192	-.311	-.275	-.344	-.364	-.325	-.267	.268	.404	.263	.371	.262	.430	.418	.392	.680	.621	
20.Vocab	-.005	-.004	-.165	-.159	-.052	-.064	-.057	.009	.227	.175	.040	.200	.066	.297	.182	.135	.305	.386	.351

VC = visual compatible, AC = auditory compatible, VA = visual arbitrary, AA = auditory arbitrary, Propo = propositional reasoning, Num Ser = number series, Arr Ser = arrow series, Know = general knowledge, Vocab = vocabulary.

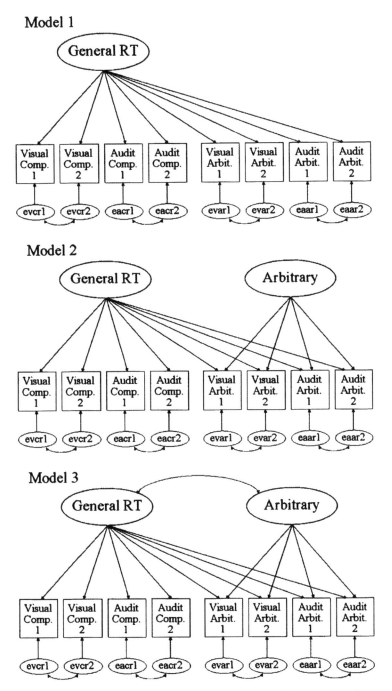

Figure 2. Family of measurement models. Large ovals represent latent factors, rectangles represent manifest (i.e., measured) variables.

allowed the error variances of the two blocks of identical tasks from the two repetitions to covary, because they probably share task-specific variance unrelated to the construct of interest.

The experimental design underlying the variables of our measurement models, together with the additive logic incorporated in models 2 and 3, implies several sets of constraints (see Oberauer et al., 2005b, for discussion). If the general factor is to reflect what tasks with compatible mappings and with arbitrary mappings have in common, and the specific factor is to capture the added costs of arbitrary mappings, then tasks differing only in S–R mapping should have the same unstandardised loading on the general factor. To incorporate this assumption, the first block of visual arbitrary mappings and the first block of visual compatible mappings was constrained to have the same unstandardised loading on the general factor. The same was done for the second administrations of these indicators, and likewise for the auditory tasks. With these constraints each person's mean RTs in blocks with arbitrary mappings are decomposed into two additive components, the mean RTs of corresponding blocks with compatible mappings plus the cost due to an arbitrary mapping. The general factor reflects the variance in the first component that is shared among all tasks; the specific factor reflects the variance in the second component that is shared among all tasks with an arbitrary mapping.[2] Introducing these constraints provides four additional degrees of freedom. Since the two models are nested, we can use the χ^2 difference test to assess whether the loss of fit due to the constraints is significant. If it is not, we accept the more constrained model because it provides a more parsimonious description of the data.

Table 5 provides a summary of the models emerging by crossing architecture (general factor, nested factor, correlated nested factor) with presence or absence of constraints on unstandardised loadings. Within the general factor models, constraints on the unstandardised loadings (model 1a) did substantial harm to the fit compared to the unconstrained model (model 1); this is not surprising because without the nested factor this model has no way to account for the mean differences between RTs with compatible and RTs with arbitrary mappings. The nested factor model with uncorrelated factors (models 2 and 2a) had convergence problems that could only be solved by adding further constraints (see notes to Table 5 for details); with these constraints the models did not fit well. Allowing a correlation between the two factors without additional constraints on loadings (model 3) also led to convergence problems. This is to be expected for this kind of model unless further constraints are introduced (see Oberauer et al., 2005b). In fact, imposing the constraints on unstandardised loadings as explained above (model 3a) removed these convergence problems. Model 3a

---

[2] The models analysed here focus on constraints on the loadings. Generally, it is possible to additionally model means and intercepts. Then the constraints additionally serve to account for mean effects.

TABLE 5
Overview of measurement models

Nr	Model	χ^2	df	p	CFI	RMSEA	AIC
1	g	33.92	16	=.001	.972	.100	73.92
1a	g	70.52	20	<.001	.921	.150	102.52
2*	nf	30.77	15	=.009	.975	.096	72.77
2a*	nf	49.51	19	<.001	.953	.119	83.51
3	nf corr	[no convergence]					
3a	nf corr	30.92	17	=.020	.978	.085	68.92

g = general factor, nf = nested factor, corr = correlated; a = constraints on unstandardised loadings: pairs of compatible and arbitrary mapping RTs had the same unstandardised loading on the general RT factor, pairs of blocks of same modality had the same unstandardised loadings on the arbitrary factor, if this factor was specified. Models 2, 2a, and 3 did not converge. For models 2 and 2a these problems could be solved by constraining all loadings on the arbitrary factor to be equal; these models are marked by *. Model 3 did not converge with these additional constraints.

provided a good fit. We also tested model versions with even stricter constraints on the loadings, but these resulted in substantial losses of fit.

Taken together there are two models with acceptable fit that support quite distinct conclusions. On the one hand there is a general factor model with freely estimated loadings (model 1). This model supports the conclusions that the communality between compatible and arbitrary indicators can be explained by a single latent factor. The various indicators do not necessarily have the same weight on this latent factor. However, the loadings are expected to be statistically different from zero and to have a sign that meets the expectations. For model 1 these expectations are met. On the other hand there is the theoretically motivated model 3a, which postulates two correlated factors—a general factor that explains the communality between all eight indicators and a nested factor for the indicators from arbitrary trials that captures the communality specific to the arbitrary indicators (see Figure 3). The unstandardised loadings of the variables on these two factors are estimated under several nontrivial constraints. Due to these constraints one parameter less is estimated in model 3a than in model 1, despite postulating an additional latent factor. Nonetheless, model 3a was the one with the better χ^2 statistic. It also had a better CFI, a better RMSEA, and a better AIC value. Therefore, we prefer model 3a over model 1.

Measurement model for fluid and crystallised intelligence. There are mainly two competing models that were proposed for the relationship of fluid and crystallised intelligence in the past. One is a nested-factor model with a general factor and a more specific factor on which only indicators of gc are permitted to load. This architecture, proposed by Gustaffson (1988; Undheim &

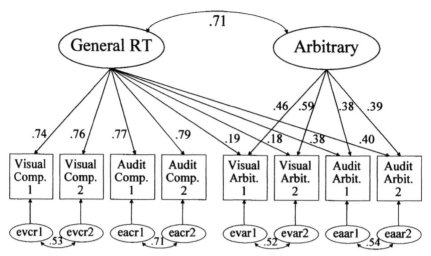

Figure 3. Measurement model with correlated nested factor and constraints on unstandardised factor loadings (model 3a). Large ovals represent latent factors, small ovals represent error terms, and rectangles represent manifest variables.

Gustafsson, 1987), identifies gf with the general factor g. The alternative is a model with two correlated factors. This model has the advantage of representing a more parsimonious measurement model. Moreover, we believe that representing fluid and crystallised intelligence as two group factors on the same level of generality comes closer to the original concepts of of fluid and crystallised intelligence, whereas the nested factor in Gustafsson's model, which measures gc only as a residual, is difficult to interpret.

We therefore decided to use a measurement model with two correlated group factors to represent the intelligence test data, as described below. We also conducted all analyses including the intelligence data with the nested-factor model proposed by Gustafsson. The fits of both models were equally good, and, extending both models along the lines described below led to the same conclusions. Therefore, we present only the results involving the correlated-factor representation of gf and gc.

The fit of this correlated group factor model was excellent, $\chi^2(26) = 25.07$, $p = .515$, CFI = 1.00, RMSEA = .000, AIC = 63.07. The loadings as well as the factor intercorrelation in this model are essentially identical to the loadings displayed in Figure 4. In this figure the measurement model for correlated group factors was extended to also include model 3a–WMC. All loadings met the expectations of having the expected sign, being of nontrivial magnitude, and being statistically different from zero. We therefore used the correlated group factors model to test our hypotheses about the relationship

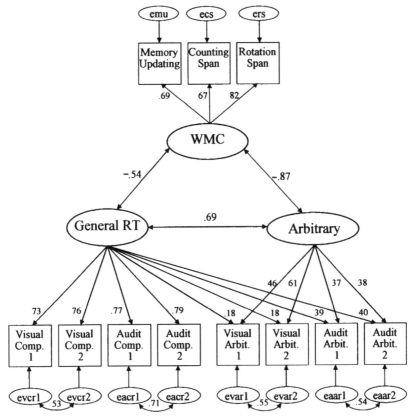

Figure 4. Structural model of general RT, arbitrary mappings RT, and working memory (model 3a–wmc). Large ovals represent latent factors, small ovals represent error terms, and rectangles represent manifest variables.

between choice RT tasks and intelligence factors. The fluid-intelligence factor is defined exclusively by reasoning tasks as indicators, so that it could also be labelled a reasoning factor. We will show that, as in previous studies, the fluid-intelligence/reasoning factor was strongly correlated with WMC, and therefore we hypothesise that the fluid-intelligence factor, too, should be correlated with arbitrary mapping RTs more than with compatible mapping RTs. We also predict that WMC will be related more to fluid than to crystallised intelligence, and therefore that the arbitrary mapping RT factor, too, will be correlated more with fluid intelligence than with crystallised intelligence. The latter relation will be larger than zero because crystallised intelligence in this model still reflects individual differences in cognitive processes that go beyond variance in knowledge alone.

Structural models. To test our hypotheses about the relationships between RT, WMC, and intellectual abilities, we extended each of the two acceptable measurement models of the RT tasks (models 1 and 3a) by additional factors. We investigated the extensions with both models in parallel to test whether the slight advantage in fit of model 3a would uphold in the context of additional variables. In a first step a latent factor for WMC, defined by the three WMC tasks, was added to both models. In a second step, the measurement model for fluid and crystallised intelligence was added. If the arbitrary factor indeed reflects the capacity to maintain bindings between stimulus and response representations it should be highly correlated with the WMC factor. The correlation between WMC and the general RT factor should be much smaller. Replicating prior research (Kane et al., 2004; Kyllonen & Christal, 1990; Süß et al., 2002) we expected a strong but not perfect correlation between the latent factors for WMC and fluid intelligence. As argued above, the arbitrary mapping factor was expected also to correlate substantially with the fluid intelligence factor, and less strongly with the crystallised intelligence factor. In the single-factor model extended by a WMC factor (model 1–wmc) the general RT factor correlated $r = .70$ with the WMC factor. The fit of this model was not very good, with $\chi^2(39) = 83.35, p < .001$, CFI = .944, RMSEA = .100, AIC = 137.35. The extended nested-factor model (model 3a–wmc) is displayed in Figure 4. The fit of this model was better, although still not excellent, $\chi^2(39) = 69.01, p = .002$, CFI = .962, RMSEA = .083, AIC = 123.06. Model 3a–wmc was superior to model 1–wmc with regard to all fit indices.

As expected, WMC was highly correlated with the nested factor reflecting the specific variance in the RT tasks with arbitrary mapping. Indeed, the correlation of $-.87$ is so close to one that it seems warranted to test whether it is different from unity. To test this hypothesis the correlation between the arbitrary mapping factor and the WMC factor was fixed to one and the correlations of these factors with the general RT factor was constrained to be equal. The resulting model did not fit significantly worse than the initial model for the two correlated nested factors, $\Delta\chi^2(2) = 4.78, p = .092$. Hence, we cannot rule out that the WMC factor and the arbitrary mapping factor are identical. We also tested whether the correlations of WMC with the two RT factors can be constrained to be equal. This constraint led to a significant loss of fit, $\Delta\chi^2(1) = 5.10, p = .013$. This implies that the correlation of WMC with the arbitrary mapping factor is significantly higher than the correlation with the general RT factor.

To summarise, the structural models so far demonstrate that—in line with our theoretical assumptions—a model with two nested and correlated factors provides a better explanation for the RT data than a one-factor model. The arbitrary mapping factor was almost perfectly correlated with the WMC factor. There was also a high correlation of WMC with the general RT factor, but it was substantially lower than that with the arbitrary mapping factor.

The second step of the structural models was to extend the models further by adding fluid intelligence and crystallised intelligence. In the extension of model 1 (called model 1–wmc-int) the general RT factor correlated $r = -.71$ with the WMC factor and $r = -.50$ with the fluid intelligence factor. The WMC factor correlated $r = .81$ with the fluid intelligence factor. Fluid and crystallised intelligence were correlated $r = .75$. The WMC factor and the general RT factor were correlated with crystallised intelligence $r = .50$ and $r = -.50$, respectively. The fit of this model was acceptable, with $\chi^2(160) = 207.10$, $p = .007$, CFI = .959, RMSEA = .051, AIC = 307.10. The extension of model 3a (model 3a–wmc-int) is displayed in Figure 5. The fit of this model was better, $\chi^2(158) = 191.88$, $p = .034$, CFI = .971, RMSEA = .044, AIC = 295.88. Although there is no large improvement compared with model 1–wmc-int, the decision in favour of the nested-factor model (model 3a–wmc-int) is unequivocally supported by all fit indices. Descriptively, the correlations met the expectations. The relation between WMC and fluid intelligence was high but not perfect. Fixing the correlation between both factors to unity and constraining correlations of these factors with other factors to equality in each case impaired the fit substantially, $\Delta\chi^2(4) = 32.61$, $p < .001$. The correlation between the WMC factor and the arbitrary mapping factor was very high; fixing this correlation to unity and constraining correlations of these factors with other factors to equality in each case again led to a just significant loss of fit, $\Delta\chi^2(4) = 9.84$, $p = .043$. Finally, the arbitrary mapping factor descriptively had a higher correlation with the WMC factor, with fluid intelligence, and with crystallised intelligence than the general RT factor. Constraining these three pairs of correlations to be equal so that the arbitrary factor and the general RT factor had identical correlations with the other three factors respectively led to a significant loss of fit, $\Delta\chi^2(3) = 23.26$, $p < .001$.

The validity of the results presented could be compromised by the relatively small sample size. The problems associated with small sample sizes are convergence problems and unreliable estimation of parameters. In order to increase the confidence in the models we computed bootstrap analyses for the three models we accept as providing viable accounts of the data (models 3a, 3a–wmc, and 3a–wmc-int). Running 10,000 bootstrap samples for each of these models with default convergence criteria and relaxed iteration limit was associated with convergence problems in 0.19%, 0%, and 0% respectively. The Bollen-Stine corrected p-values show close fit for all three models ($p = .125$, $p = .078$, and $p = .323$ for models 3a, 3a–wmc, and 3a–wmc-int, respectively). The confidence intervals around factor covariances in all three accepted models are sufficiently small to exclude zero covariances as plausible results in all cases. Because bootstrapping is a good method if the multivariate normality assumption is violated—which is almost inevitable when analysing reaction times—these analyses further increase the confidence in the multivariate results substantially.

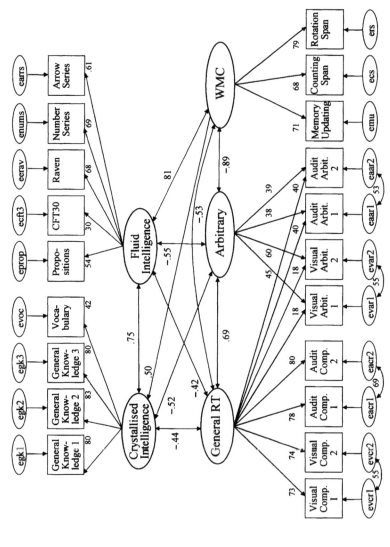

Figure 5. Structural model of general RT, arbitrary mappings RT, working memory, fluid and crystallised intelligence (model 3a–wmc-int). Large ovals represent latent factors, small ovals represent error terms, and rectangles represent manifest variables.

42

DISCUSSION

In this study we tested one hypothesis about why WMC is highly correlated with various indicators of mental speed, among them choice RT tasks. Since WMC is strongly correlated with reasoning ability, our results are also relevant for the relationship of reasoning ability or fluid intelligence with the speed of simple cognitive operations. Our basic assumption is that WMC reflects the ability to establish and maintain temporary bindings between arbitrary representational elements. We applied this assumption to choice RT tasks by assuming that WMC is needed to establish and maintain bindings between stimulus and response representations. Such bindings will be particularly important when the mapping between stimuli and responses is arbitrary, so that the cognitive system cannot use preexisting associations to translate a stimulus into its corresponding response. We therefore predicted that reaction times on choice RT tasks with arbitrary S–R mappings would be correlated higher with measures of WMC than RTs from tasks with compatible S–R mappings. The hypothesis was tested in three steps.

The first step was to fit a measurement model to the RT data that incorporated a factorial distinction between general speed on choice RT tasks on the one hand, and the specific variance due to an arbitrary S–R mapping on the other hand. We succeeded to establish such a measurement model after introducing theoretically motivated constraints on the loadings. This model provided a better fit to the data than a model with only a single general factor accounting for all the common variance among the RT variables. We should add, however, that the general-factor model was not unambiguously rejected by the data and a nested-factor model without constraints on the loadings (model 2) did not fit significantly better. Therefore, we are not completely confident that RTs from tasks with arbitrary S–R mappings actually reflect a substantial amount of specific variance that is not shared with RTs from tasks with compatible mappings.

The second step was to test the relationship of the two RT factors with a latent factor reflecting WMC. The structural equation models confirmed our prediction that WMC was more strongly related to the factor reflecting RT with arbitrary mapping than with the factor reflecting general choice RT speed. In fact, we were barely able to reject the hypothesis that the correlation between WMC and the arbitrary mapping factor was perfect. This result is remarkable for two reasons. First, it demonstrates a correlation between a factor based on latency measures with a factor based on accuracy measures. To our knowledge, there is no precedent in the literature of such a high correlation between a latency-based and an accuracy-based factor. Second, the arbitrary mapping factor represented the residuals of RTs after extracting the variance of a general RT factor. The residuals are relatively pure measures of the costs associated with an arbitrary mapping compared to a compatible mapping as baseline. This is what makes residuals or other cost indices (e.g., difference scores) from experimental tasks particularly attractive to researchers. Unfortunately, previous attempts to correlate intelligence or WMC with residuals or cost indices from RT tasks (e.g., estimates of the slope in the Sternberg task, or of switching costs in the task-set switching paradigm) have been largely unsuccessful (Lohman, 1994; Neubauer, 1997; Oberauer, Süß, Wilhelm, & Wittmann, 2003). The finding of a nearly perfect correlation between WMC and the residuals of RTs from arbitrary mapping therefore provides particularly strong evidence that WMC is related specifically to whatever sets RT tasks with arbitrary mappings apart from RT tasks with compatible mappings. In our view, this is the requirement to establish arbitrary S–R bindings. We want to add, however, that with larger samples it should be expected that, *ceteris paribus*, there will be a statistically unequivocal distinction between the arbitrary RT factor and WMC.

Nonetheless, the correlation of WMC with the general RT factor was surprisingly high. How can we explain this? If we assume that the cognitive system deals with compatible S–R mappings through the associative path exclusively, we should not expect any correlation between WMC and RTs from tasks with compatible mappings. The RTs should then depend only on the strength of the associations between stimuli and responses, and on the basic speed of information transmission along such associations. The exclusivity assumption, however, is unrealistic. When confronted with a speeded task, people will most likely mobilise all resources available to them. As long as their working memory is not completely occupied by other activities, they will bring its capacity to bear on the task by establishing temporary bindings between stimuli and responses even when the mapping is compatible. People then have both the associative and the rule-based path available. We need only assume that the two paths operate in parallel, and it follows that RTs will be shorter when using both paths than with just one of them.[3] Therefore, using WMC to establish S–R bindings pays off even when the S–R mapping is compatible. This implies that people with higher WMC will benefit even on tasks with compatible mappings: The contribution of the rule-based path to overall performance is faster for them. Variance in the efficiency of the rule-based path is only one of two sources of variance that affect RT on compatible tasks, whereas it is the only source of variance for RT on arbitrary tasks. Therefore, we should expect WMC to be correlated with RTs on compatible tasks, but to a lesser degree than with RTs on arbitrary tasks. This is exactly what we found.

---

[3] There are two models to consider here. In one, the outputs of the two paths race against each other; the one who finishes first determines the response and its time. With two horses in the race, the average finishing time is shorter than with a single horse. The other model assumes that both paths continuously contribute evidence to a common accumulator. The combined output of two paths converging on the same response obviously brings the accumulator to threshold faster than the output from a single path.

In a third step, we extended our structural model to integrate fluid and crystallised intelligence. In line with theories distinguishing two very general group factors below a higher order general factor (Carroll, 1993) we used a model with correlated group factors for fluid and crystallised intelligence. Fluid intelligence was strongly correlated with WMC, replicating previous studies (Kane et al., 2004; Süß et al., 2002; see also Ackerman, Beier, & Boyle, 2005; Oberauer, Schulze, Wilhelm, & Süß, 2005a; see also Cornoldi, 2006 this issue, for a theoretical discussion). In addition, fluid intelligence was strongly correlated with the arbitrary mapping factor. Although fluid intelligence was also strongly correlated with the general RT factor the pattern is descriptively similar to the findings with WMC. The arbitrary mapping factor was more highly correlated with the WMC factor, the fluid intelligence factor, and the crystallised intelligence factor than the general RT factor. Constraining both factors to have relations of equal magnitude to the three other factors impaired model fit. Therefore the arbitrary mapping factor was more strongly correlated with relevant criteria than the general RT factor. Pending replication, we tentatively extend our hypothesis to fluid intelligence: Fluid intelligence (in particular reasoning ability) is strongly correlated with choice RT because they share the requirement of building and maintaining temporary bindings. In other words: Bindings are the glue that binds WMC, fluid intelligence, and choice reaction speed together.

A single study is clearly not sufficient to establish a new explanation of the nature of the common variance among WMC, choice RT speed, and fluid intelligence. Our study has several limitations. One is the restricted sample of tasks to measure the effect of S–R compatibility. Both our tasks involved four manual responses and both used a spatial dimension as the relevant feature dimension. Moreover, because we wanted the compatible and the arbitrary task versions to differ in as little as possible apart from the nature of the S–R mapping, we used arbitrary mapping tasks in which the relevant stimulus dimension (i.e., spatial location of the stimuli in the visual task, spatial orientation of the spoken words in the auditory task) overlapped with a response dimension (i.e., spatial location of the keys). In other words, dimensional overlap was high in both the compatible and the arbitrary mapping tasks. This implies that there is an associative mapping from stimuli to responses even in the tasks with arbitrary mapping, only that the instructed mapping does not match the preexisting mapping. The tasks with arbitrary mapping therefore might involve an element of conflict between the rule-based path and the associative path, and speed on the arbitrary mapping tasks might reflect in part the ability to overcome this conflict. One question for future research therefore is whether our results generalise to tasks without dimensional overlap, and hence without conflict between the rule-based and the associative path. Tasks without dimensional overlap necessarily involve an arbitrary mapping between stimuli and responses and therefore should also correlate higher with WMC and reasoning than compatible-mapping tasks. Testing this prediction it is important to distinguish our account from that of Engle et al. (1999), who would predict a relatively high correlation with WMC for RT tasks involving conflict, and hence for tasks with dimensional overlap and arbitrary mapping, but not for RT tasks without dimensional overlap.

Another limitation of our study is the relatively small sample size. One consequence of this is that all estimates of relations between manifest and latent variables and between any two latent variables are associated with large standard errors. Consequently, there are substantial confidence intervals around the path coefficients. All the reported coefficients are distinct from zero. When two coefficients are tested against each other, however, or when a model with constraints on unstandardised loadings is compared to a model without such constraints, it is important to bear in mind that the power to detect differences can be very low. Hence, absence of statistically significant differences does not imply absence of differences in these or similar data. Finally, the results presented here are without precedence. In order to increase the confidence in the conclusions a replication and possibly an extension is desirable.

Despite these methodological issues we consider our results very encouraging. Bringing together strategies of experimental and correlational research we were able to shed some light on the question why WMC and reasoning ability are strongly related to speed in relatively simple RT tasks. The relationship seems to be particularly strong when the RT task relies on an arbitrary S–R mapping, supporting our hypothesis that the ability to establish and maintain temporary bindings is the common denominator of choice RT tasks, WMC, and reasoning (Oberauer et al., in press).

Our results also bring some substance to the complexity hypothesis regarding the relationship between RT and intelligence. Several authors have concluded from their reviews of available evidence that the correlation between speed measures and intelligence test scores increases as a function of complexity of the speed task (e.g., Danthiir et al., 2005a; Jensen, 1998), at least up to a point on the complexity continuum. *Complexity* in this context is not used as a theoretical concept—it is simply defined as the mean reaction time in a given speed task or an experimental condition. There are various factors that affect the mean RT in a speeded task—some of them might also affect the correlation of RT with intelligence or WMC, whereas others might not. Experimentally disentangling these factors and their effect on the RT–intelligence link could help to move the complexity hypothesis from an empirical generalisation to a theoretically motivated hypothesis. Our study is a start in that direction. The nature of the S–R mapping is one particularly powerful factor affecting mean RTs, and hence the task's complexity. We have shown that this factor indeed affects the relationship between RT and WMC, and probably also the relationship between RT and fluid and crystallised intelligence. So far, this has not been demonstrated for any other specific factor affecting the complexity of RT tasks. Therefore, we believe that our research represents a substantial step toward understanding the relationship between RT and complex cognitive abilities. It provides an example for how to unpack the "complexity" of RT tasks by experimentally varying individual factors that affect mean RTs and investigating how they affect the correlation of RTs with intelligence and WMC. This research strategy will certainly help to distinguish between the various explanations for the link between mental speed and complex cognitive abilities. It might eventually even help to understand the nature of intelligence.

REFERENCES

Ackerman, P. L., Beier, M. E., & Boyle, M. O. (2002). Individual differences in working memory within a nomological network of cognitive and perceptual speed abilities. *Journal of Experimental Psychology: General, 131*, 567–589.

Ackerman, P. L., Beier, M. E., & Boyle, M. O. (2005). Working memory and intelligence: The same or different constructs? *Psychological Bulletin, 131*, 30–60.

Amthauer, R., Brocke, B., Liepmann, D., & Beauducel, A. (1999). *Intelligenz-Struktur-Test 2000* [Intelligence Structure Test 2000]. Göttingen, Germany: Hogrefe.

Beauducel, A., & Kersting, M. (2002). Fluid and crystallized intelligence and the Berlin Model of Intelligence Structure (BIS). *European Journal of Psychological Assessment, 18*, 97–112.

Barrouillet, P., Bernardin, S., & Camos, V. (2004). Time constraints and resource sharing in adults' working memory spans. *Journal of Experimental Psychology: General, 133*, 83–100.

Borella, E., Carretti, B., & Mammarella, I. M. (2006). Do working memory and susceptibility to interference predict individual differences in fluid intelligence? *European Journal of Cognitive Psychology, 18*(1), 51–69.

Carroll, J. B. (1993). *Human cognitive abilities: A survey of factor-analytic studies*. Cambridge, MA: Cambridge University Press.

Cattell, R. B., & Weiss, R. H. (1971). *Grundintelligenztest Skala 3 (CFT 3)* [Culture Fair Test 3]. Göttingen, Germany: Hogrefe.

Cohen, J., & Cohen, P. (1983). Applied multiple regression/correlation analysis for the behavioral sciences (2nd ed.). Hillsdale, NJ: Lawrence Erlbaum Associates, Inc.

Cohen, J. D., & Servan-Schreiber, D. (1992). Context, cortex, and dopamine: A connectionist approach to behavior and biology in schizophrenia. *Psychological Review, 99*, 45–77.

Conway, A. R. A., Cowan, N., Bunting, M. F., Therriault, D. J., & Minkoff, S. R. B. (2002). A latent variable analysis of working memory capacity, short-term memory capacity, processing speed, and general fluid intelligence. *Intelligence, 30*, 163–183.

Cornoldi, C. (2006). The contribution of cognitive psychology to the study of human intelligence *European Journal of Cognitive Psychology, 18*(1), 1–17.

Danthiir, V., Roberts, R. D., Schulze, R., & Wilhelm, O. (2005a). Mental speed: On frameworks, paradigms, and a platform for the future. In O. Wilhelm & R. W. Engle (Ed.), *Understanding and measuring intelligence* (pp. 27–46). Thousand Oaks, CA: Sage.

Danthiir, V., Wilhelm, O., & Schacht, A. (2005b). Decision speed in intelligence tasks: Correctly an ability? *Psychology Science, 47*, 200–229.

Dempster, A. P., Laird, N. M., & Rubin, D. B. (1977). Maximum likelihood estimation from incomplete data via the EM algorithm (with discussion). *Journal of the Royal Statistical Society B, 39*, 1–38.

De Ribaupierre, A., & Lecerf, T. (2006). Relationships between working memory and intelligence from a developmental perspective: Convergent evidence from a neo-Piagetian and a psychometric approach. *European Journal of Cognitive Psychology, 18*(1), 109–137.

Dutta, A., & Proctor, R. W. (1992). Persistence of stimulus–response compatibility effects with extended practice. *Journal of Experimental Psychology: Learning, Memory, and Cognition, 18,* 801–809.

Elliott, E. M., Barrilleaux, K. M., & Cowan, N. (2006). Individual differences in the ability to avoid distracting sounds. *European Journal of Cognitive Psychology, 18*(1), 90–108.

Engle, R. W., Kane, M. J., & Tuholski, S. W. (1999). Individual differences in working memory capacity and what they tell us about controlled attention, general fluid intelligence, and functions of the prefrontal cortex. In A. Miyake & P. Shah (Eds.), *Models of working memory: Mechanisms of active maintenance and executive control* (pp. 102–134). Cambridge, UK: Cambridge University Press.

Fry, A., & Hale, S. (1996). Processing speed, working memory, and fluid intelligence. *Psychological Science, 7,* 237–241.

Gustafsson, J. E. (1988). Hierarchical models of individual differences in cognitive abilities. In R. J. Sternberg (Eds.), *Advances in the psychology of human intelligence* (Vol. 4, pp. 35–71). Hillsdale, NJ: Lawrence Erlbaum Associates, Inc.

Halford, G. S., Wilson, W. H., & Phillips, S. (1998). Processing capacity defined by relational complexity: Implications for comparative, developmental, and cognitive psychology. *Behavioral and Brain Sciences, 21,* 803–864.

Hu, L. T., & Bentler, P. M. (1995). Evaluating model fit. In R. H. Hoyle (Ed.), *Structural equation modelling: Concepts, issues, and applications* (pp. 76–99). London: Sage.

Hu, L. T., & Bentler, P. M. (1999). Cutoff criteria for fit indexes in covariance structure analysis: convenctional criteria versus new alternatives. *Structural Equation Modeling, 6,* 1–55.

Hummel, J. E., & Holyoak, K. J. (1997). Distributed representations of structure: A theory of analogical access and mapping. *Psychological Review, 104,* 427–466.

Jäger, A. O., & Althoff, K. (1983). *Der WILDE-Intelligenz-Test: Ein Strukturdiagnostikum* [The WILDE intelligence test: A structural test]. Göttingen, Germany: Hogrefe.

Jensen, A. R. (1993). Spearman's g: Links between psychometrics and biology. *Annals of the New York Academy of Sciences, 702,* 103–129.

Jensen, A. R. (1998). *The g factor.* Westport, CT: Praeger.

Kail, R., & Salthouse, T. A. (1994). Processing speed as a mental capacity. *Acta Psychologica, 86,* 199–225.

Kane, M. J., & Engle, R. W. (2002). The role of prefrontal cortex in working-memory capacity, executive attention, and general fluid intelligence: An individual-differences perspective. *Psychonomic Bulletin and Review, 9,* 637–671.

Kane, M. J., & Engle, R. W. (2003). Working-memory capacity and the control of attention: The contributions of goal neglect, response competition, and task set to Stroop interference. *Journal of Experimental Psychology: General, 132,* 47–70.

Kane, M. J., Hambrick, D. Z., Tuholski, S. W., Wilhelm, O., Payne, T. W., & Engle, R. E. (2004). The generality of working-memory capacity: A latent-variable approach to verbal and visuo-spatial memory span and reasoning. *Journal of Experimental Psychology: General, 133,* 189–217.

Kornblum, S., Hasbroucq, T., & Osman, A. M. (1990). Dimensional overlap: Cognitive basis for stimulus–response-compatibility—a model and taxonomy. *Psychological Review, 97,* 253–270.

Kranzler, J. H., & Jensen, A. R. (1991). The nature of psychometric g: Unitary process or a number of independent processes? *Intelligence, 15,* 397–422.

Kyllonen, P. C. (1994). Aptitude testing inspired by information processing: A test of the four-sources model. *Journal of General Psychology, 120,* 375–405.

Kyllonen, P. C., & Christal, R. E. (1990). Reasoning ability is (little more than) working-memory capacity?! *Intelligence, 14,* 389–433.

Lewandowsky, S., Duncan, M., & Brown, G. D. A. (2004). Time does not cause forgetting in short-term serial recall. *Psychonomic Bulletin and Review, 11,* 771–790.

Li, S. C., & Sikström, S. (2002). Integrative neurocomputational perspectives on cognitive aging, neuromodulation, and representation. *Neuroscience and Biobehavioral Reviews, 26,* 795–808.

Lien, M.-C., & Proctor, R. W. (2002). Stimulus–response compatibility and psychological refractory period effects: Implications for response selection. *Psychonomic Bulletin and Review, 9*, 212–238.

Lohman, D. F. (1994). Component scores as residual variation (or why the intercept correlates best). *Intelligence, 19*, 1–11.

Marsh, H. W., Balla, J. R., & McDonald, R. P. (1988). Goodness of fit indexes in confirmatory factor analysis: The effect of sample size. *Psychological Bulletin, 103*, 391–410.

Miller, E. M. (1994). Intelligence and brain myelination: A hypothesis. *Personality and Individual Differences, 17*, 803–832.

Miller, L. T., & Vernon, P. A. (1992). The general factor in short-term memory, intelligence, and reaction time. *Intelligence, 16*, 5–29.

Neubauer, A. C. (1997). The mental speed approach in the assessment of intelligence. In W. Tomic (Ed.), *Advances in cognition and education: Reflections on the concept of intelligence* (pp. 149–173). Greenwich, CT: JAI Press.

Neubauer, A. C., & Bucik, V. (1996). The mental speed–IQ relationship: Unitary or modular? *Intelligence, 22*, 23–48.

Oberauer, K. (2002). Access to information in working memory: Exploring the focus of attention. *Journal of Experimental Psychology: Learning, Memory, and Cognition, 28*, 411–421.

Oberauer, K., Demmrich, A., Mayr, U., & Kliegl, R. (2001). Dissociating retention and access in working memory: An age-comparative study of mental arithmetic. *Memory and Cognition, 29*, 18–33.

Oberauer, K., Schulze, R., Wilhelm, O., & Süß, H.-M. (2005a). Working memory and intelligence—their correlation and their relation: A comment on Ackerman, Beier, and Boyle (2005). *Psychological Bulletin, 131*, 61–65.

Oberauer, K., Süß, H-M., Schulze, R., Wilhelm, O., & Wittmann, W. W. (2000). Working memory capacity: Facets of a cognitive ability construct. *Personality and Individual Differences, 29*, 1017–1045.

Oberauer, K., Süß, H.-M., Wilhelm, O., & Sander, N. (in press). Individual differences in working memory capacity and reasoning ability. In A. R. A. Conway, C. Jarrold, M. J. Kane, A. Miyake, & J. N. Towse (Eds.), *Variation in working memory*. New York: Oxford University Press.

Oberauer, K., Süß, H.-M., Wilhelm, O., & Wittmann, W. W. (2003). The multiple faces of working memory—storage, processing, supervision, and coordination. *Intelligence, 31*, 167–193.

Oberauer, K., Wilhelm, O., & Schmiedek, F. (2005b). Experimental strategies in multivariate research. In A. Beauducel, B. Biehl, M. Bosniak, W. Conrad, G. Schönberger, & D. Wagener (Eds.), *Festschrift on multivariate research strategies*. Maastricht, The Netherlands: Shaker Publishing.

Raven, J. C., Raven, J. E., & Court, J. H. (1998). *Progressive matrices*. Oxford, UK: Oxford Psychologists Press.

Roberts, R. D., & Stankov, L. (1999). Individual differences in speed of mental processing and human cognitive abilities: Toward a taxonomic model. *Learning and Individual Differences, 11*, 1–120.

Roberts, R. D., & Stankov, L. (2001). *Omnibus Screening Protocol*. Sydney: E-ntelligent Testing Products.

Saito, S., & Miyake, A. (2004). An evaluation of the task switching account of working memory span scores: Evidence against a temporal decay assumption. *Journal of Memory and Language, 50*, 425–443.

Salthouse, T. A. (1992). Influence of processing speed on adult age differences in working memory. *Acta Psychologica, 84*, 95–110.

Salthouse, T. A. (1996). The processing speed theory of adult age differences in cognition. *Psychological Review, 103*, 403–428.

Schafer, J. L., & Graham, J. W. (2002). Missing data: Our view of the state of the art. *Psychological Methods, 7*, 147–177.

Shah, P., & Miyake, A. (1996). The separability of working memory resources for spatial thinking and language processing: An individual differences approach. *Journal of Experimental Psychology: General, 125*, 4–27.

SPSS, Inc. (2004). *SPSS missing value analysis 12.0.* Chicago: Author.

Süß, H.-M., Oberauer, K., Wittmann, W. W., Wilhelm, O., & Schulze, R. (2002). Working memory capacity explains reasoning ability—and a little bit more. *Intelligence, 30*, 261–288.

Undheim, J. O., & Gustafsson, J.-E. (1987). The hierarchical organization of cognitive abilities: Restoring general intelligence through the use of linear structural relations. *Multivariate Behavior Research, 22*, 149–171.

Vernon, P. A. (1983). Speed of information processing and general intelligence. *Intelligence, 7*, 53–70.

Vernon, P. A., & Mori, M. (1992). Intelligence, reaction times, and peripheral nerve conduction velocity. *Intelligence, 16*, 273–288.

Vernon, P. A., Nador, S., & Kantor, L. (1985). Reaction time and speed of processing: Their relationship to timed and untimed measures of intelligence. *Intelligence, 9*, 357–374.

Wickett, J. C., & Vernon, P. A. (1994). Peripheral nerve conduction velocity, reaction time, and intelligence: An attempt to replicate Vernon and Mori (1992). *Intelligence, 18*, 127–131.

Wilhelm, O. (2005). Measuring reasoning ability. In O. Wilhelm & R. W. Engle (Eds.), *Understanding and measuring intelligence* (pp. 373–392). London: Sage.

Wilhelm, O., & Schulze, R. (2002). The relation of speeded and unspeeded reasoning with mental speed. *Intelligence, 30*, 537–554.

EUROPEAN JOURNAL OF COGNITIVE PSYCHOLOGY
2006, 18 (1), 51–69

Do working memory and susceptibility to interference predict individual differences in fluid intelligence?

Erika Borella, Barbara Carretti, and Irene C. Mammarella

Department of General Psychology, Padova, Italy

In the current study we examined the relationship between working memory capacity, inhibition/susceptibility to interference and fluid intelligence, measured by the Raven's Progressive Matrices (PM38), comparing groups of young (aged 18–35), young-old (aged 65–74), and old-old (aged 75–86) participants. Groups were administered two working memory tasks tapping into different mechanisms involved in working memory. The ability to control for irrelevant information was measured both considering memory errors (intrusion errors) in a working memory task and an index of susceptibility to interference obtained with a variant of the Brown-Peterson task. Regression analyses showed that the classical working memory measure was the most potent predictors of the Raven's score. Susceptibility to interference and intrusions errors contributed, but to a lower extent, to the Raven explained variance. These results confirm that working memory shares cognitive aspects with the fluid intelligence measure considered, whereas the role of inhibition to Raven scores is still in need of better evidence.

Working memory refers to the ability to temporarily maintain information for use in ongoing mental operations (Baddeley & Hitch, 1974). Since its introduction, Baddeley and Hitch's model has been exposed to several reconceptualisations. Some authors suggest that working memory has to be considered as a unitary system regulated by attentional resources (e.g., Engle, Tuholski, Laughlin, & Conway, 1999), while others stress the modality specific nature of some of its processes (Baddeley & Logie, 1999; Cornoldi & Vecchi, 2003). Nevertheless it is possible to draw some common points between the various models proposed (Miyake & Shah, 1999). Firstly, it is well-accepted that the working memory capacity is limited in nature and its limitations are due to different factors such as trace decay (Baddeley & Logie, 1999), susceptibility to interference (Engle et al., 1999; Hasher & Zacks, 1988; see also Elliott, Barrilleaux, & Cowan, 2006 this issue) and processing speed (Salthouse & Meinz, 1995; see also de Ribaupierre & Lecerf, 2006 this issue; Wilhelm & Oberauer,

Correspondence should be addressed to Erika Borella, Dipartimento di Psicologia Generale, Via Venezia, 8, 35131 Padova, Italy. Email: erika.borella@unipd.it

2006 this issue). Secondly, the management of attentional resources is a distinctive feature of working memory functioning and it could be considered the point of conjunction between working memory and complex cognitive processes, such as reading comprehension (Daneman & Merikle, 1996; De Beni, Palladino, Pazzaglia, & Cornoldi, 1998), problem solving (Passolunghi, Cornoldi, & De Liberto, 1999; Passolunghi & Siegel, 2001), note taking (Kiewra & Benton, 1988), and fluid intelligence abilities (Engle et al., 1999; Kane et al., 2004).

Within this framework, working memory capacity appears as an important source of individual differences. Indeed, a large number of studies have shown that working memory capacity is useful in distinguishing learning-disabled children from normal students (Swanson & Ashbaker, 2000; for a review, see Swanson & Siegel, 2001) and older adults from younger adults (Jenkins, Myerson, Hale, & Fry, 1999). One of the researchers' aims has been to determine which aspects of working memory better account for these differences in performance. Individual differences in working memory can be conceptualised in terms of the ability to monitor attentional resources (Engle et al., 1999), the amount of available resources (Daneman & Tardif, 1987; Engle et al., 1999), and the efficacy of the inhibitory mechanisms (May, Hasher, & Kane, 1999). In the last few years, the latter explanation has gained greater relevance (Friedman & Miyake, 2004).

According to Hasher and Zacks (1988), inhibition is involved in different kinds of control functions that allow people: to determine which activated representations gain entrance into working memory, to suppress those representations that are no longer relevant for the current goal, and to prevent predominant but inappropriate responses (Hasher & Zacks, 1988; Hasher, Zacks, & May, 1999). When inhibitory mechanisms are inefficient, a broader range of information will enter in working memory. Information no longer relevant continues to remain active and the frequency of overt inappropriate responses and of irrelevant or marginally relevant momentary thoughts will increase (Hasher, Quig, & May, 1997). As a consequence working memory becomes saturated. Several studies have shown that older adults, as well as low working memory span young adults (Conway & Engle, 1994; Kane & Engle, 2000; Rosen & Engle, 1997, 1998), are less likely to inhibit irrelevant items and are more likely to retrieve them (e.g., Hamm & Hasher, 1992; Hartman & Dusek, 1994; Hartman & Hasher, 1991). Furthermore, Engle and colleagues have demonstrated that the performance of low span participants under interference conditions can be simulated by dividing the attention of high span participants, consistently with the idea that the attention-control ability is the source of individual differences between high and low working memory participants. Thus in these studies, the presence of interfering material in working memory is interpreted in terms of inefficient inhibitory mechanisms that produce proactive interference.

Several researchers, using the Brown-Peterson task, have shown larger proactive interference effects in older adults compared to younger adults (Lustig, May, & Hasher, 2001; May et al., 1999; Winocur & Moscovitch, 1983). Unfortunately, the data are not entirely consistent. Indeed some authors have shown a higher susceptibility to interference for the elderly (Schonfield, Davidson, & Jones, 1983), while others have not (Craik, 1977; Dobbs, Aubrey, & Rule, 1989). This inconsistency could be due to differences in the procedure used. The Brown-Peterson task requires listening to lists of words and subsequently recalling the words contained in the lists; in addition, between the encoding and the retrieval phases, participants are usually required to do a rehearsal prevention task that allows the prolonging of the retention interval. In some cases the interval duration can go beyond the typical interval for working memory tasks. This can also have a consequence on the age effects (Inman & Parkinson, 1983), since it has been shown that the elderly are less impaired in long term memory recall and by long term memory interference. Conversely one would expect older adults to show a poorer recall and a higher susceptibility to interference compared to younger participants when recall relies on the working memory components.

Another measure that is often considered as an expression of the efficient/inefficient inhibitory mechanism is the number of intrusion errors in a working memory task (De Beni et al., 1998). This measure is conceived of as the ability to manage information currently in the focus of working memory on the basis of its relevance to the task goal (Carretti, Cornoldi, De Beni, & Palladino, 2004; De Beni et al., 1998; Palladino, Cornoldi, De Beni, & Pazzaglia, 2001). It has been suggested that a poor performance in working memory tasks is associated with an increased number of intrusion errors and that the probability of intrusions of irrelevant items is a function of the degree of item activation: The more the items are activated (stressed intrusion), the more they are likely to be erroneously included in the set of items to be recalled (De Beni et al., 1998; Oberauer, 2001; Osaka, Nishizaki, Komori, & Osaka, 2002). Some authors have shown a specific increase in stressed intrusion errors in the older adults' performance (De Beni & Palladino, 2004; Palladino & De Beni, 1999); however, others have not (McCabe & Hartman, 2003; Schelstraete & Hupet, 2002).

Palladino et al. (2001) suggested a distinction between intrusion errors that arise from items belonging to the list currently being processed (i.e., intrusion of items that are in the focus of attention) and intrusion of items that belong to the previous lists (probably due to some proactive interference effect). Palladino et al. highlighted that young participants with reading comprehension difficulties made more intrusions of the first kind, concluding that they had a specific impairment in managing information in working memory. Also in the case of elderly participants, De Beni and Palladino (2004) showed that intrusions of items from the current lists were more frequent in the older adults' performance than other kinds of errors. These data suggest that interference from a preceding list or from the same list in a short-term memory task do not necessarily measure the same type of susceptibility to interference.

WORKING MEMORY, PROACTIVE INTERFERENCE, AND INTELLIGENCE

A common assumption of working memory models is that working memory is at the service of complex cognition (Miyake & Shah, 1999). The maintenance aspects of the working memory capacity together with its processing functions allow to store and manipulate information during complex cognitive activities. Engle et al. (1999) argued that individual differences in performance on complex span tasks are primarily due to differences in the central executive component of working memory, whereas in the case of simple span task performance they are primarily due to differences in domain-specific abilities such as chunking and rehearsal (in the case of verbal span tasks). This reflection was confirmed by a structural equation modelling analysis that demonstrated that a latent variable derived from the complex span task predicts general fluid intelligence performance (measured by Raven's and Cattell's tests), whereas the latent variable derived from the simple span tasks does not. Furthermore, Engle et al. (1999) found that in removing the variance common to the working memory latent variable and the short-term memory latent variable, the relationship between working memory and fluid intelligence was still significant. In addition, Kane et al. (2004) demonstrated that this relation was independent of the type of material used (verbal or visuospatial). They provided evidence that the increase in attentional resources necessary to carry out typical working memory span tasks causes the disappearance of domain specific differences, since all the working memory measures are loaded on a single general common factor (see also Cornoldi, 2006 this issue).

Taken together these findings suggest that the request of the executive control is critical to the utility of the working memory span in predicting complex cognition (Conway, Cowan, Bunting, Therriault, & Minkoff, 2002; Cornoldi & Vecchi, 2003; Kane & Engle, 2002).

More recently, a meta-analysis conducted by Ackerman, Beier, and Boyle (2005) showed that working memory and fluid intelligence are not isomorphic constructs (see also de Ribaupierre & Lecerf, 2006 this issue) contrary to the hypothesis advanced by Kane and Engle (2002). In addition, Ackerman et al. did not confirm the complete amodal nature of the relationship between working memory and fluid intelligence since they found that the correlations between tasks that had an overlapping content for working memory and fluid intelligence were higher than for nonoverlapping tasks.

However, it is not clear which specific function of the central executive is involved in the relationship with fluid intelligence. In the past few years, in contrast with a unitary view of the central executive, data supporting the possibility of fractionating the central executive has been collected (Letho, 1996;

Miyake et al., 2000). Furthermore, it has been demonstrated that different executive functions make different contributions in explaining complex task performance (see Miyake et al., 2000).

From another viewpoint, Dempster and Corkill (1999) suggested that inhibitory mechanisms play an important role in predicting fluid intelligence performance. Their proposal was to show that differences in the Raven's performance could be due to the efficiency/deficit in controlling previously learned information or previously used rules. Thus a low scoring participant would be less susceptible to proactive interference than a high scoring participant. Though correlational studies with young participants have confirmed Dempster's hypothesis (Brewin & Beaton, 2002), the evidence collected with older participants is discrepant. As regards the relationship between fluid intelligence and age, there are numerous studies indicating that there are large adult age differences on the Raven test, with correlations normally ranging from about − .49 to − .64 (Babcock, 1994; Hooper, Hooper, & Colbert, 1984; Schultz, Kaye, & Hoyer, 1980). Several researchers have offered possible explanations for age-related differences in the Raven score, such as differences in memory (Bromley, 1953; Chown, 1961), in the ability to determine relevant dimensions of the problem (Anderson, Hartley, Bye, Harber, & White, 1986), and in the ability to ignore irrelevant dimensions (Hoyer, Rebok, & Sved, 1979).

An interesting contribution to the analysis of the relationship between working memory and fluid intelligence was made by Carpenter, Just, and Shell (1990). The authors developed two simulation models to specify the processes engaged in solving the Raven's Advanced Progressive Matrices problems (Raven, 1965): the FAIRAVEN and BETTERAVEN, which correspond respectively to the median or the highest performance. According to these authors, the FAIRAVEN needed the inclusion of the working memory construct, in order to store rules and partial products in an active state thus available for further manipulation. However, the BETTERAVEN performance was simulated adding the, so-called, "goal monitoring module" that allows the setting of strategic goals, monitoring of progress towards them, and adjustment of the goals if necessary. Thus, to reach the highest performance in the Raven test the working memory measure is to be considered necessary but not sufficient for the BETTERAVEN performance. They concluded that one of the main distinctions between higher scoring participants and lower scoring participants was the higher scoring participants' ability to successfully generate and manage their problem-solving rules in working memory.

Objective of the study

To summarise, several authors found evidence of a relationship between resistance to interference and fluid intelligence scores (Brewin & Beaton, 2002; Dempster & Corkill, 1999). At the same time, recent research showed that people with high susceptibility to interference have lower working memory capacity (Friedman & Miyake, 2004; Kane & Engle, 2000). Thus, it is possible to argue that resistance to interference could represent a crucial aspect both in working memory task and in fluid intelligence measures. However, different measures of working memory and susceptibility to interference in working memory do not seem to tap identical processes.

The objective of the current study was to examine the independent role of working memory and susceptibility to interference in the Raven's test performance, deeply analysing which processes make working memory important for fluid intelligence. To this aim participants of different ages were compared. Groups were administered two working memory tasks tapping into different mechanisms involved in working memory functioning. In the first task (derived from De Beni et al., 1998), in which the procedure used was the same as in the most classical working memory tasks (like the listening span; Daneman & Carpenter, 1980), participants were required to simultaneously maintain and process information, selecting relevant items and suppressing irrelevant ones. In the second task, a modified version of the Brown-Peterson paradigm, participants were invited to recall a series of lists, and the effect of susceptibility to proactive interference on recall was also measured (Kane & Engle, 2000).

METHOD

Participants

Two age groups of participants, 30 young adults and 60 older adults took part in this study (see Table 1). The young participants were aged between 18 and 27 years (25 females and 5 males) and were University of Padova undergraduates; the older participants were aged between 65 and 86 years. The group of older adults was spilt into two groups: Participants with an age range of 64–74 years' old comprised the young-old group ($n = 30$; 23 females, 7 males), while participants older than 74 years were allocated to the old-old group ($n = 30$; 18 females, 12 males).

Participants were all Italian native speakers and volunteered to the study. Older adults were selected on the basis of a physical and a health questionnaire.

TABLE 1
Participants' characteristics (means and standard deviations)
by age group

	Young		Young-old		Old-old	
	M	SD	M	SD	M	SD
Age	20.23	2.36	67.20	2.89	78.60	2.97
Education	14.23	2.35	7.57	3.44	6.53	3.62

Older participants were active in the cultural and social activities of the neighbourhood.

Educational level was significantly different across age groups, $F(1, 87) = 51.44$, $p < .001$, $p\eta^2 = .54$. Post hoc comparison using Tukey's method showed that young adults had a higher educational level than the young-old ($p < .01$) and old-old ($p < .01$). The difference between the young-old and the old-old was not significant. Since the difference in educational level was not relevant for the measures considered this variable was not taken into account in the following analyses.[1]

Materials

Categorisation working memory span task (De Beni et al., 1998). A modified version of the original working memory task was used. The materials consisted of six sets of stimuli, each composed of three series containing a growing number (from 4 to 6) of strings of words. Each string contained five words rated for familiarity by five independent judges. Strings contained zero, one, or two body-part nouns, which could be presented in various locations, including the final position. Of the total number of words (450) included in the task, 69 were body-part nouns (11 in final positions). An example of a string is the following: house, mother, *head*, word, **night**.

Subjects heard the strings of words presented at a rate of approximately 1 s per word and were required to tap their hand on the table whenever they heard a body-part word. At the end of the set subjects recalled the last word of each string in serial order. The total number of correctly recalled words was considered as being the measure of their working memory capacity.

The number of intrusion errors (i.e., nonfinal words incorrectly recalled) was computed distinguishing between intrusions of words belonging to previous lists and intrusions of words belonging to the current list. In the latter category we further distinguished the mean percentage of intrusions of stressed words (body parts) and nonstressed words (all other words).[2]

Moreover the total number of tapping errors was calculated, to be sure that all participants are carrying out a double task.

Proactive interference (PI) task. Three blocks, of four lists of words, composed the task (based on Kane & Engle, 2000). Words presented belonged to three different categories: animals, occupations, and countries. Each block consisted of three lists of eight words from the same category (e.g., animals) and the last one, which served as the "release from PI" list, from another category

---

[1] ANCOVA analyses conducted with education level as a covariate on the measures used confirmed this assumption, showing that it did not affect cognitive performance.

[2] The percentage of errors was calculated dividing the total number of intrusions by the total number of correct words recalled, thus considering the individual working memory capacity.

(e.g., countries). The lists were presented orally, with a rate of one word per second. Between the presentation of each list and the recall, participants performed a rehearsal-prevention task.

Upon hearing a letter paired with a two-digit number ranging from 10 to 90 (e.g., *G–36*), participants alternated between counting aloud from the letter and number for 16 s, starting with the pair provided ("G–36, H–37, I–38," etc.). Participants were instructed to count aloud quickly and accurately. At the end of the rehearsal prevention task, participants had 20 s to recall as many words as possible in any order, and they were encouraged to continue attempting to recall for the entire 20 s. A practice block with two lists from unrelated categories was administered.

The mean percentage of recalled words for each list summed across the three blocks was used as dependent variable. In addition, a measure of total recall was computed averaging the percentage of recall across the lists.

Moreover, in agreement with previous findings (e.g., Friedman & Miyake, 2004; Kane & Engle, 2000, Exp. 2; Wickens, Born, & Allen, 1963) we calculated for each participant two indexes of interference susceptibility, considering the recall in list 1 as baseline in the assessment of the proactive interference build-up. Susceptibility to PI for lists 2 and 3 was estimated using the formula [(list1– list2) / list1)], [(list1– list3) / list1)]. List 4 was used as a control for the appearance of the release of proactive interference.

Raven's Progressive Matrices.   In this standardised test (Raven, Court, & Raven, 1977) participants were presented with 60 matrices, grouped in five series of 12 matrices each. The matrices were similar to a puzzle with a piece missing from the bottom right corner. For each matrix six pieces that could fill in the missing part of the puzzle were presented. The participants had to choose the one that completed the figure showing consistency between different elements. They were not allowed to use paper to work out any of the problems and they were instructed to answer each question before moving to the next picture. No time limits were given. The total number of correct solutions was used as a measure of fluid intelligence.

RESULTS

The reliability of our experimental measures was assessed by calculating Cronbach's alpha over items. The reliability coefficients were satisfactory: categorisation working memory span task (correct recall), $\alpha = .98$; PI task (correct recall), $\alpha = .95$; Raven's matrices (PM38), $\alpha = .94$.

Post hoc analyses were conducted using either Dunnett's T3 or Tukey's HSD statistic. The post hoc method was adopted after considering whether or not measures violated the homogeneity of variance assumption, according to Levene's test. For all the analyses the alpha value was set at .05.

Categorisation working memory span task

Errors in the tapping task

To be sure that all the participants carried out the processing task (tapping on the table when a body part noun occurred), the rate of errors between groups of participants were compared. Results did not show any group effect (Table 2).

Correct recall

A one-way ANOVA on the total number of words recalled in the correct order was performed. The main effect of group was significant, $F(2, 87) = 153.20$, $p < .001$, $p\eta^2 = .78$. The group of young participants recalled a significantly higher number of words than the young-old and the old-old that differed significantly from each other (Table 2).

Intrusion errors

A 3 × 2 repeated-measures ANOVA with mixed design with group (young, young-old, old-old) as between-subjects factor and type of intrusion (same vs. previous list) as within factor was conducted. Results indicated a main effect of the type of intrusion, $F(1, 87) = 15.96$, $p < .001$, $p\eta^2 = .155$, but not of the group's age. Independently of the age, the frequency of intrusions from the same list was higher than intrusions from the previous lists. However, the significant interaction Group × Type of intrusion, $F(1, 87) = 3.64$, $p < .05$, $p\eta^2 = .08$, revealed that the age-related differences emerged

TABLE 2

Descriptive statistics (means and standard deviations) for all measures of the study by age group

	Young		Young-old		Old-old	
	M	SD	M	SD	M	SD
CWMS task						
% WM recall	77.62	13.46	36.44	12.85	23.33	11.19
% Intrusion of stressed words	0.95	1.59	1.28	2.87	4.43	9.03
% Intrusion of nonstressed words	2.31	2.47	2.14	3.78	5.36	10.02
Errors in the tapping task	4.57	2.90	2.83	2.60	3.63	3.26
PI task						
% Proactive interference recall	52.67	10.43	34.58	8.92	26.35	9.69
Errors in the rehearsal prevention task	1.27	1.93	2.50	2.45	3.27	2.49
Raven's Progressive Matrices						
% Raven score	86.78	7.55	53.67	17.14	40.44	15.86

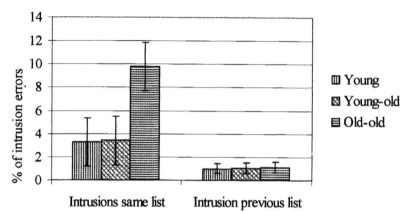

Figure 1.   Mean percentage of working memory intrusion errors by type of intrusions (same vs. previous list) and age group.

only when intrusion errors from the same list were considered. The groups of young and young-old differed significantly from the old-old group (Tukey's post-hoc analysis, $p < .05$). (See Figure 1.)

Moreover, we distinguished errors within the category of intrusion from the same list on the basis of activation of stressed and nonstressed items. Two one-way ANOVA tests were conducted to examine the effects of group (young, young-old, old-old) on the two types of intrusion calculated in percentage (stressed words and nonstressed words). There was a main group effect in the case of stressed intrusions, $F(2, 87) = 3.59$, $p < .05$, $p\eta^2 = .08$. A Tukey's post hoc analysis yielded a unique age difference: Old-old participants made significantly more intrusion errors for stressed words than the young adults ($p < .05$) (Table 2). On the contrary, the group effect was not significant for the nonstressed intrusions.

Proactive interference task

Errors in the rehearsal prevention task

The comparison of accuracy on the rehearsal prevention task yielded a main group effect, $F(2, 87) = 5.76$, $p < .01$, $p\eta^2 = .11$, with old-old adults committing a higher number of errors ($M = 3.27$, $SD = 2.49$) than the young adults ($M = 1.27$, $SD = 1.92$).

Correct recall

A repeated-measures ANOVA with group as between factor (young, young-old, and old-old) and list recall in percentage as within factor (list 1, list 2, list 3, list 4) was conducted.

The result showed a main effect for group, $F(2, 87) = 57.82$, $p < .001$, $p\eta^2 = .57$, and list, $F(3, 261) = 109.86$, $p < .001$, $p\eta^2 = .56$. Tukey's post hoc analyses yielded significant age differences: The young recalled a greater number of words than the young-old ($p < .001$) and the old-old ($p < .001$). Moreover participants recalled more words in list 1 than in the other lists. The Group × List interaction was significant, $F(6, 261) = 29.28$, $p < 001$, $p\eta^2 = .40$. The interaction arises from the observation that the two groups of elderly showed, contrary to the young adults, an inverse pattern in the percentage of recalled words from list 2 to list 3. Tukey's post hoc analyses revealed that both the young-old and the old-old recalled, in percentage, more words in list 3 than in list 2 ($p < .01$). Moreover for the two groups of older participants the rate of recall from list 3 to list 4 did not increase significantly, showing a lack of release of proactive interference in the last list.

Significant age differences favouring young adults, and confirming the above results, were obtained on the total recall measure computed for the words recalled across the four lists, $F(2, 87) = 57.82$, $p < .001$, $\eta^2 = .57$ (Table 2).

Proactive interference indexes

A one-way ANOVA was used to examine the effects of group on the proportional proactive interference effect on list 2 and list 3 and on the prevention rehearsal task (Figure 2).

The main effect of group on the index computed for list 2 was significant, $F(2, 87) = 3.96$, $p < .05$, $p\eta^2 = .08$. Post hoc comparison using Tukey's test

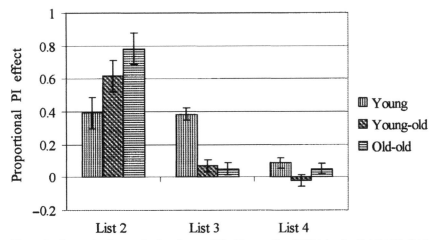

Figure 2. Proportional proactive interference (PI) effects on lists 2 [(list 1 − list 2) / list 1)], list 3 [(list 1 − list 3) / list 1)] and list 4 [(list 1 − list 4) / list 1)] by age group. Vertical lines depict standard errors of the mean.

yielded the following results. The old-old and marginally the young-old showed a higher susceptibility to interference than the young ($p < .05$ and $p = .07$, respectively). The mean difference between the young-old and the old-old was not significant.

The main effect of group was also significant on the index computed for list 3, $F(2, 87) = 24.30$, $p < .001$, $p\eta^2 = .36$, revealing a substantial difference favouring between the two groups of elderly participants, that did not differ from each other, compared to the group of young. Unexpectedly, neither the young-old nor the old-old participants present proactive interference on this index. This effect could be due to the lower percentage of words recalled by the elderly participants. In the case of the older participants' performance on list 2 was so poor that there was virtually no recall to interfere with performance on list 3. On the contrary the higher rate of words recalled on list 1, compared to words recalled on list 2, produced an interference effect.

If in one case (list 2 index) it is necessary for elderly participants, especially for old-old ones, to resist interfering items coming for list 1, this seems not the case for list 3. The resources consumed in storing words from list 1 could have limited, on one hand, the storage process for list 2 words and, on the other hand, the resistance to interference.

Another crucial aspect regarding these outcomes, which will be discussed further on, is the role potentially played by the secondary task on recall performance.

Raven's Matrices

A one-way ANOVA on the total number of correct responses on the Raven task yielded a main effect of age, $F(2, 87) = 85.06$, $p < .001$, $p\eta^2 = .66$, with significant main differences obtained for young and old-old adults and for young-old and old-old adults (Table 2).

Correlational analyses

Correlations were computed in order to examine the relationship among the following variables: the index list 2 of the PI task, the combined score of words recalled on PI task, working memory recall, working memory intrusion errors, the total number of correct responses in the Raven test, and age.

Though the crucial role of stressed intrusion errors in highlighting age-related differences, the working memory intrusion error (stressed and nonstressed) measures were collapsed to obtain a more robust index. In fact both these measures, taken independently, were necessarily weak due to the low number of observations and the high correlation between the two measures ($r = .86$) made plausible to merge the two types of measure. The same was not possible in the case of PI indexes since only the index computed for list 2

TABLE 3
Intercorrelations among measures used

	1	2	3	4
1. PI index (list 2)	—			
2. PI recall	−.60**	—		
3. WM recall	−.40**	.85**		
4. WM intrusion same list	.13	−.24*	−.30***	—
5. Raven	−.26**	.65**	.76***	−.15

$N = 90$. **$p < .01$, *$p < .05$. PI = proactive interference.

emerged as a proper measure of interference for the three age groups considered.

Correlations between the above mentioned measures were first computed within each age group to assess the measure of similarity between the three different patterns of results. Since results showed a similar pattern of correlations independently of the age group considered, we calculated a global correlation matrix for the whole sample (Table 3). The correlations ranged from small to large (Morse, 1998).

Working memory measures were highly correlated. On the contrary interference measures showed a lower relationship but in the expected direction: intrusion errors correlated negatively with the PI tasks. This confirms our hypothesis: Participants who suppressed irrelevant information more efficiently are the ones who are less sensitive to interference effects, recalling in percentage more correct words in the PI task. Moreover, the efficacy in suppressing irrelevant information from the contents of working memory is also significantly correlated with a higher working memory capacity. Globally, correlations showed that a lower susceptibility to interference is associated with a higher working memory capacity, higher scores on the Raven's test and a higher number of words recalled in the PI task. Nevertheless intrusion errors did not correlate with the PI index.

Regression analysis

Two distinct hierarchical regression analyses were used to examine the contribution of the two working memory tasks on the Raven's performance.

In a regression analysis the recalled words at the categorisation working memory span task and the words recalled on PI task (combined scores) were entered as predictors. Working memory measures accounted for 58% of the variance in the Raven's performance and the recalled words in the categorisation working memory span task ($\beta = .76$, $p < .001$) were the only salient predictor.

In the second regression analysis the susceptibility to interference (list 2 PI index) and the intrusion measure (combined score between the stressed and nonstressed intrusions errors) were entered as predictors. Interference measures accounted for a very limited part of the variance (less than 1%) of the Raven's performance and only susceptibility to interference contributed significantly towards the Raven's performance.

GENERAL DISCUSSION

The current study is an attempt to understand the links between three important aspects of cognition, i.e., the working memory capacity, susceptibility to interference, and fluid intelligence (measured by the Raven's test) in function of age-related changes. To this aim we firstly compared groups of participants of different ages in tasks that are considered as representative of these cognitive processes. The following step was to establish the role of working memory and susceptibility to interference in explaining the variation in a task measuring fluid intelligence.

The group comparison results substantially replicated well-known findings with only slight differences. The working memory task differentiated clearly between groups: Both groups of elderly participants reached a very low level of correctly recalled words compared to the younger adults. Differences were also found within the group of the elderly, with young-adults outperforming the old-old group. Analyses on intrusion errors, measuring the efficacy of the inhibitory processes, showed that old-old participants were less able to control for irrelevant information in comparison with young adults and young-old (De Beni & Palladino, 2004). This was true only when intrusion errors from the same list were considered, suggesting that old-old adults are specifically impaired in controlling information in working memory. Moreover, this result was confirmed by the further analysis of the category of the "same list" intrusion errors. The differences between old-old group and the other two groups were found only in the case of highly activated words, i.e., stressed words (body nouns), but not for other kinds of intrusion, i.e., nonstressed words. Thus, these results support the idea that the older adults have difficulty in monitoring the permanence of information in working memory depending on its relevance (De Beni & Palladino, 2004). In the case of the elderly participants, their inhibitory mechanism seems to show a deficit especially for those items that were more active in memory (De Beni & Palladino, 2004; Palladino & De Beni, 1999). The lack of differences between the young and the young-old adults suggests that the age-related differences in the inhibitory mechanisms are not the crucial aspect in the decline of the working memory capacity (Gamboz, Russo, & Fox, 2002). However, the results concerning intrusion errors have to be considered with caution, since, especially in the case of the elderly groups, their row scores were rather low.

The recall in the PI task revealed again a poorer performance in the memory task for older adults compared to young adults; indeed both the groups of elderly participants obtained a performance always below 50%. Since the interval between the presentation of the stimuli and recall was set at 16 s, we can assume that recalling activities rely on primary memory (Floden, Stuss, & Craik, 2000), i.e., on the working memory capacity. Thus, the older adults' lower performance could be ascribed to their working memory capacity deficit, as suggested by the correlational analyses. However, in the case of this task, it is likely that other aspects negatively influenced the elderly participants' performance. Some authors have pointed out that the level of difficulty of the secondary task could be one of the crucial aspects in influencing the older adults' performance (Inman & Parkinson, 1983; Parkinson, Inman, & Dannenbaum, 1985). Indeed a more complex secondary task heightened the difficulty in successfully encoding information in memory, producing poorer memory traces. The encoding difficulty resulting from a more complex secondary task could also account for the low rate of intrusion errors in this task. In the case of the index of resistance to interference, our results highlighted significant differences for the index computed for list 2 in that the young differed significantly from the old-old but only marginally from the young-old group in the susceptibility to interference. In addition older participants showed a comparable level of susceptibility. However, the index computed in list 3 showed a heavy reduction in susceptibility to interference in both the elderly groups. In our opinion, this finding could be a product of the impressively low level of recall performance reached by the elderly groups in list 2. This could suggest that list 2 is better in highlighting age-related differences in susceptibility to interference. It is worth noticing that this hypothesis has been made in the case of results obtained with younger adults (see, for example, Friedman & Miyake, 2004).

Finally, as expected, in the Raven's test the young adults outperformed both groups of elderly participants. Furthermore, similarly with findings obtained in the working memory task, we found differences also within the elderly group with a better performance for the young-old adults in comparison with the old-old participants.

The second part of the study aimed to understand the relationship between these aspects of cognition. The literature reports correlations that vary remarkably in strength between working memory, fluid intelligence (measured with the Raven's test) and resistance to interference. In the present study, the regression analyses showed that measures expressing the ability to control for interference (PI index) and intrusion errors are weakly related with the Raven scores. In contrast, working memory capacity emerged as powerful predictors in explaining a significant and consistent part of the variance of fluid intelligence as measured by the Raven test. Despite the fact that the two working memory tasks we used, the categorisation working memory span task and the PI task, come from different paradigms and seem to rely on partially different functions, in the present study they seemed to share the largest part of the variance in the Raven test. Concerning the memory performance the categorisation working memory span test appeared a better predictor of fluid intelligence than recall in the PI task, whereas—with respect to susceptibility of interference—the proactive interference index appeared preferable to the intrusion measure. However the two measures of susceptibility to interference did not appear particularly powerful. Before concluding that susceptibility to interference is not a good predictor of fluid intelligence, further stronger evidence is necessary. In fact, our two measures, intrusions and PI, were based on a low number of observations and this could have affected the general pattern of data. More robust measures and a larger number of tasks could disambiguate more precisely the relationship between fluid intelligence (in this study measured only with the Raven task), working memory, and susceptibility to interference.

To summarise, our study confirmed the important role of working memory and highlighted the weak contribution of the ability to control for irrelevant interfering information in a measure of fluid intelligence, the Raven test.

REFERENCES

Ackerman, P. L., Beier, M. E., & Boyle, M. O. (2005). Working memory and intelligence: The same or different constructs? *Psychological Bulletin, 131*, 30–60.

Anderson, J. W., Hartley, A. A., Bye, R., Harber, K. D., & White, O. L. (1986). Cognitive training using self-discovery methods. *Educational Gerontology, 12*, 159–171.

Babcock, R. L. (1994). Analysis of adult age differences on the Raven's Advanced Progressive Matrices test. *Psychology and Aging, 9*, 303–314.

Baddeley, A. D., & Hitch, G. J. (1974). Working memory. In G. Bower (Ed.), *The psychology of learning and motivation* (Vol. 8, pp. 47–90). New York: Academic Press.

Baddeley, A. D., & Logie, R. H. (1999). Working memory: The multiple-component model. In A. Miyake & P. Shah (Eds.), *Models of working memory* (pp. 28–61). Cambridge, UK: Cambridge University Press.

Brewin, C. R., & Beaton, A. (2002). Thought suppression, intelligence, and working memory capacity. *Behaviour Research and Therapy, 40*, 923–930.

Bromley, D. B. (1953). Primitive forms of response to the matrices test. *Journal of Mental Sciences, 99*, 374–393.

Carpenter, P. A., Just, M. A., & Shell, P. (1990). What one intelligence test measures: A theoretical account of the processing in the Raven Progressive Matrices test. *Psychological Review, 97*, 404–431.

Carretti, B., Cornoldi, C., De Beni, R., & Palladino, P. (2004). What happens to information to be suppressed in working memory tasks? Short and long term effects. *Quarterly Journal of Experimental Psychology, 57A*, 1059–1084.

Chown, S. M. (1961). Age and the rigidities. *Journal of Gerontology, 16*, 353–362.

Conway, A. R. A., Cowan, N., Bunting, M. F., Therriault, D. J., & Minkoff, S. R. B. (2002). A latent variable analysis of working memory capacity, short-term memory capacity, processing speed, and general fluid intelligence. *Intelligence, 30*, 163–183.

Conway, A. R. A., & Engle, R. W. (1994). Working memory and retrieval: a resource-dependent inhibition model. *Journal of Experimental Psychology: General, 123*, 354–373.

Cornoldi, C. (2006). The contribution of cognitive psychology to the study of human intelligence *European Journal of Cognitive Psychology, 18*(1), 1–17.

Cornoldi, C., & Vecchi, T. E. (2003). *Visuo-spatial working memory and individual differences.* Hove, UK: Psychology Press.

Craik, F. I. M. (1977). Age differences in human memory. In J. E. Birren & K. W. Schaie (Eds.), *Handbook of the psychology of aging* (pp. 384–420). Englewood Cliffs, NJ: Prentice Hall.

Daneman, M., & Carpenter, P. A. (1980). Individual differences in working memory and reading. *Journal of Verbal Learning and Verbal Behavior, 19,* 450–466.

Daneman, M., & Merikle, P. M. (1996). Working memory and language comprehension: A meta-analysis. *Psychonomic Bulletin and Review, 3,* 422–433.

Daneman, M., & Tardif, T. (1987). Working memory and reading skill reexamined. In M. Coltheart (Ed.), *Attention and performance XII: The psychology of reading* (pp. 491–508). Hove, UK: Lawrence Erlbaum Associates Ltd.

De Beni, R., & Palladino, P. (2004). Decline in working memory updating through ageing: Intrusion error analyses. *Memory, 12,* 75–89.

De Beni, R., Palladino, P., Pazzaglia, F., & Cornoldi, C. (1998). Increases in intrusion errors and working memory deficit of poor comprehenders. *Quarterly Journal of Experimental Psychology, 51A,* 305–320.

Dempster, F. N., & Corkill, A. J. (1999). Individual differences in susceptibility to interference and general cognitive ability. *Acta Psychologica, 10,* 395–416.

De Ribaupierre, A., & Lecerf, T. (2006). Relationships between working memory and intelligence from a developmental perspective: Convergent evidence from a neo-Piagetian and a psychometric approach. *European Journal of Cognitive Psychology, 18*(1), 109–137.

Dobbs, A. R., Aubrey, J. B., & Rule, B. G. (1989). Age-associated release from proactive interference: A review. *Canadian Psychology, 30,* 588–595.

Elliott, E. M., Barrilleaux, K. M., & Cowan, N. (2006). Individual differences in the ability to avoid distracting sounds. *European Journal of Cognitive Psychology, 18*(1), 90–108.

Engle, R. W., Tuholski, S. W., Laughlin, J. E., & Conway, A. R. A. (1999). Working memory, short-term memory and general fluid intelligence: A latent variable approach. *Journal of Experimental Psychology: General, 128,* 309–331.

Floden, D., Stuss, D. T., & Craik, F. I. M. (2000). Age differences in performance on two versions of the Brown-Peterson task. *Aging, Neuropsychology and Cognition, 7,* 245–259.

Friedman, N. P., & Miyake, A. (2004). The relations among inhibition and interference control functions: A latent-variable analysis. *Journal of Experimental Psychology: General, 133,* 101–135.

Gamboz, N., Russo, R., & Fox, E. (2002). Age differences and the identity negative priming effect: An updated meta-analysis. *Psychology and Aging, 17,* 525–531.

Hamm, V. P., & Hasher, L. (1992). Age and the availability of inferences. *Psychology and Aging, 7,* 56–64.

Hartman, M., & Dusek, J. (1994). Direct and indirect memory tests: What they reveal about age differences in interference. *Aging and Cognition, 1,* 292–309.

Hartman, M., & Hasher, L. (1991). Aging and suppression: Memory for previously relevant information. *Psychology and Aging, 6,* 587–594.

Hasher, L., Quig, M. B., & May, C. P. (1997). Inhibitory control over no-longer-relevant information: Adult age differences. *Memory and Cognition, 25,* 286–295.

Hasher, L., & Zacks, R. T. (1988). Working memory, comprehension and aging: A review and new view. In G. H. Bower (Ed.), *The psychology of learning and motivation* (pp. 193–225). San Diego, CA: Academic Press.

Hasher, L., Zacks, R. T., & May, C. P. (1999). Inhibitory control, circadian arousal, and age. In D. Gopher & A. Koriat (Eds.), *Attention and performance XVII: Cognitive regulation of performance: Interaction of theory and application* (pp. 653–675). Cambridge, MA: MIT Press.

Hooper, F. H., Hooper, J. O., & Colbert, K. C. (1984). *Personality and memory correlates of intellectual functioning: Young adulthood to old age.* Basel, Switzerland: Karger.

Hoyer, J. W., Rebok, G. W., & Sved, S. M. (1979). Effects of varying irrelevant information on adult age differences in problem solving. *Journal of Gerontology, 34,* 553–560.

Inman, V. W., & Parkinson, S. R. (1983). Differences in Brown-Peterson recall as a function of age and retention interval. *Journal of Gerontology, 38*, 58–64.

Jenkins, L., Myerson, J., Hale, S., & Fry, A. F. (1999). Individual and developmental differences in working memory across the life span. *Psychonomic Bulletin and Review, 6*, 28–40.

Kane, M. J., & Engle, R. W. (2000). Working-memory capacity, proactive interference, and divided attention: Limits on long-term memory retrieval. *Journal of Experimental Psychology: Learning, Memory, and Cognition, 26*, 336–358.

Kane, M. J., & Engle, R. W. (2002). The role of prefrontal cortex in working-memory capacity, executive attention, and general fluid intelligence: An individual-differences perspective. *Psychonomic Bulletin and Review, 9*, 637–671.

Kane, M. J., Hambrick, D. Z., Wilhelm, O., Payne, T., Tuholski, S., & Engle, R. W. (2004). The generality of working memory capacity: A latent variable approach to verbal and visuo-spatial memory span and reasoning. *Journal of Experimental Psychology: General, 133*, 189–217.

Kiewra, K. A., & Benton, S. L. (1988). The relationship between information processing ability and notetaking. *Contemporary Educational Psychology, 13*, 33–44.

Letho, J. (1996). Are executive function tests dependent on working memory capacity? *Quarterly Journal of Experimental Psychology, 49*, 29–50.

Lustig, C., May, C. P., & Hasher, L. (2001). Working memory span and the role of proactive interference. *Journal of Experimental Psychology: General, 30*, 199–207.

May, C. P., Hasher, L., & Kane, M. J. (1999). The role of interference in memory span. *Memory and Cognition, 27*, 759–767.

McCabe, J., & Hartman, M. (2003). Examining the locus of age effects on complex span tasks. *Psychology and Aging, 18*, 562–572.

Miyake, A., Friedman, N. P., Emerson, M. J., Witzki, A. H., Howerter, A., & Wager, T. (2000). The unity and diversity of executive functions and their contributions to complex "frontal lobe" tasks: A latent variable analysis. *Cognitive Psychology, 41*, 49–100.

Miyake, A., & Shah, P. (1999). *Models of working memory*. Cambridge, UK: Cambridge University Press.

Morse, D. T. (1998). MINSIZE: A computer program for obtaining minimum sample size as an indicator of effect size. *Educational and Psychological Measurement, 58*, 142–153.

Oberauer, K. (2001). Removing irrelevant information from working memory: A cognitive aging experiment with the modified Sternberg task. *Journal of Experimental Psychology: Learning, Memory, and Cognition, 27*(4), 948–957.

Osaka, M., Nishizaki, Y., Komori, M., & Osaka, N. (2002). Effect of focus on verbal working memory: Critical role of the focus word in reading. *Memory and Cognition, 30*(4), 562–571.

Palladino, P., Cornoldi, C., De Beni, R., & Pazzaglia, F. (2001). Working memory and updating processes in reading comprehension. *Memory and Cognition, 29*, 344–354.

Palladino P., & De Beni, R. (1999). Short term and working memory in aging: Maintenance and suppression. *Aging, Clinical and Experimental Research, 11*, 301–306.

Parkinson, S. R., Inman, V. W., & Dannenbaum, S. E. (1985). Adult age differences in short-term forgetting. *Acta Psychologica, 60*, 83–101.

Passolunghi, M. C., Cornoldi, C., & De Liberto, S. (1999). Working memory and intrusions of irrelevant information in a group of specific poor problem solvers. *Memory and Cognition, 27*, 779–790.

Passolunghi, M. C., & Siegel, L. S. (2001). Short-term memory, working memory, and inhibitory control in children with difficulties in arithmetic problem solving. *Journal of Experimental Child Psychology, 80*, 44–57.

Raven, J. C. (1965). *Advanced Progressive Matrices, Sets I and II*. London: H. K. Lewis.

Raven, J. C., Court, J. H., & Raven, J. (1977). *Standard Progressive Matrices*. London: H. K. Lewis.

Rosen, V. M., & Engle, R. W. (1997). The role of working memory capacity in retrieval. *Journal of Experimental Psychology: General, 126*, 211–227.

Rosen, V. M., & Engle, R. W. (1998). Working memory capacity and suppression. *Journal of Memory and Language, 39*, 418–436.

Salthouse, T. A., & Meinz, E. J. (1995). Aging, inhibition, working memory, and speed. *Journals of Gerontology: Series B. Psychological Sciences and Social Sciences, 50B*, 297–306.

Schelstraete, M., & Hupet, M. (2002). Cognitive aging and inhibitory efficiency in the Daneman and Carpenter's working memory task. *Experimental Aging Research, 28*, 269–279.

Schonfield, A. E. D., Davidson, H., & Jones, H. (1983). An example of age-associated interference in memorizing. *Journal of Gerontology, 38*, 204–210.

Schultz, N. R., Kaye, D. B., & Hoyer, W. J. (1980). Intelligence and spontaneous flexibility in adulthood and old age. *Intelligence, 4*, 219–231.

Swanson, H. L., & Ashbaker, M. H. (2000). Working memory, short-term memory, speech rate, word recognition and reading comprehension in learning disabled readers: Does the executive system have a role? *Intelligence, 28*, 1–30.

Swanson, H. L., & Siegel, L. (2001). Learning disabilities as a working memory deficit. *Issues in Education, 7*, 1–48.

Wickens, D. D., Born, D. G., & Allen, C. K. (1963). Proactive inhibition and item similarity in short-term memory. *Journal of Verbal Learning and Verbal Behavior, 2*, 440–445.

Wilhelm, O., & Oberauer, K. (2006). Why are reasoning ability and working memory capacity related to mental speed? An investigation of stimulus–response compatibility in choice reaction time tasks. *European Journal of Cognitive Psychology, 18*(1), 18–50.

Winocur, G., & Moscovitch, M. (1983). Paired-associate learning in institutionalized and non-institutionalized old people: An analysis of interference and context effects. *Journal of Gerontology, 38*, 455–464.

EUROPEAN JOURNAL OF COGNITIVE PSYCHOLOGY
2006, 18 (1), 70–89

Intellectual functioning of deaf adults and children: Answers and questions

Marc Marschark

Center for Education Research Partnerships, National Technical Institute for the Deaf, Rochester Institute of Technology, New York USA, and Department of Psychology, University of Aberdeen, UK

Intelligence has long been seen as linked to the spoken and written word. Because most deaf people have poor spoken language skills and find reading a significant challenge, there is a history in both psychology and education of considering deaf individuals to be less intelligent or less cognitively flexible than hearing individuals. With progress in understanding natural signed languages and cognitive abilities of individuals who lack spoken language, this perspective has changed. We now recognise, for example, that deaf people have some advantages in visuospatial ability relative to hearing people, and there is a link between the use of natural signed languages and enhanced visuospatial abilities in several domains. Such findings contrast with results found in memory, where the modality of mental representation, experience, and organisation of knowledge lead to differences in performance between deaf and hearing individuals, usually in favour of the latter. Such findings demonstrate that hearing loss and use of a natural sign language can influence intellectual abilities, including many tapped by standardised IQ tests. These findings raise interesting questions about the place of spoken language in our understanding of intelligence and ways in which we can use basic research for applied purposes.

Understanding intellectual functioning in special populations is a difficult undertaking—or should be. That is, there is a natural tendency for individuals in majority populations to view those in minority or special populations as varying quantitatively from the norm (indicated by means or standard deviations) rather

Correspondence should be addressed to Marc Marschark, Center for Education Research Partnerships, National Technical Institute for the Deaf, 96 Lomb Memorial Drive, Rochester, NY 14623, USA. Email: Marc.Marschark@RIT.EDU or m.marschark@abdn.ac.uk

Preparation of this report was supported by grant nos. REC-0207394 and REC-0307602 from the National Science Foundation. Any opinions, findings and conclusions, or recommendations expressed in this material are those of the authors and do not necessarily reflect the views of the National Science Foundation.

DOI:10.1080/09541440500216028

than qualitatively. Anthropologists and sociologists have learned the dangers of such ethnocentric interpretations of data, and yet in psychology it seems that the lesson may still be in need of teaching.

One place where such instruction is readily available is in efforts to understand and describe intellectual functioning of deaf individuals, both those who are children of deaf parents (less than 5% of all deaf individuals; Mitchell & Karchmer, 2004) and deaf children of hearing parents raised with sign language rather than spoken language. This is not a new endeavour and, indeed, many early nonverbal intelligence tests originally were constructed specifically for the purpose of being able to test deaf as well as hearing individuals (e.g., Binet & Simon, 1909; Pintner & Patterson, 1916, 1917). Yet even while developing instruments that do not depend on language, such enquiries never resolved the questions of the extent to which intelligence depends on language and how it might differ qualitatively or quantitatively with the use of spoken versus other forms of language. In this regard, research involving deaf individuals can be most informative.

This paper seeks to highlight some of the apparent answers to questions concerning the cognitive abilities of deaf individuals as demonstrated via standard psychological paradigms. More importantly, it will point up the variety of remaining questions concerning interactions of language and cognition and the ways in which our formal and informal views of intelligence are influenced by our emphasis on spoken language—appropriately or not. Throughout most of this discussion, *intellectual functioning* rather than *intelligence* will be used for reasons that go beyond psychological accuracy, and bear on some of the cultural and historical issues that make this such a difficult area of investigation and an even more difficult area in which to obtain consensus. This review thus has three primary goals. One of these is to provide a critical analysis of the possible role(s) of spoken language as a necessary condition for intellectual functioning, together with potential implications for perspectives on deaf individuals. As a corollary, the paper also will consider the view that signed languages and spoken languages are fully comparable in their support of intellectual functioning. In order to understand both the history of these two perspectives and the ways in which they have guided both research involving individuals and the education of deaf children, it is essential to recognise that it was only in 1960 that the first study revealed American Sign Language (ASL) to be a "true" language rather than a gestural system (Stokoe, 1960/2005). Therefore, what had previously been considered an issue of "thinking without language" (Furth, 1966), is now seen as a question of how spoken and signed language may differentially affect cognitive functioning (Marschark, 2003). The paper thus offers a historical sketch of research on deafness, language, and intelligence, followed by consideration of several specific areas of relevant research, and then implications for future research and practice.

WHAT WE CAN LEARN FROM HISTORICAL STUDIES OF DEAFNESS, LANGUAGE, AND INTELLIGENCE

Historical descriptions of deaf individuals and their communities (e.g., Groce, 1985; Lang, 2003; Woll & Ladd, 2003) provide us with some understanding of their social and linguistic functioning, including some notion of how they and their signed languages were viewed by others as effective means of both communication and learning. In Plato's *Cratylus* (360 BC), for example, Socrates poses the question "Suppose that we had no voice or tongue and wanted to indicate objects to one another. Should we not, like the deaf and dumb, make signs with the hands, head, and the rest of the body?" In the fourth century AD, Saint Augustine, wrote in *De Quantitate Animae* and *De Magistro* about deaf people's use of gestures and signs in discussing learning of the Gospel. He asked: "Have you never noticed how men converse, as it were, with deaf people by gestures and how the deaf themselves in turn use gestures to ask and answer questions, to teach and to make known either all their wishes or, at least, a good many of them?"

If Plato and St. Augustine saw deaf people as educational examples, Sultans of the Ottoman Court saw them as a valuable resource, as deaf people lived at court and taught sign language to those who were not permitted to speak in front of the Sultan (Woll & Ladd, 2003). In the late seventeenth century, one of the best known historical examples of a signing deaf community was established in America. A large deaf population had emigrated from a deaf community in Kent, England, and after settling in Scituate and other New England towns, eventually gathered at Martha's Vineyard (Massachusetts) (Groce, 1985). There, intermarriage led to an extremely high rate of deafness and sign language was a natural and accepted form of communication.

Together with early reports from philosophers, physicians, and scientists, such descriptions provide a better understanding of deaf people and sign language throughout history. From the Venerable Bede's history of the English people, *The Ecclesiastical History of the English Nation*, written around 700 AD, to William Harvey's 1636 observations (when he was not working on the human circulatory system) of deaf siblings signing to each other, there were questions about how the lack of spoken language and/or the presence of sign language might affect knowledge and thinking (Marschark, Lang, & Albertini, 2002, chap. 2). Clearly, at least some signing and nonsigning deaf people were accepted members of both the community and scientific circles, and there was a variety of internationally prominent deaf individuals who were artists and scientists, like Sir John Gaudy, a signing deaf artist knighted in Britain in the late seventeenth century (Evelyn, 1955); and his contemporaries French Academy member Guillaume Amontons, recognised as a pioneer in optical telegraphy and for laying the foundation for the study of temperature, and Leo Lesquereux, a paleobiologist who was the first member of the (US) National Academy of Sciences (Lang & Meath-Lang, 1995).

By the late 1800s, scientific observations of deaf children were undertaken to better understand "the deaf-mute language" (which actually differed in each country) and its relation to higher mental functioning. Sign language was being used in schools for the deaf in France, the Netherlands, and the United States at a time when psychology was struggling to decipher the relations of language, images, and thought (Marschark & Spencer, 2006). On one side were com- mentators like Bartlett (1850), who argued that "an intelligent person ... entirely destitute of all knowledge of language [is] an impossibility" (p. 86). Preyer (1882) took up a similar position, arguing that deaf children may understand a variety of complex concepts and abstractions of a lower order, but that without speech could not have many more of higher order abstractions "than very intelligent animals".

Such notions had been dismissed as early as the 1600s by investigators who had observed the behaviour of signing deaf adults (Stokoe, 1960/2005), and careful observations and analyses of deaf individuals by investigators like William James (1893), demonstrated that although higher mental processes might often be accompanied by spoken language, they did not require it. Nevertheless, the belief that normal cognitive development depends on the acquisition of spoken language persisted in many places through to the end of the twentieth century (see Spencer & Marschark, 2006, for reviews).

INTELLIGENCE, IQ, AND DEAF CHILDREN

The spoken language–sign language controversy has not gone away. Following more than 100 years of spoken language dominance in deaf education (led early on by Alexander Graham Bell, e.g., 1898/2005); however, recognition that signed languages were "true" languages, beginning in the 1960s (Stokoe, 1960/2005), led to their scientific study and their renewed use in educational settings. Importantly, today as 100 years ago, most deaf children have hearing parents who generally lack good sign skills or other means to effectively communicate with them. In the absence of access to early communication and language despite intensive "oral" training, most deaf children thus enter school with language delays of up to 2 years, and these lags often become greater with age (Geers, 2006). To early investigators who observed such delays (e.g., Pintner & Patterson, 1916, 1917), it often appeared that the lack of *spoken* language was the cause of academic and intellectual challenges—not that it was the failure to acquire appropriate language skills in any mode that created barriers to deaf children's learning. Indeed, there was ample evidence then (see Lang, 2003) and there is now (see Marschark et al., 2002) that natural signed languages (like American Sign Language [ASL], Italian Sign Language [LIS], and British Sign Language [BSL]) can provide deaf children with normal developmental trajectories and academic achievement. Yet, only about 25% of deaf children develop intelligible speech (Beattie, 2006; Cole & Paterson, 1984), and specific difficulties with spoken language—and with speech-dependent literacy skills (Traxler, 2000) led to considerable difficulty in assessing deaf children's intellectual functioning using traditional tests and measurements.

One difficulty in this regard is the lack of sign language translations of intelligence and achievement tests. About 1 in 1000 infants in Western countries is born with a severe to profound hearing loss (≥ 60 dB in the better ear), and the (US) National Center for Health Statistics (NCHS) reported over 965,000 children between 3 and 17 years of age with some degree of hearing loss, with more than 210,000 of them classified as deaf (NCHS, 1999). Cone-Wesson (2003) noted that this is "an exceptionally high prevalence for a potentially disabling condition". However, it is still not high enough to justify test publishers creating sign language versions of most IQ tests, and ad hoc translations used in several studies have not yet been validated. Thus, while deaf children tend to score below hearing children by about 1 standard deviation on verbal intelligence scales even when the effects of language skill are controlled (Braden, 1994; Braden, Kostrubala, & Reed, 1994), it is unclear whether those tests are inappropriate for deaf individuals or whether hearing loss necessarily affects verbal intelligence independent of language fluencies.

Lacking consensus on the above issue, most investigators currently make use of nonverbal, performance IQ tests with deaf children (e.g., Vernon, 1967, 1968/ 2005; see Maller, 2003, for a review). But even with performance tests, it is unclear how the language and cognitive disadvantages experienced by most deaf children in early childhood affect test validity. In a still influential review article, Vernon (1968/2005) reported that deaf and hard-of-hearing individuals had essentially the same distribution of nonverbal intelligence as the general population and only deaf children with other disabilities tended to score lower than hearing peers. More recently, studies involving deaf children have found nonverbal IQ to vary widely as a function of both the tests involved and the greater heterogeneity of deaf children relative to hearing children (Marschark, 1993b). Maller (2003, pp. 452–453) provided one review of such studies in which deaf children were reported to obtain IQ scores comparable to hearing peers on the Kaufman Assessment Battery for Children (K-ABC), but lower scores than hearing peers on the Leiter International Performance Scale–Revised (LIPS-R), the Comprehensive Test of Nonverbal Intelligence (CTONI), and the Universal Nonverbal Intelligence Test (UNIT).

Differences between deaf and hearing children on both verbal and nonverbal intelligence tests traditionally have been interpreted in terms of delayed cognitive development due to impoverished early language environments and reduced early stimulation or a direct consequence of separate, nonstandard education (Pintner & Patterson, 1917; Raviv, Sharan, & Strauss, 1973). During the 1950s and 1960s, when maternal rubella epidemics resulted in large numbers of deaf children, tests specifically designed for deaf children were popular (see Blennerhassett, 2000, for a review). Such tests are now outdated and no longer used, although some investigators argue that special norms are necessary so that deaf children can be compared only to other deaf children (Vernon & Andrews, 1990). This view may appeal to some notions of equality, but the position has been shown to be psychometrically and conceptually invalid (Braden, 2001; Jensen, 1980).

More recently, it has been argued that both assessment tools and teaching methods designed for hearing children may not match the cognitive abilities and knowledge of deaf children (Marschark & Lukomski, 2001; Zweibel, 1987). This situation may argue for the inappropriateness of particular tests, but it also may be that the general findings are valid with respect to deaf children's cognitive abilities relative to hearing age-mates, indicating the need for a greater understanding of educational practice at home and at school. Indeed, variability is so great among deaf children, that assessment involving only a single cognitive test may well misrepresent an individual child's abilities (Marschark, 1993b, chap. 7; Pizzuto, Ardito, Caselli, & Volterra, 2001; Rönnberg, 2003). Consideration of intelligence among deaf individuals also is complicated by the fact approximately 30–40% of them have some other syndromic or nonsyndromic condition that might affect test performance or related prior learning (Cone-Wesson, 2003). The variability contributed by such conditions could be partially responsible for any apparent overall, quantitative differences between deaf and hearing samples or qualitative differences in the configuration of abilities within the deaf population (Braden, 1994; Marschark, 1993b, chaps. 7–9; Ulissi, Brice, & Gibbins, 1990). Alternatively, it has been suggested that deafness, and especially hereditary deafness, might confer some intellectual advantages.

Kusché, Greenberg, and Garfield (1983), for example, examined nonverbal intelligence and verbal achievement in four groups of deaf high school students, conforming to a 2 (deaf or hearing parents) × 2 (genetic or nongenetic deafness) design and found that students with genetic deafness had higher mean scores (112 according to WISC-R and WAIS norms) than their matched groups with nongenetic deafness (101 and 102 on the WISC-R and WAIS, respectively). Because only one of two genetically deaf groups had hearing parents, Kusché et al. ruled out early language stimulation and quality of parental communication as possible loci of the IQ differences and suggested "natural, cultural, and/or historical selection" (p. 464) instead, a conclusion also reached by Zweibel (1987) in a study of Israeli children. More recently, Akamatsu, Musselman, and Zweibel (2000) found in a Canadian longitudinal study that IQs of deaf school children with nonsyndromic, hereditary deafness were equal to or higher than those of hearing peers.

Typically, however, differences in cognitive performance between deaf and hearing children, favouring the latter group, emerge as the gap between their linguistic and academic competencies increases, especially with regard to literacy skills. It thus may be that the intellectual development of deaf children is impeded by their relatively poor reading and writing skills (Traxler, 2000), a suggestion consistent with the positive relation found between the verbal scales of the WISC and literacy measures in deaf children (e.g., Geers & Moog, 1989; Moores & Sweet, 1990). Alternatively, the link between print literacy and intelligence might be viewed as creating qualitative rather than quantitative differences between deaf and hearing children. In this view, deaf children may gain much less from reading than hearing peers, and thus become more reliant on perceptually based reasoning rather than the abstract reasoning that is promoted by print literacy (Zweibel & Mertens, 1985), an orientation that could affect their performance in a variety of other cognitive domains (Marschark, 2005; McEvoy, Marschark, & Nelson, 1999).

LANGUAGE, EXPERIENCE, AND COGNITION IN DEAF ADULTS AND CHILDREN

Given the environments in which most deaf children grow up, it is not surprising that they are cognitively and intellectually more heterogeneous than hearing peers. Antia, Stinson, and Gaustad (2002) argued that as a result of their early environments, deaf children are likely to encounter "unfamiliar situations" more frequently than hearing peers and thus may have a greater need for precisely those problem-solving skills they lack. The issue of familiarity of task environments and the extent to which they elicit knowledge and strategies in deaf children's repertoires has arisen not only in cognitive tasks that demand explicit problem-solving strategies (e.g., Furth, 1966; Marschark & Everhart, 1999) but also in tasks that implicitly tap similar knowledge and skills (memory, associative learning, reading, etc.). In short, it appears that both growing up deaf and growing up with language skills 2–4 years behind those of hearing peers (Geers, 2006) has both general and specific effects on cognition. Some differences observed between deaf and hearing individuals now are understood to be related to sign language use rather than hearing loss *per se*. Other differences appear directly linked to a relative lack of auditory experience or a relative dependence on visual experience.

Language fluency and memory

Links between language and memory in deaf individuals have been of particular interest to psychological investigators for more than 100 years and, aside from literacy, memory has been the single most studied aspect of psychological functioning in deaf children (see Marschark, 1993b, chaps. 8 and 9). At a general level, Marschark (1993a) suggested that language fluency and, in turn, social interaction during childhood could have an influence on the structure and contents of semantic memory and other cognitive skills (e.g., working memory), even into adulthood. He argued that children with better communication skills would be more likely to have interactions with others from whom memory strategies and memory-relevant content knowledge can be learned, either explicitly or implicitly, and those children also are more likely to have interactions with diverse individuals with whom remembering things might be important. In all of these respects, Marschark argued that sign language and spoken language were fully comparable, given interactions with adults who possess fluent language skills.

At a more specific level, in contrast, a variety of investigators have argued that memory in deaf children is closely linked to their spoken language skill and, not coincidentally perhaps, inversely linked to their degree of hearing loss (e.g., Conrad, 1970, 1979). We have long known, for example, that hearing adults and children have longer memory spans than deaf individuals, and that those deaf individuals who use spoken language have longer spans than those who use sign language (Mayberry & Eichen, 1991; Pintner & Patterson, 1917). However, the consistent finding that deaf individuals tend to demonstrate equal forwards and backwards memory spans (e.g., Wilson, Bettger, Niculae, & Klima, 1997)—contrasting with the usual finding from hearing individuals that backwards span is significantly more difficult—signals the fact that there are qualitative as well as quantitative differences to be considered.

Studies conducted over the past decade have now demonstrated a connection between spoken language skill and linguistic working memory in deaf individuals. Using a variety of paradigms involving, for example, oral versus manual articulatory suppression and words that sound or are signed similarly, investigators have shown that deaf individuals may make use of either speech-based or sign-based codes in working memory (Lichtenstein, 1998; MacSweeney, Campbell, & Donlan, 1996; Marschark & Mayer, 1998; Wilson & Emmorey, 1997). Because individual signs take longer to articulate than individual words, however, speech skill generally is found to be positively related to working memory capacity in deaf individuals. Lichtenstein (1998), for example, demonstrated positive relations between working memory, speech, and reading among deaf college students; and Marschark and Mayer (1998) reported both a positive relation between working memory and speech skill and a negative relation between working memory and sign skill (where skill was presumed to reflect relative reliance on one language or the other).

Language skills aside, deaf students are rarely as efficient in their memory strategies as hearing peers and typically show significantly lower serial recall across a wide range of stimulus materials regardless of their preferred language modality (Krakow & Hanson, 1985; Lichtenstein, 1998; Logan, Mayberry, & Fletcher, 1996; O'Connor & Hermelin, 1973). Although this difference may be in part a consequence of the greater demands on cognitive capacity of either sign-based coding (greater memory demands) or speech-based coding (lesser fluency) relative to hearing peers, there are other cognitive differences that may reflect more generalised divergence in intellectual processing by deaf and hearing individuals.

Strategic and content differences in memory and cognition

The finding of both qualitative and quantitative differences in memory, as well as other differences in basic cognitive functioning between deaf and hearing individuals has been a source of considerable controversy in the field of deafness (see Marschark, 2003; Moores, 2001) in large part because claims of *differences* have often been taken as claims of *deficiencies*. There now appear to be data which directly indicate that language fluencies of deaf individuals can have positive as well as negative consequences for various cognitive processes. Courtin (1997), for example, suggested that the morphological structure of sign language might provide deaf children with a cognitive advantage with regard to concept formation. His reasoning followed from the fact that in French Sign Language (Langue des Signes Français, LSF), as in other sign languages, signs below the *basic* level (e.g., "tree") often do not exist (e.g., "maple", "oak"). In order to specify a maple tree in ASL, for example, one would first sign TREE and then fingerspell "maple". Courtin noted that basic-level, "generic" signs in LSF often have iconic or metonymic characteristics. Accordingly, he suggested that a generic sign sometimes refers to the prototypical element of the category, having a representative shape of exemplars in the category. But generic signs also refer to the intentional properties of the category in that they encompass some of the characteristic properties (e.g., the trunk and branches). Courtin therefore argued that categorisation might be easier for a deaf child who is a native user of LSF than for a hearing child.

Courtin (1997) conducted an experiment involving hearing children of hearing parents and deaf children of deaf parents, all aged 5–6 years, who were shown pictures sharing either a superordinate category and a generic, to-be-instantiated sign (e.g., a cake and a strawberry tart) or a "schematic" conceptual relation (e.g., a pudding and a dessert spoon, both related to desserts). He found that the deaf children were more likely to match pictures on the basis of categorical choices than schematic choices, whereas the reverse was true for hearing children (cf. Marschark, Convertino, McEvoy, & Masteller, 2004). Deaf children did not show greater overall categorisation abilities that hearing peers, but the underlying commonality in sign concepts clearly facilitated their application of a categorical strategy (cf. Marschark & Everhart, 1999). Courtin did not evaluate children of hearing parents who were acquiring sign language, but recent findings involving college students who were already skilled in sign language have indicated no difference in the frequency with which deaf and hearing students provide superordinate responses in a single-word free association task (Marschark et al., 2004).

If such results suggest interactions of language and concept learning in deaf children, there was already abundant evidence for qualitative differences in conceptual organisation in semantic memory between deaf and hearing individuals. Studies of semantic memory organisation during the 1970s—usually attempts to explain observed quantitative differences in recall—typically revealed considerable overlap in deaf and hearing students' associative knowledge, and concluded that there was little if any difference in memory organisation (e.g., Hoemann, Andrews, & DeRosa, 1974; Koh, Vernon, & Bailey, 1971; Liben, 1979). More recently, studies have revealed significant differences in the strength and spread of associations among concepts that seem likely to affect functioning in a variety of cognitive and academic domains (e.g., Marschark et al., 2004; McEvoy et al., 1999).

McEvoy et al. (1999), for example, examined the organisation of conceptual knowledge in deaf and hearing college students using a single-word association task. They found high overlap in primary associates for the two groups ($r = .77$), but significant differences on several dimensions indicated that hearing students had greater coherence and consistency in conceptual organisation relative to deaf students. Marschark et al. (2004) obtained similar results using category names and category exemplars as stimuli. Deaf and hearing students again showed high overlap in their associative responses, as they produced the same primary associates for 82% of the stimuli. Contrary to their predictions, Marschark et al. found that deaf students were significantly less likely than hearing peers to respond to a category name with an exemplar, even while the two groups were equally likely to respond to an exemplar with a category name. This result indicates asymmetric category-exemplar relations in semantic memory for deaf but not hearing students (see also Liben, 1979).What evidence is available therefore suggests that despite considerable similarity in the knowledge organisation of deaf and hearing individuals, there are consistent differences that can influence intellectual functioning. Still unclear, however, is the locus of results indicating differences in cognitive organisation. Marschark, Convertino, and LaRock (in press) have argued that such findings reflect both developmental and educational factors, rather than being a consequence of hearing loss *per se*. Indeed, there are several general differences in information processing between deaf and hearing individuals that appear to reflect very different orientations to learning, memory, and cognition. One of these relates to an emphasis on relational versus individual item information.

Deaf learners and relational processing

Ottem (1980) was the first to point out a difference between deaf and hearing individuals in their relational versus individual-item information processing, in his review of over 50 studies of concept learning, conservation, classification, memory, and problem solving. He observed that when tasks had involved only a single dimension (e.g., size or number), deaf individuals usually performed comparably to hearing age-mates. However, when tasks required simultaneous consideration of two or more dimensions (e.g., size and shape), the performance of hearing adults and children usually surpassed that of deaf peers. Such findings reflect differing orientations towards relational versus individual-item processing, a dimension known to affect performance in a variety of cognitive tasks. In a study exploring deaf children's memory for text, for example, Banks, Gray, and Fyfe (1990) found that deaf and hearing children recalled equal amounts of text, but deaf children's recall tended to be composed of disjointed parts rather than whole idea units. Similar findings were obtained by Marschark, De Beni, Polazzo, and Cornoldi (1993) in a study in which deaf and hearing students were matched either for age or reading ability and read reading-level appropriate passages. Overall, the deaf adolescents recalled significantly less than their hearing age-mates, but more than the younger reading-matched children. When recall was scored for the number of relational units or individual words recalled, deaf students were found to remember proportionately fewer relations than words, while the reverse was true for both groups of hearing students. Consistent with the Banks et al. findings, these results were interpreted as indicating that deaf students tend to focus on the meanings of individual words or pieces of text rather than taking a more relational, holistic approach to reading (see Wilhelm & Oberauer, 2006 this issue).

The finding that deaf individuals tend not to automatically apply relational processing strategies also may help to explain the consistent finding of poorer serial recall for word, sign, and picture stimuli relative to hearing age-mates. The lack of strong associative bonds in semantic memory may result in less relational processing in both episodic memory (e.g., list learning) and reading, where deaf students are seen to adopt more word-by-word strategies and typically fail to make either text-connecting or gap-filling inferences even when they have the linguistic and world knowledge necessary to do so (Strassman, 1997). Indeed, the lack of an integrative orientation may be at the root of deaf students' performance below hearing age-mates on a variety of memory, problem solving, and academic tasks.

From this perspective, the findings with regard to spoken language and tasks involving temporal or sequential information may be seen as indicating that deaf individuals have alternative ways of coding and remembering information rather than any generalised cognitive deficits. Unfortunately, some of those alternatives may not be as appropriate or successful as the codes and strategies employed by hearing individuals in academic and other settings, but deaf individuals may have advantages in domains that take advantage of their greater reliance on visuospatial information.[1] Either as one component of higher order cognitive processing, or in and of itself, this point of divergence in deaf and hearing individuals may help to clarify our understanding of intellectual processes in deaf adults and children. It therefore will be worthwhile studying their visuospatial functioning in more detail.

VISUOSPATIAL COGNITION IN DEAF INDIVIDUALS: HEARING LOSS OR SIGN LANGUAGE USE?

The arguments of Akamatsu et al. (2000), Zweibel (1987), and others suggesting hereditary advantages in IQ for deaf individuals, as well as those suggesting alternative information processing strategies, indicate that a full understanding of the intellectual functioning of deaf adults and children must include attention to cultural, environmental, and neuropsychological contributions to development. Beyond interactions of language development, cognitive development, and heredity, early experience clearly has impact on the development of the nervous system and organisation within the brain which, in turn, will influence learning in some subtle and not so subtle ways. Although it is still unclear whether the observed neuropsychological (Corina, 1998; Emmorey, 2001; Rönnberg, 2003) and behavioural (Marschark et al., in press) differences observed in the laboratory have any functional effects in real-world activities, several such differences have been identified that appear to influence and reflect differences in intellectual functioning.

Todman and Cowdy (1993) and Todman and Seedhouse (1994), for example, found that profoundly deaf children, aged 6–16 years, surpassed hearing peers on the Compound Stimulus Visual Information (CSVI) task. The CSVI test requires short-term memory of complex visual figures and subsequent performance of actions based on different dimensions of the figures. The only case in which the performance of hearing children exceeded that of deaf children is when the task involved serial presentation of parts of a stimulus and serial (ordered) recall. Belmont, Karchmer, and Bourg (1983), however, warned that the heterogeneity in deaf children's early experiences would likely affect coding strategies and preferences. They presented 16 deaf and 16 hearing 11-year-olds with computer-generated stimulus arrays differing in spatial and temporal order; the children then recalled the digits or were asked to choose the presented sequences from a pair of alternatives. Belmont et al. found that all the hearing children adopted temporal coding strategies, whereas nine deaf children adopted spatial coding strategies and seven adopted temporal strategies. After

---

[1] In fact, the majority of deaf individuals do have some residual hearing, but there have been few attempts to discern the extent to which their technologically aided or unaided hearing influences performance in either cognitive tasks or academic settings.

determining children's coding preferences, Belmont et al. used a task that required children to switch to the alternate, spatial or temporal, strategy. The switch reduced performance by both deaf and hearing children, but only hearing children showed a recovery of performance after several trials.

Unfortunately, the Belmont et al. (1983) study did not distinguish between children who relied on sign language versus spoken language, a dimension now recognised as influencing visuospatial performance in several domains. On average, for example, deaf adults and children have been found to surpass hearing individuals in visuospatial such as mental rotation (Emmorey, Kosslyn, & Bellugi, 1993), face recognition (Bellugi et al., 1990), mental image generation (Emmorey & Kosslyn, 1996), detecting motion (Neville et al., 1997), and sign language (Swisher, 1993) in peripheral vision, and redirecting visual attention from one location to another (Corina, Kritchevsky, & Bellugi, 1992; Rettenback, Diller, & Sireteanu, 1999). However, some of those advantages are now recognised to be due to the use of a natural, visuospatial sign language rather than a function of hearing loss. Emmorey and Kosslyn (1996) and Emmorey et al. (1993), for example, found that both deaf and hearing signers were faster in generating complex (but not simple) mental images than non-signing peers; and in a two-dimensional rotation task, Emmorey et al. found deaf and hearing signers to have faster response times than hearing nonsigners.[2] Chamberlain and Mayberry (1994) further demonstrated that deaf individuals who relied on spoken language did not differ from hearing nonsigners on the mental rotation task, while Talbot and Haude (1993) showed that level of sign language expertise (but not age of acquisition) affected mental rotation performance with three-dimensional block figures.

Bettger, Emmorey, McCullough, and Bellugi (1997) hypothesised that the experience of people who use ASL in discriminating facial expressions that have linguistic interpretations also might enhance their ability to discriminate among faces. In three experiments involving adults, they demonstrated a significant advantage supporting their prediction. Importantly, however, only those aspects of face processing related to ASL grammar and lipreading enhanced performance, and there was no general enhancement of visual discrimination (e.g., for inverted faces). Bettger et al. also examined the perceptual abilities of 6- to 9-year-old deaf children with deaf or hearing parents. These "early signers" and "late signers" were compared to a group of hearing children with hearing parents using the Benton Faces Test, a task in which a model photograph of a face must be compared to other photographs which may be of the same or different people (seen from the front, in profile, or in shadow). Bettger et al. found that deaf

---

[2] The difference observed by Emmorey et al. (1993) was apparently due to deaf people being faster in making judgements about normal versus mirror-image orientation, rather than in rotation speed *per se*.

children with deaf parents consistently scored significantly higher than either the hearing children or the deaf children with hearing parents, who did not differ significantly from each other. These results indicate that individuals who are native signers develop face-specific perceptual abilities, reflecting a specific link between language and visuospatial abilities (McCullough & Emmorey, 1997).

Although other visuospatial abilities still appear to be a function of hearing loss rather than sign skill (e.g., sensitivity to motion in peripheral vision), results of this sort emphasise that interactions of hearing loss, language, and experience must be considered if we are to fully understand the intellectual abilities of deaf children and adults. Even if there are few, if any, generalised advantages for deaf individuals by virtue of hearing losses alone, better understanding of those domains in which they differ from hearing peers in qualitative and quantitative ways—including domains in which sign language confers some advantage— may offer insights into methods for improving deaf children's academic learning, thus bridging research and practice.

CONCLUSIONS AND IMPLICATIONS

For those interested in intelligence and the relations of verbal and nonverbal processes, deaf individuals have always presented a puzzling case. When non-verbal, performance intelligence tests are used, deaf and hearing individuals generally perform similarly. Verbal intelligence tests developed for hearing individuals may not be appropriate for use with deaf individuals, but not only because of the language barrier involved. To the extent that deaf children have different patterns of early socialisation and diversity of experiences from hearing peers, as well as exposure to variable quality in academic instruction, standardised verbal intelligence tests may not be "culture fair". What then are we to make of the fact that deaf adults and children may employ fundamentally different coding strategies than hearing peers—due either to hearing loss or their reliance on signed languages? In cases where their performance falls below that of hearing peers, many educators and investigators suggest that the tests appropriately indicate a lack of "normal" cognitive-academic skills (e.g., Luetke-Stahlman & Luckner, 1991; Sharpe, 1985; see also, Cornoldi, 2006 this issue). Yet there have been few attempts to demonstrate superior performance by deaf individuals in domains where they appear to have cognitive advantages.

It is not surprising that children growing up without hearing or with diminished hearing are more dependent of visual information than normally hearing peers, and it thus should not be surprising if there are neurological and neuropsychological correlates of such differences early in development. What is surprising is how little we make use of those findings in either theorising about intellectual functioning of deaf individuals or in seeking to meet demonstrated needs in their academic performance. In the educational sphere, Detterman and Thompson (1997, p. 1083) argued that "lack of understanding of the cognitive skills underlying educational interventions is the fundamental problem in the development of special education. Without understanding the full complexity of cognitive abilities, special educational methods can never be special.'' With regard to intelligence and intellectual functioning, however, reliance on spoken language and performance comparable to hearing children often is still considered the ''gold standard''. Admittedly, this situation is largely a consequence of parental wishes that their deaf child appear as ''normal'' as possible, but more than 150 years of research concerning language, cognition, and intellectual functioning among deaf individuals—and an equal period of trying to make them speak, read, and perform academically like their hearing siblings—should be enough to tell us that this is unlikely to occur.

The fact that deaf individuals both have a greater reliance on visual information than hearing peers and have to deal with visual and verbal (also via the visual modality) information consecutively rather than simultaneously (e.g., in naming and explanations of ongoing events) clearly will result in their having different perceptual and cognitive strategies than those who can draw on both visual and auditory input. Furthermore, most deaf children are raised in environments in which their parents cannot effectively communicate with them and in which there is a mandate for education in a system that is designed for hearing children. Such environments would not be particularly sensitive to the special needs of visuospatial learners. Yet, little attention has been given to how deaf individuals come to accommodate this situation and often succeed despite the barriers placed before them.

Attempts over the years to alter the landscape for deaf children by requiring intensive oral-only education or placing them in regular local classrooms have done little to improve literacy and other academic skills or to make deaf children look more like hearing children (Traxler, 2000). Perhaps it is time to follow Detterman and Thompson's (1997) suggestion that we need to better understand the normal intellectual functioning of deaf children in order to adapt our instructional methods to match their strengths and needs. This seems a far better use of psychological research than gratuitously attempting to make deaf children adopt the learning behaviours of hearing children (some years delayed). We already have many of the answers; it seems that our problem lies in finding the right questions.

REFERENCES

Akamatsu, C. T., Musselman, C., & Zweibel, A. (2000). Nature vs. nurture in the development of cognition in deaf people. In P. Spencer, C. Erting, & M. Marschark (Eds.), *Development in context: The deaf children in the family and at school* (pp. 255–274). Mahwah, NJ: Lawrence Erlbaum Associates, Inc.

Antia, S. D., Stinson, M. S., & Gaustad, M. G. (2002). Developing membership in the education of deaf and hard of hearing students in inclusive settings. *Journal of Deaf Studies and Deaf Education, 7*, 214–229.

Banks, J., Gray, C., & Fyfe, R. (1990). The written recall of printed stories by severely deaf children. *British Journal of Educational Psychology, 60*, 192–206.

Bartlett, D. E. (1850). The acquisition of language. *American Annals of the Deaf and Dumb, 3*, 83–92.

Beattie, R. (2006). The oral methods and spoken language acquisition. In P. E. Spencer & M. Marschark (Eds.), *Advances in spoken language development of deaf and hard-of-hearing children* (pp. 103–135). New York: Oxford University Press.

Bell, A. G. (2005). The question of sign-language and the utility of signs in the instruction of the deaf. *Journal of Deaf Studies and Deaf Education, 10*, 111–121. (Original work published 1898.)

Bellugi, U., O'Grady, L., Lillo-Martin, D., O'Grady, M., van Hoek, K., & Corina, D. (1990). Enhancement of spatial cognition in deaf children. In V. Volterra & C. J. Erting (Eds.), *From gesture to language in hearing and deaf children* (pp. 278–298). New York: Springer-Verlag.

Belmont, J. M., Karchmer, M. A., & Bourg, J. W. (1983). Structural influences on deaf and hearing children's recall of temporal/spatial incongruent letter strings. *Educational Psychology, 3*, 259–274.

Bettger, J. G., Emmorey, K., McCullough, S. H., & Bellugi, U. (1997). Enhanced facial discrimination: Effects of experience with American Sign Language. *Journal of Deaf Studies and Deaf Education, 2*, 223–233.

Binet, A., & Simon, T. (1909). Peut-on enseigner la parole aux sourds-muets. *L'année Psychologique, 15*, 373–396.

Blennerhassett, L. (2000). Psychological assessments. In P. A. Hindley & N. Kitson (Eds.), *Mental health and deafness* (pp. 185–205). London: Whurr.

Braden, J. (1994). *Deafness, deprivation, and IQ*. New York: Plenum Press.

Braden, J. (2001). The clinical assessment of deaf people's cognitive abilities. In M. D. Clark, M. Marschark, & M. Karchmer (Eds.), *Context, cognition, and deafness* (pp. 14–37). Washington, DC: Gallaudet University Press.

Braden, J. P., Kostrubala, C., & Reed, J. (1994). Why do deaf children score differently on performance v. motor-reduced nonverbal intelligence tests? *Journal of Psychoeducational Assessment, 12*, 250–265.

Chamberlain, C., & Mayberry, R. I. (1994, May). *Do the deaf "see" better? Effects of deafness on visuospatial skills*. Poster presented at TENNET V meetings, Montreal, Canada.

Cole, E., & Paterson, M. (1984). Assessment and treatment of phonologic disorders in the hearing-impaired. In J. Castello (Ed.), *Speech disorders in children* (pp. 93–127). San Diego, CA: College Hill Press.

Cone-Wesson, B. (2003). Screening and assessment of hearing loss in infants. In M. Marschark & P. E. Spencer (Eds.), *Oxford handbook of deaf studies, language, and education* (pp. 420–433). New York: Oxford University Press.

Conrad, R. (1970). Short-term memory processes in the deaf. *British Journal of Psychology, 61*, 179–195.

Conrad, R. (1979). *The deaf school child: Language and cognition*. London: Harper & Row.

Corina, D. P. (1998). Studies of neural processing in deaf signers: Toward a neurocognitive model of language processing in the deaf. *Journal of Deaf Studies and Deaf Education, 3*, 35–48.

Corina, D. P., Kritchevsky, M., & Bellugi, U. (1992). Linguistic permeability of unilateral neglect: Evidence from American Sign Language. In *Proceedings of the cognitive science society* (pp. 384–389). Hillsdale, NJ: Lawrence Erlbaum Associates, Inc.

Cornoldi, C. (2006). The contribution of cognitive psychology to the study of human intelligence *European Journal of Cognitive Psychology, 18*(1), 1–17.

Courtin, C. (1997). Does sign language provide deaf children with an abstraction advantage? Evidence from a categorization task. *Journal of Deaf Studies and Deaf Education, 2*, 161–171.

Detterman, D. K., & Thompson, L. A. (1997). What is so special about special education? *American Psychologist, 52*, 1082–1090.

Emmorey, K. (2001). *Language, cognition, and the brain: Insights from sign language research.* Mahwah, NJ: Lawrence Erlbaum Associates, Inc.

Emmorey, K., & Kosslyn, S. (1996). Enhanced image generation abilities in deaf signers: A right hemisphere effect. *Brain and Cognition, 32,* 28–44.

Emmorey, K., Kosslyn, S., & Bellugi, U. (1993). Visual imagery and visual-spatial language: Enhanced imagery abilities in deaf and hearing ASL signers. *Cognition, 46,* 139–181.

Evelyn, J. (1955). *The diary of John Evelyn.* Oxford, UK: Clarendon Press.

Furth, H. G. (1966). *Thinking without language.* New York: Free Press.

Geers, A. (2006). Spoken language in children with cochlear implants. In P. E. Spencer & M. Marschark (Eds.), *Advances in spoken language development of deaf and hard-of-hearing children* (pp. 244–270). New York: Oxford University Press.

Geers, A. E., & Moog, J. S. (1989). Factors predictive of the development of literacy in profoundly hearing-impaired adolescents. *Volta Review, 91,* 69–86.

Groce, N. E. (1985). *Everyone here spoke sign language: Hereditary deafness at Martha's Vineyard.* Cambridge, MA: Harvard University Press.

Hoemann, H., Andrews, C., & DeRosa, D. (1974). Categorical encoding in short-term memory by deaf and hearing children. *Journal of Speech and Hearing Research, 17,* 426–431.

James, W. (1893). Thought before language: A deaf-mute's recollections. *American Annals of the Deaf and Dumb, 18,* 135–145.

Jensen, A. R. (1980). *Bias in mental testing.* New York: Free Press.

Koh, S. D., Vernon, M., & Bailey, W. (1971). Free-recall learning of word lists by prilingual deaf subjects. *Journal of Verbal Learning and Verbal Behavior, 10,* 542–547.

Krakow, R. A., & Hanson, V. L. (1985). Deaf signers and serial recall in the visual modality: Memory for signs, fingerspelling, and print. *Memory and Cognition, 13,* 265–272.

Kusché, C. A., Greenberg, M. T., & Garfield, T. S. (1983). Nonverbal intelligence and verbal achievement in deaf adolescents: An examination of heredity and environment. *American Annals of the Deaf, 128,* 458–466.

Lang, H. G. (2003). Perspectives on the history of deaf education. In M. Marschark & P. E. Spencer (Eds.), *Oxford handbook of deaf studies, language, and education* (pp. 9–20). New York: Oxford University Press.

Lang, H. G., & Meath-Lang, B. (1995). *Deaf persons in the arts and sciences: A biographical dictionary.* Westport, CT: Greenwood Press.

Liben, L. S. (1979). Free recall by deaf and hearing children: Semantic clustering and recall in trained and untrained groups. *Journal of Experimental Child Psychology, 27,* 105–119.

Lichtenstein, E. (1998). The relationships between reading processes and English skills of deaf college students. *Journal of Deaf Studies and Deaf Education, 3,* 80–134.

Logan, K., Mayberry, M., & Fletcher, J. (1996). The short-term memory of profoundly deaf people for words, signs, and abstract spatial stimuli. *Applied Cognitive Psychology, 10,* 105–119.

Luetke-Stahlman, B., & Luckner, J. (1991). *Effectively educating students with hearing impairments.* New York: Longman.

MacSweeney, M., Campbell, R., & Donlan, C. (1996). Varieties of short-term memory coding in deaf teenagers. *Journal of Deaf Studies and Deaf Education, 1,* 249–262.

Maller, S. J. (2003). Intellectual assessment of deaf people: A critical review. In M. Marschark & P. E. Spencer (Eds.), *Oxford handbook of deaf studies, language, and education* (pp. 451–463). New York: Oxford University Press.

Marschark, M. (1993a). Origins and interactions in language, cognitive, and social development of deaf children. In M. Marschark & D. Clark (Eds.), *Psychological perspectives on deafness* (pp. 7–26). Hillsdale, NJ: Lawrence Erlbaum Associates, Inc.

Marschark, M. (1993b). *Psychological development of deaf children.* New York: Oxford University Press.

Marschark, M. (2003). Cognitive functioning in deaf adults and children. In M. Marschark & P. E. Spencer (Eds.), *Oxford handbook of deaf studies, language, and education* (pp. 464–477). New York: Oxford University Press.

Marschark, M. (2005). Developing deaf children or deaf children developing? In D. Power & G. Leigh (Eds.), *Educating deaf students: Global perspectives* (pp. 13–26). Washington, DC: Gallaudet University Press.

Marschark, M., Convertino, C., & LaRock, D. (in press). Assessing cognition, communication, and learning by deaf students. In C. Hage, B. Charlier, & J. Leybaert (Eds.), *L'évaluation de la personne sourde.* Brussels: Mardaga.

Marschark, M., Convertino, C., McEvoy, C., & Masteller, A. (2004). Organization and use of the mental lexicon by deaf and hearing individuals. *American Annals of the Deaf, 149,* 51–61.

Marschark, M., de Beni, R., Polazzo, M. G., & Cornoldi, C. (1993). Deaf and hearing-impaired adolescents' memory for concrete and abstract prose: Effects of relational and distinctive information. *American Annals of the Deaf, 138,* 31–39.

Marschark, M., & Everhart, V.S. (1999). Problem solving by deaf and hearing children: Twenty questions. *Deafness and Education International, 1,* 63–79.

Marschark, M., Lang, H. G., & Albertini, J. A. (2002). *Educating deaf students: From research to practice.* New York: Oxford University Press.

Marschark, M., & Lukomski, J. (2001). Cognition, literacy, and education. In M. D. Clark, M. Marschark, & M. Karchmer (Eds.), *Context, cognition, and deafness* (pp. 71–87). Washington, DC: Gallaudet University Press.

Marschark, M., & Mayer, T. (1998). Mental representation and memory in deaf adults and children. In M. Marschark & M. D. Clark (Eds.), *Psychological perspectives on deafness* (Vol. 2, pp. 53–77). Mahwah, NJ: Lawrence Erlbaum Associates, Inc.

Marschark, M., & Spencer, P. E. (2006). Spoken language development of deaf and hard-of-hearing children: Historical and theoretical perspectives. In P. E. Spencer & M. Marschark (Eds.), *Advances in the spoken language development of deaf and hard-of-hearing children* (pp. 3–21). New York: Oxford University Press.

Mayberry, R. I., & Eichen, E. B. (1991). The long-lasting advantage of learning sign language in childhood: Another look at the critical period for language acquisition. *Journal of Memory and Language, 30,* 486–512.

McCullough, S., & Emmorey, K. (1997). Face processing by deaf ASL signers: Evidence for expertise in distinguishing local features. *Journal of Deaf Studies and Deaf Education, 2,* 212–233.

McEvoy, C., Marschark, M., & Nelson, D. L. (1999). Comparing the mental lexicons of deaf and hearing individuals. *Journal of Educational Psychology, 91,* 1–9.

Mitchell, R. E., & Karchmer, M. A. (2004). Chasing the mythical ten percent: Parental hearing status of deaf and hard of hearing students in the United States. *Sign Language Studies, 4,* 138–163.

Moores, D. F. (2001). *Educating the deaf: Psychology, principles, and practices.* Boston: Houghton Mifflin.

Moores, D. F., & Sweet, C. (1990). Factors predictive of school achievement. In D. F. Moores & K. P. Meadow-Orlans (Eds.), *Educational and developmental aspects of deafness* (pp. 154–201). Washington, DC: Gallaudet University Press.

National Center for Health Statistics. (1999). *Vital and health statistics, Series 10, No. 194.* Retrieved 20 April 2005 from http://www.cdc.gov/nchs/data/series/sr_10/sr10_194.pdf

Neville, H. J., Coffey, S. A., Lawson, D., Fischer, A., Emmorey, K., & Bellugi, U. (1997). Neural systems mediation American Sign Language: Effects of sensory experience and age of acquisition. *Brain and Language, 57,* 285–308.

O'Connor, N., & Hermelin, B. M. (1973). Short-term memory for the order of pictures and syllables by deaf and hearing children. *Neuropsychologia, 11,* 437–442.

Ottem, E. (1980). An analysis of cognitive studies with deaf subjects. *American Annals of the Deaf, 125,* 564–575.

Pintner, R., & Patterson, D. (1916). A measure of the language ability of deaf children. *Psychology Review, 23*, 413–436.

Pintner, R., & Patterson, D. (1917). A comparison of deaf and hearing children in visual memory for digits. *Journal of Experimental Psychology, 2*, 76–88.

Pizzuto, E., Ardito, B., Caselli, M. C., & Volterra, V. (2001). Cognition and language in Italian deaf preschoolers of deaf and hearing families. In M. D. Clark, M. Marschark, & M. Karchmer (Eds.), *Context, cognition, and deafness* (pp. 49–70). Washington, DC: Gallaudet University Press.

Preyer, W. (1882). *Die Seele des Kindes*. Leipzig, Germany.

Raviv, S., Sharan, S., & Strauss, S. (1973). Intellectual development of deaf children in different educational environments. *Journal of Communication Disorders, 6*, 29–36.

Rettenback, R., Diller, G., & Sireteanu, R. (1999). Do deaf people see better? Texture segmentation and visual search compensate in adult but not in juvenile subjects. *Journal of Cognitive Neuroscience, 11*, 560–583.

Rönnberg, J. (2003). Working memory, neuroscience, and language: Evidence from deaf and hard-of-hearing individuals. In M. Marschark & P. E. Spencer (Eds.), *Oxford handbook of deaf studies, language, and education* (pp. 478–490). New York: Oxford University Press.

Sharpe, S. L. (1985). The primary mode of human communication and complex cognition. *American Annals of the Deaf, 130*, 39–46.

Spencer, P. E., & Marschark, M. (Eds.). (2006). *Advances in the spoken language development of deaf and hard-of-hearing children*. New York: Oxford University Press.

Stokoe, W. C. (2005). *Sign language structure: An outline of the visual communication system of the American deaf* (Studies in Linguistics, Occasional Papers 8). Buffalo, NY: Department of Anthropology and Linguistics, University of Buffalo. Reprinted in *Journal of Deaf Studies and Deaf Education, 10*, 3–37. (Original work published 1960)

Strassman, B. (1997). Metacognition and reading in children who are deaf: A review of the research. *Journal of Deaf Studies and Deaf Education, 2*, 140–149.

Swisher, M. V. (1993). Perceptual and cognitive aspects of recognition of signs in peripheral vision. In M. Marschark & M. D. Clark (Eds.), *Psychological perspectives on deafness* (pp. 229–265). Hillsdale, NJ: Lawrence Erlbaum Associates, Inc.

Talbot, K. F., & Haude, R. H. (1993). The relationship between sign language skill and spatial visualizations ability: Mental rotation of three-dimensional objects. *Perceptual and Motor Skills, 77*, 1387–1391.

Todman, J., & Cowdy, N. (1993). Processing of visual-action codes by deaf and hearing children: Coding orientation or capacity? *Intelligence, 17*, 237–250.

Todman, J., & Seedhouse, E. (1994). Visual-action code processing by deaf and hearing children. *Language and Cognitive Processes, 9*, 129–141.

Traxler, C. B. (2000). Measuring up to performance standards in reading and mathematics: Achievement of selected deaf and hard-of-hearing students in the national norming of the 9th Edition Stanford Achievement Test. *Journal of Deaf Studies and Deaf Education, 5*, 337–348.

Ulissi, S. M., Brice, P. J., & Gibbins, S. (1990). Use of the Kaufman-Assessment Battery for Children with the hearing impaired. *American Annals of the Deaf, 135*, 283–287.

Vernon, M. (1967). Relationship of language to the thinking process. *Archives of General Psychiatry, 16*, 325–333.

Vernon, M. (2005). Fifty years of research on the intelligence of deaf and hard of hearing children: A review of literature and discussion of implications. *Journal of Rehabilitation of the Deaf, 1*, 1–12. (Original work published 1968)

Vernon, M., & Andrews, J. F. (1990). *The psychology of deafness*. New York: Longman.

Wilhelm, O., & Oberauer, K. (2006). Why are reasoning ability and working memory capacity related to mental speed? An investigation of stimulus–response compatibility in choice reaction time tasks. *European Journal of Cognitive Psychology, 18*(1), 18–50.

Wilson, M., Bettger, J. G., Niculae, I., & Klima, E. S. (1997). Modality of language shapes working memory: Evidence from digit span and spatial span in ASL signers. *Journal of Deaf Studies and Deaf Education, 2,* 152–162.

Wilson, M., & Emmorey, K. (1997). A visuo-spatial "phonological loop" in working memory: Evidence from American Sign Language. *Memory and Cognition, 25,* 313–320.

Woll, B., & Ladd, P. (2003). Deaf communities. In M. Marschark & P. E. Spencer (Eds.), *Oxford handbook of deaf studies, language, and education* (pp. 151–163). New York: Oxford University Press.

Zweibel, A. (1987). More on the effects of early manual communication on the cognitive development of deaf children. *American Annals of the Deaf, 132,* 16–20.

Zwiebel, A., & Mertens, D. M. (1985). A comparison of intellectual structure in deaf and hearing children. *American Annals of the Deaf, 130,* 27–32.

EUROPEAN JOURNAL OF COGNITIVE PSYCHOLOGY
2006, 18 (1), 90–108

Individual differences in the ability to avoid distracting sounds

Emily M. Elliott and Katie M. Barrilleaux

Louisiana State University, Baton Rouge, USA

Nelson Cowan

University of Missouri-Columbia, USA

The present work aims to establish a greater understanding of the cognitive mechanisms involved in avoiding distraction from speech and nonspeech sounds. Although mixed results have been presented by research investigating the hypothesis that individuals with superior working memory abilities are better able to avoid acoustic distraction, we found that working memory correlated with some aspects of performance during distraction when carefully examined. This is consistent with the view that working memory involves resisting interference. In a large sample, we examined two different tasks accompanied by acoustic distraction—serial recall and rapid colour naming—as well as two different measures of working memory (operation span and running span). We show that the previous inability to find relations between working memory and avoidance of distraction may stem from the use of inadequate correlational techniques. Additionally, the level of difficulty of the serial recall task may be an important factor. The results illustrate that commonly used statistical techniques can be misleading and furthermore that the ability to avoid distraction from irrelevant items may not be a unitary construct.

The question of how much cognitive control we can exert in the face of distraction from stimuli in the environment is one that has generated a considerable amount of interest. Early research in this topic examined the capabilities of the selective attention system by examining the performance of participants in dichotic-listening tasks, often with the requirement that one channel of input be shadowed to control the direction of attention (Treisman, 1960). This type of research helped to define the limits of the cognitive system. More recently, researchers have examined the role of attention in cognition by asking

Correspondence should be addressed to Emily Elliott, Department of Psychology, Louisiana State University, 236 Audubon Hall, Baton Rouge, LA 70803, USA. Email: eelliott@lsu.edu

This work was supported by a grant from the Louisiana Board of Regents, awarded to the first author, and NIH Grant R01 HD-21338 awarded to the third author.

DOI:10.1080/09541440500216044

participants to perform complex memory span tasks in which some elements of both storage and processing are required (Turner & Engle, 1989). Current theoretical views describe attention as an important component of working memory function (Cowan, 1995; Engle, Kane, & Tuholski, 1999). This study is an attempt to integrate findings from different tasks with the goal of understanding the ability to avoid distraction from irrelevant sounds. Two measures of working memory will be utilised, along with two different measures of performance in the presence of irrelevant sounds. Past work with complex span measures and distraction-based tasks will be discussed, and then the design of the current study will be described.

Uniting the literature from the dichotic-listening and complex span paradigms, Conway, Cowan, and Bunting (2001) examined the relationship between individual differences in working memory performance and the ability to detect one's name in the unattended channel (the task of Moray, 1959; Wood & Cowan, 1995). Working memory span was measured using the operation span task (Turner & Engle, 1989), in which participants were asked to complete arithmetic problems between items presented for later serial recall. (This task will be discussed in more detail in the Method section.) Their findings revealed that those participants with operation spans in the lowest quartile were much *more* likely to report hearing their name in the unattended channel than those participants in the highest quartile (65% vs. 20%). The results clearly indicated that the ability to avoid distraction from irrelevant auditory material (in this case, the participant's own name) was related to working memory, a finding that is consistent with other evidence that high span individuals better control attention (e.g., Kane, Bleckley, Conway, & Engle, 2001).

However, recent work with a different type of task using irrelevant auditory materials has been somewhat of a puzzle, as the expected pattern of results has not been obtained. Beaman (2004) examined the role of working memory in individual differences in the ability to avoid distraction from irrelevant sounds while engaging in a serial recall task. This work, known as the irrelevant-speech effect (Colle & Welsh, 1976; Salamé & Baddeley, 1982), refers to the finding that performance on a serial recall task decreases in the presence of irrelevant speech that participants are instructed to ignore. Because it can occur also with nonspeech distracting sounds (Jones & Macken, 1993), it has more recently been termed the irrelevant-sound effect (ISE). Beaman also used the operation span task as a measure of working memory, and he did not find evidence for a relationship between the magnitude of the ISE and working memory span. Two studies found no relationship even between serial recall and the ISE (Ellermeier & Zimmer, 1997; Neath, Farley, & Surprenant, 2003).

This issue was examined once more by Elliott and Cowan (2005) in their study of individual and developmental differences in the ISE using both speech and tone stimuli. Although a few correlations were found between measures of memory span and the ISE, the correlations were in the positive direction (larger irrelevant-sound effects for higher span individuals), which was unexpected. The findings were interpreted in light of the role of rehearsal in the performance of both memory span tasks and the serial recall task used to measure the ISE. Prominent theories of the ISE discuss the importance of rehearsal of the relevant items for disruption from the irrelevant items to occur (e.g., Beaman & Jones, 1997, 1998). In those theories, it is assumed that the irrelevant sounds, even if they are nonspeech sounds, interfere with the rehearsal process and the episodic record that it creates in working memory. Those participants who are likely to be successful in a complex memory span task are likely to make heavy use of rehearsal of the to-be-remembered items. These same participants, as a consequence, by these assumptions would be likely to show large detrimental effects of irrelevant speech on their serial recall performance. Thus, a positive correlation could result if participants with a higher score on a working-memory measure, by engaging in more rehearsal, created more opportunities for corruption of the episodic record by irrelevant sounds.

One reason for the absence of a more consistent pattern of correlations is that they depend on individual ISE scores obtained by subtracting a speech condition from a no-speech control condition. In order for two measures to correlate, both must be sufficiently reliable. Elliott and Cowan (2005) showed that, even when the raw measures are quite reliable, the difference scores tend to be much less reliable. The highest reliability alpha coefficient obtained to date for an ISE may be that of Ellermeier and Zimmer (1997), and that coefficient was only .55. To illustrate the effect of this unreliability, according to the formula for correction of the attenuation of correlations caused by unreliability of the measures, $r_{corrected} = r_{xy} / (r_{xx} * r_{yy})$, if the true population correlation between the ISE and a working memory measure were .40 and the reliability of the two measures to be correlated were .55 and .90, respectively, then the observed correlation would be only .28. Elliott and Cowan (2005) solved this unreliability problem by using stepwise regressions on the raw measures, rather than calculating a subtraction for the ISE. If the irrelevant-sound condition accounts for significant variance in the working memory measure even after the variance from the silent control condition has been taken out, then it can be said that the irrelevant-sound effect is related to working memory. Elliott and Cowan still found inconsistent results with this regression method, but the question will be reexamined in the present paper using a different set of ISE conditions.

Another area of the literature that has shown relationships between working memory and performance in the presence of distracting stimuli is the traditional Stroop task, in which participants are asked to name the ink colour of an incongruent colour word (Stroop, 1935). Kane and Engle (2003) used the operation span task and a version of the Stroop task that also included some congruent trials (e.g., the word *red* written in red ink). When the proportion of congruent trials included in the experiment was high, participants with a low score on the working memory task were more likely to show interference effects from the incongruent stimuli (as revealed by either errors or changes in their response times to name the ink colour, depending on the experiment in the series). This was interpreted with respect to the goal maintenance necessary in the face of distraction. With a greater number of congruent trials, the goal of naming the ink colour became more difficult because the same result could be achieved by reading the word instead.

One limitation of the procedure of Kane and Engle (2003) is that it reflects a situation in which it is exceedingly difficult to ignore the distracting stimuli (printed colour words often matching the colours). Under such circumstances, participants may instead have to process them fully and actively suppress them, or prevent them from affecting the response. What is not yet clear is whether working memory performance is related to the effects of distracting colour words when the identity of the colour word is not so often tied to the identity of the printed colour. Also, it is not yet clear whether working memory performance is related to performance on a version of Stroop-type test in which the distracting words are presented in the auditory modality (Cowan & Barron, 1987; Elliott & Cowan, 2001; Elliott, Cowan, & Valle-Inclan, 1998), providing a closer analogue to the ISE.

Finally, in addition to the operation span task (Turner & Engle, 1989) described above, which is a measure of working memory commonly used in recent literature, we also used an older task termed running memory span (Pollack, Johnson, & Knaff, 1959). In this task, participants are asked to attend to a string of items without knowing when the items will stop (i.e., with a variable and unpredictable number of stimuli), and are then asked to remember a set amount of items from the end of the list (e.g., the last six or eight items). This type of task, like operation span, correlates with mental aptitudes more highly than does the typical digit span test, and correlates well with other working memory tasks (Cowan, Elliott, & Saults, 2002; Mukunda & Hall, 1992).

The running span task, as we administered it, had several attributes that made it very different from the operation span task. First, whereas operation span was administered visually, running span was administered with a list of spoken digits to be recalled, at a rapid rate of four digits per second. The acoustic presentation is important because, if correlations between memory span and acoustic distraction are driven by individual differences in individuals' tendency to attend to visual versus auditory stimuli, operation span and running span should not yield similar results. The rapid presentation also is important because it allows a clean interpretation of processes involved in running span. In a particularly elegant investigation of running span, Hockey (1973) varied the rate of presentation and also varied the processing instructions. With slow presentations, participants did best when instructed to try to rehearse; they presumably used a method in which the series to be remembered was continually updated in working memory. However, with fast presentations, participants did better when instructed simply to listen passively until the list ended. At that point, they presumably had to focus attention on an auditory sensory memory stream in order to extract the last few digits into working memory (see Cowan et al., 2002). Thus, unlike the operation span task, in our running span task attention is used at a specific, well-defined point in time. Correlations between operation span and running span, despite these substantial differences in procedure, presumably occur because there is a core ability common to them, such as the scope or agility of attention (Cowan, 2001).

In sum, the present study represents an attempt to integrate the findings discussed above in an investigation of individual differences in the ability to avoid distraction from irrelevant sounds. It is perhaps the first study to use multiple measures of auditory distraction and multiple measures of working memory to examine individual differences. Several different irrelevant-sound tasks were used: three conditions in a serial recall task (silence, irrelevant speech, and irrelevant tones) and several in a speeded colour-naming task (silence, noncolour words, and colour words, with the words at two timing intervals). Working memory was measured in two tasks (operation span and running memory span). We will attempt to answer four specific questions: (1) whether the ISE, measured using both speech and tones as distracting auditory stimuli, is related to working memory; (2) whether the cross-modal Stroop effect is related to working memory; (3) whether the two irrelevant-sound tasks are related to each other, and related to working memory in the same way; and (4) whether the two measures of working memory tap into the same abilities and therefore yield the same patterns of correlations. To foreshadow our results a bit, it appears that the ability to avoid distraction from irrelevant sounds may not be a unitary construct, as different elements of working memory abilities may be called upon as task demands change. Findings from this research can help to inform our understanding of the factors that contribute to individual differences in performance in the presence of irrelevant sounds.

METHOD

Participants

One hundred and twenty undergraduate students from Louisiana State University participated in exchange for extra credit in Psychology courses. Of these, two participants reported hearing loss, and four were not native speakers of English. Additionally, four participants were lost due to computer error (two in the operation span task and two in the running memory span task). With those exclusions, 110 were eligible to be included in the data analyses. From that sample, initial screening of the data was done based on the level of arithmetic accuracy in the operation span task. Participants had to achieve at least 80% accuracy on the arithmetic problems to be included in subsequent analyses. This criterion resulted in the removal of nine more participants. These deletions left a total sample of 101 participants (19 male) with data in all tasks. Although this is skewed towards more females in the sample, past research has not shown any gender differences in the ISE (Ellermeier & Zimmer, 1997).

Design, apparatus, and stimuli

A total of six tasks were administered in individual sessions lasting approximately 1 hour and 45 min. Two of the tasks were measures of test anxiety, which will not be discussed here. There were two task orders, with the goal of balancing the order of the two irrelevant-sound tasks. The running memory span task was always first, followed by the operation span task second. In the first task order, the irrelevant-sounds serial recall task was third, whereas, in the second task order, the cross-modal colour naming task was third. The fourth and fifth tasks were the test anxiety measures, and the sixth and final task was the other irrelevant-sounds task, depending on whether a participant was randomly assigned to the first or second task order.

Participants were run on Dell Dimension desktop computers equipped with 17-inch monitors and all programs were presented with E-Prime programming software (Schneider, Eschman, & Zuccolotto, 2002). Each task will be described separately.

Running memory span task. Participants were presented with a fixation cross on the centre of the screen to orient them to the beginning of each trial. Following this, a random list of the digits 1–9 was presented through headphones at the rate of four per second. The spoken digits were recorded in a male voice and were digitally compressed. Although the rate was very rapid, the digits were easy to comprehend. The sound level was measured to be 64 dB(A) with an earphone coupler and a Quest sound-level meter, using the fast setting. The list length was randomly varied to avoid participants' prediction of the end of the list, and five list lengths were presented (12, 14, 16, 18, and 20 digits per list). Participants were instructed to listen carefully to the digits and then try to recall just the last six digits. They had use of a placeholder when typing their response. Strict serial order was emphasised and participants were given practice trials to be sure they understood the instructions. The experimenter made sure the participants understood that they were to recall only the last six digits before continuing on to the test trials. There were three practice trials followed by 40 test trials, including eight repetitions of each of the five list lengths. Each block of five trials included all five list lengths in a random order.

Operation span task. This task was taken from the Conway and Engle (1996) version of the operation span (Ospan) task that is posted on the website for the System of Teaching Experimental Psychology (http://step.psy.cmu.edu). This version of the program presented a two-step arithmetic problem of the type $[(2/2) + 2 = 3?]$, which participants were to assess as true or false. Immediately after their response to each arithmetic problem, a word was presented. Participants were instructed to remember the words for later recall, and to make a concentrated effort to solve the arithmetic problems correctly. All material in this task was read aloud by the participants, so that the experimenter could monitor their compliance with instructions. After receiving the items for a given trial, recall of the words was cued and participants typed in their recall response. There were three sets of items randomly presented, ranging from two to six trials in length, for a total of 60 recall responses across the 15 trials.

Irrelevant-sounds serial recall task.   Participants were asked to recall eight-item lists of the consonants *f, k, l, m, q, r, s, t,* while ignoring any sounds heard through the headphones. Each trial began with a fixation cross for 750 ms and was followed by presentation of the to-be-remembered (TBR) items at the rate of 1 per second. This was followed by an 8 s retention interval before the cue to recall was given. Participants were asked to type in their response, and strict serial recall was emphasised. The keys on the keyboard that were not part of the current response were disabled, so that participants could only type in letters that were part of the presented list. Sounds were presented either simultaneously with the TBR items, or afterwards in the retention interval.

There were three types of auditory distractor conditions, silence as a baseline measure of serial recall performance, tones, and speech. The tones were a random selection of 500 ms sine waves of 87, 174, 266, 348, 529, 696, 788, 880, and 972 Hz, and were the same tones used in Elliott and Cowan (2005). The speech tokens were one-syllable adjectives that did not begin with the same consonants as the TBR items: *bad, cold, due, hot, nice, plus, vast, warm.* The speech sounds were digitised in a female voice and were 310–500 ms in duration. The rate of presentation was equivalent to the visual stimuli at 1 per second, and when presented together the auditory and visual stimuli had simultaneous onsets. The sounds were measured with a Quest sound-level meter and earphone coupler, using the fast setting, and were determined to be within the range of 66–72 dB(A). The sounds also were judged to be subjectively equal in intensity.

Five trial types were included (silence, speech during or after the list, and tones during or after the list) and the task contained 65 trials. The first five trials were practice, and included one of each type of trial. The test trials were broken up into two blocks of 30 trials each, with the opportunity for a break between blocks. The total number of test trials consisted of 12 repetitions of each possible trial type (6 in the first block and 6 in the second).

Cross-modal Stroop task.   This colour-naming task was modelled after the task used by Elliott et al. (1998), with the main change being the inclusion of congruent trials. Participants were first presented with a 500 ms fixation cross and were asked to name the colour square that appeared on the screen as quickly as possible. Responses were spoken into a headset microphone connected to a response box that recorded the vocal reaction time. The experimenter keyed in the spoken response, and also keyed in special notation if the participant made a false start (such as saying "gree...blue" or if the experimenter made an error. The colours *red, green, blue,* and *yellow* were used to make up the 4.4 cm × 4.4 cm colour squares. There were three auditory conditions, silence as a baseline measure of reaction time to name the colour squares, colour words, and non-colour words. These were digitised words in a female voice, 210–500 ms long. However, on different trials of the present experiment, there could be either a match or a mismatch between the colour square and the spoken colour word. The colour words came from the same set as the visually presented colour squares, and the noncolour words came from the set of *tall, long, short,* and *big.* These words were used in Elliott and Cowan (2001) and were equated for frequency with the colour words.

In addition to the manipulation of type of auditory distractor, there was a manipulation of the presentation timing. The onset of the auditory distractor was either simultaneous with the presentation of the colour square (0 ms SOA) or the onset of the auditory distractor preceded the presentation of the colour square by 500 ms (500 ms SOA). The manipulation of SOA and the type of auditory distractor created six unique trial types. Participants began with 12 practice trials in which colour squares were presented in silence for practice with the microphone. There were two blocks of 104 test trials, each of which included 24 incongruent- and 16 congruent-colour word trials, 32 noncolour-word trials, and 32 trials with silence. Within each such condition, half of the trials occurred at a 0 ms SOA and half occurred at a 500 ms SOA. For the silent condition, a 500 ms SOA meant that 500 ms elapsed between the end of the fixation cross and the beginning of the colour square.

RESULTS

Descriptive statistics are presented in Table 1. Analyses for each task will be discussed individually, to be followed by correlation and regression analyses across tasks.

Working memory measures

Operation span task. The operation span task was scored in two different ways. One method of scoring produced a span score and the other produced a measure of the proportion of items correctly recalled (see Kane et al., 2004, for a discussion of scoring). Both methods rely on strict serial recall. In the span score method, lists that are recalled correctly are given one point and this is multiplied by the list length. The points for each list are then summed to provide a total score of the number of items correctly recalled across the task. For example, a person correctly responding to all three lists at length 2 would receive six points,

TABLE 1
Descriptive statistics for memory measures and auditory distraction tasks

Task	Measure	Mean	Range	Standard error
Operational span	Span score	19.35	2.00–50.00	1.07
	Proportion score	0.57	0.24–0.94	0.02
	Math accuracy	0.94	0.80–1.00	0.01
Running span	LL average	0.52	0.22–0.86	0.01
Serial recall	Silence	0.57	0.22–0.98	0.02
	Speech during	0.51	0.18–0.96	0.02
	Speech after	0.51	0.22–0.92	0.02
	Tone during	0.55	0.20–0.94	0.02
	Tone after	0.55	0.19–0.96	0.02
Colour naming	Colour 0 ms inc	570	421–750	6.41
	Colour 0 ms con	537	404–733	6.72
	Noncolour 0 ms	553	406–758	6.83
	Silence 0 ms	506	385–703	5.93
	Colour 500 ms inc	482	323–656	5.22
	Colour 500 ms con	458	357–600	4.76
	Noncolour 500 ms	474	376–612	4.65
	Silence 500 ms	489	378–620	4.75

$N = 101$. The units for the means are the proportions recalled, except for span score (number recalled) and colour naming conditions (reaction time in ms). "During" and "after'" refer to whether the sound was presented during or after the list to be recalled. "Inc" and "con" refer to colour words that were inconsistent or consistent with the colours on the computer screen.

and this would be added to the points from any additional lists answered correctly. The proportion correct measure does not depend upon the entire list being answered correctly for the participant to earn credit for that list. The proportion of items correctly recalled in each list is averaged across lists, to produce a total proportion correct score.

Running memory span task. The running span task contained five list lengths, and the proportion correct scores for all list lengths were entered into a one-way, repeated-measures ANOVA. The results of this analysis indicated that performance did not differ among list lengths, and in the remaining results the average of the list lengths will be used.

Auditory distraction tasks

Cross-modal Stroop task. Data from the cross-modal Stroop task were examined to determine the number of responses coded as incorrect (the wrong colour was named), false starts ("blu...green"), or experimenter errors. Less than 1% of all trials were answered incorrectly. False starts were made on 1.5%, and experimenter errors were made on less than 0.5% of all trials. After removing those trials, the remaining trials were used to calculate the median response time for each condition. These were then entered into analyses to determine if the Stroop interference effect occurred.

First a 2 (SOA) × 4 (auditory condition: colour incongruent, colour congruent, noncolour, or silence) ANOVA of the eight different conditions in the cross-modal Stroop task was conducted. There was a significant main effect of SOA, $F(1, 100) = 428.07$, $MSE = 2054$, $p < .01$, reflecting faster overall response times in the 500 ms condition ($M = 476$ ms) than in the 0 ms condition ($M = 542$ ms). The main effect of SOA is consistent with previous findings in this task, and has been interpreted as a warning effect (Elliott et al., 1998). The main effect of auditory condition was also significant, $F(3, 300) = 73.90$, $MSE = 534$, $p < .01$. Response times were fastest in the silence and congruent colour word conditions ($M = 497$ ms for both), followed by the noncolour word condition ($M = 513$ ms). The slowest responding occurred in the incongruent colour word condition ($M = 526$ ms). Finally, the Auditory condition × SOA interaction was significant as well, $F(3, 300) = 126.01$, $MSE = 428$, $p < .01$.

To investigate this interaction, the analysis was followed by separate one-way analyses of each SOA condition. The analysis of the 0 ms SOA conditions was significant, $F(3, 300) = 122.30$, $MSE = 617$, $p < .01$, and Bonferroni post hoc testing was done to determine the differences among the conditions. All four of the 0 ms SOA conditions differed significantly (all $ps < .01$). The patterns of response times indicated a significant interference effect in the presence of incongruent colour words and a significant facilitation effect in the presence of congruent colour words (relative to the performance in the noncolour word condition). The analysis of the 500 ms SOA conditions was also significant, $F(3, 300) = 52.12$, $MSE = 345$, $p < .01$, and was also followed by Bonferroni post hoc testing. The results indicated that all comparisons were significantly different, with the exception of the comparison of the incongruent colour word condition and the silent condition. Consistent with the interpretation of a warning effect, response times were slowest in the silent condition. The fastest response times were seen in the congruent colour word condition, but the interpretation of a facilitation effect is confounded with the presence of the warning effect. To summarise, for the 0 ms SOA, silent < consistent < noncolour < inconsistent, whereas, for the 500 ms SOA, consistent < noncolour < inconsistent = silent.

Serial recall task. The dependent variable in the serial recall task with irrelevant sounds was the proportion of correct responses. The five auditory conditions were entered into a one-way, repeated-measures ANOVA to determine if an ISE occurred. This analysis was significant, $F(4, 400) = 11.85$, $MSE = 0.0059$, $p < .01$, and was followed by a Bonferroni post hoc test. The pattern of performance indicated by this test was that performance in silence was best and did not differ significantly from performance in the two tone conditions (tone during and tone after); however, performance in the two speech conditions was significantly lower than in both silence and tones. The two speech conditions did not differ significantly (speech during and speech after).

Due to the absence of an effect of the presentation timing of the distractors, the conditions were collapsed across trials in which the irrelevant sounds occurred during versus after the list. The remaining three conditions were then analysed to determine if the silent control condition differed significantly from the average of the speech and tone conditions. This analysis produced a significant result, $F(2, 200) = 23.69$, $MSE = 0.0038$, $p < .01$, which was then followed by a Bonferroni post hoc test that followed the same pattern as the analyses above. Tones and silence did not differ significantly, although performance in speech was significantly lower than the other two conditions. This absence of an irrelevant tone effect is inconsistent with previous work (see individual experiments within Elliott & Cowan, 2005) and is puzzling due to other published reports of irrelevant tone effects (Jones & Macken, 1993; LeCompte, Neely, & Wilson, 1997). However, as we will see, one explanation is that individuals differed in their ability to overcome the effects of irrelevant tones, in a systematic rather than random manner.

Correlations and regression analyses

Correlations.   Correlations among the working memory measures and the irrelevant-sound tasks are presented in Table 2. Inspection of this table reveals the clear relationships among the working memory measures and the conditions of the serial recall task, but no relationships among the working memory measures and the conditions of the colour-naming task. The colour and non-colour conditions in the Stroop task produced significant negative correlations with serial recall; the correlations were negative because faster performance (lower RTs) in the colour-naming task went with higher serial recall scores.

The absence of any significant relationship between working memory measures and colour-naming speeds in Table 2 is difficult to interpret because the attentional control factor in colour naming should be found only in the subtraction of the colour conditions from the corresponding noncolour conditions, or possibly in the subtraction of the noncolour conditions from the silent condition. We have noted that these subtractions do not result in very reliable measures. In fact, Cronbach's alpha measures of reliability for the effect of speech during or after the list and tones during or after the list, as subtractions from the silent control condition, were all .23 or lower, despite the high reliabilities for individual conditions shown in Table 2; and those for subtractive measures in the Stroop task were lower still. Indeed, there were no significant correlations between working memory measures and any of the difference scores, in either the serial recall task or in the colour-naming task.

TABLE 2
Correlations with working memory measures and irrelevant-sounds tasks

Task	1	2	3	4	5	6	7	8	9	10	11	12	13	14
Working memory														
OspanScore (1)	*.73*													
OspanProp (2)	.90**	*.71*												
RunSpan (3)	.31**	.34**	*.90*											
Serial recall														
Silence (4)	.36**	.36**	.59**	*.85*										
Speech average (5)	.35**	.36**	.54**	.86**	*.91*									
Tone average (6)	.43**	.42**	.58**	.88**	.92**	*.90*								
Colour naming														
Colour0Inc (7)	−.14	−.11	−.16	−.26*	−.29*	−.29*	*.83*							
Colour0Con (8)	−.11	−.05	−.19	−.18	−.21*	−.20*	.84**	*.67*						
Noncolour (9)	−.06	−.03	−.17	−.25*	−.25*	−.21*	.89**	.83**	*.90*					
Silence0 (10)	−.13	−.10	−.10	−.19	−.23*	−.19	.89**	.81**	.89**	*.88*				
Colour500Inc (11)	−.09	−.05	−.15	−.23*	−.26*	−.26*	.78**	.72**	.74**	.79**	*.83*			
Colour500Con (12)	−.10	−.02	−.19	−.24*	−.31*	−.28*	.73**	.70**	.70**	.75**	.82**	*.44*		
Noncolour500 (13)	−.11	−.05	−.10	−.19	−.24*	−.23*	.79**	.72**	.79**	.81**	.87**	.83**	*.87*	
Silence500 (14)	−.07	−.02	−.16	−.21*	−.25*	−.22*	.83**	.78**	.83**	.87**	.89**	.82**	.90**	*.89*

$N = 101$. Ospan = operation span, Prop = proportion, RunSpan = running span. Colour0Inc = colour naming with a 0 ms interval and inconsistency between the colour and spoken word; Con = consistent; and so on. Numbers in italics are chronbach's alpha measure of reliability. In the colour naming task, reliability measures were based on mean reaction times with the exclusion of data points below 100 ms or above 2 s; these were highly (> .93) correlated with the median reaction times, which were used for the reported correlations.

$*p < .05$, $**p < .001$.

101

Regressions.   Past research in the area of individual differences in the ISE has used difference scores to measure the magnitude of the disruption, typically subtracting performance in the presence of speech from performance in silence. However, the low reliability of difference scores can be problematic (Elliott & Cowan, 2005). Given this difficulty, regression analyses were used to partition the variance from the silent condition separately from the conditions with irrelevant sounds, thus removing the variance due to the baseline measure.

In the first regression analysis, operation span scores were used as the dependent variable with the silent control condition entered in first, producing a significant $R^2 = .13, p < .001$. When the average of the irrelevant-tone condition was added in second, the result was a significant $\Delta R^2 = .06, p < .01$. This same analysis was done in the reverse order and the average of the tone condition accounted for 19% of the variance, $p < .001$. When the silent control condition was added in second it did not account for any additional variance. To ascertain the direction of this relationship, partial correlations were calculated. The correlation between the operation span score and the silent control condition, with the tone average condition partialled out, was $r_p = -.05$, n.s. However, the correlation between the operation span score and the irrelevant-tone condition average, with the silent control condition partialled out, was $r_p = .26, p < .01$. This indicates an effect of the tones in the serial recall task that is larger for low span individuals than for high span individuals; the high span individuals do better in the tone condition than one would predict on the basis of their silent control condition scores. This appears to be one consequence of the better attentional-control capabilities of high span individuals.

In order to clarify the significant regression effects, results were examined separately in the 26 individuals with the highest and 26 individuals with the lowest operation spans (approximately the top and bottom quartiles). For high spans, the proportions correct in the silence and tone conditions were nearly identical at .69 and .68, respectively. In the low spans, they were also nearly identical, at .48 and .47, respectively. However, the relation between silence and tone conditions appeared to differ between these groups. For high spans, the regression equation was: "tones = .72 (silence) + .18". For low spans, however, it was "tones = .78 (silence) + .10". It was almost identical to this for the middle-span subjects: "tones = .77 (silence) + .10". An informal description of these results is that, in high span individuals, performance in the presence of tones was more protected than it was in other participants, even when performance in silence was relatively low.

Regression analyses comparable to those for the tone conditions were conducted with the average of the irrelevant-speech conditions. Speech consistently accounted for nonsignificant amounts of variance beyond what was accounted for by the silent control condition. The implications are that the dual-task nature of the serial recall task with irrelevant sounds may differ depending on whether the sounds are speech or tones. The tone condition accounts for extra variance.

Very similar patterns of results were obtained when the operation span proportion score was used. Perhaps, unlike tones, irrelevant speech cannot be blocked by the mechanisms of attention, even in high span individuals.

Also, comparable analyses were conducted with running memory span, as opposed to operation span, as the criterion variable, but the results were not the same. The silent control condition accounted for a great deal of the variance in running memory span, $R^2 = .35$, $p < .001$. When the irrelevant-tone condition was added in second it only accounted for a nonsignificant 2% of additional variance. When the irrelevant-tone condition was entered into the equation first, it produced $R^2 = .34$, $p < .001$, and the silent control condition produced $\Delta R^2 = .03$, $p < .05$. Similarly, the irrelevant-speech condition added no variance when entered after the silent control condition. The speech condition entered first accounted for $R^2 = .28$, $p < .001$, and the silent condition added afterward contributed $\Delta R^2 = .06$, $p < .01$. Thus, for running span, the irrelevant-sound conditions accounted for less variance than the silent control condition. One possible theoretical interpretation of these results is consistent with the idea that the running span task is performed in a very different manner than the operation span task, thus leading to the differences between the regression results for these two working memory tasks. The running span task relies more heavily on participants drawing the responses from the focus of attention, as compared to the operation span task, which involves reactivating items that are no longer in the focus of attention. We will return to this matter of the differences between the two working memory tasks in the final discussion.

All eight Stroop-task measures (0 ms and 500 ms presentations of inconsistent colour words, consistent colour words, noncolour words, and silence) also were examined, but even the combination of all of them did not account for a significant amount of variance in regressions on operation span or running span.

DISCUSSION

This study represents the first attempt to compare different types of measures of distraction by irrelevant sounds, both to each other and to individual difference measures of working memory. Several previous studies have looked for positive relations between working memory and the ability to overcome effects of irrelevant sounds, which would be manifest as negative correlations between working memory task performance and the magnitude of the ISE (Beaman, 2004; Ellermeier & Zimmer, 1997; Elliott & Cowan, 2005; Neath et al., 2003). This relation would be expected on the grounds that high working memory indicates the ability to control attention and filter out distraction (e.g., Conway et al., 2001; Kane et al., 2001). Nevertheless, an effect of that nature still has never been obtained for the irrelevant-speech effect of Salamé and Baddeley (1982), and the present study is the first one to find such a relation in the context of the irrelevant-sound effect of Jones and Macken (1993), with tone distractors. There is convergent evidence in developmental work; Elliott (2002) found that young children had larger ISEs than adults, for both speech and tone distractors.

The significant relation between working memory and the irrelevant-tone effect on serial recall observed in the present study was relatively weak, but it still is of considerable theoretical importance that the expectation was confirmed. One account of the present results is that attention can be used to filter out distracting tones, though only by individuals with high working memory span. In contrast, it may not be possible even for them to filter out distracting speech sounds, which may automatically enter the phonological loop and contaminate memory for printed verbal items, as suggested by Salamé and Baddeley (1982). In a very different experimental procedure that does not involve serial recall, Conway et al. (2001) found a relation between working memory and the ability to filter out irrelevant speech, but that was when the relevant and irrelevant channels were speech streams to opposite ears and the relevant channel only had to be repeated, not retained.

There are several reasons why previous studies may not have obtained the expected relations between working memory and irrelevant-sound effects. The first is the poor reliability of difference scores that are taken as the proper measures of irrelevant-sound effects. That problem can be overcome through regressions using combinations of the raw scores instead of correlations between difference scores, as Elliott and Cowan (2005) have already pointed out. It was that regression technique that was successful here. Second, though, Elliott and Cowan noted psychometric properties that could tend to cancel out the desired relation. Individuals who perform better in the silent condition of serial recall have further for their scores to drop in the presence of irrelevant sounds. Third, most previous studies of individual differences did not include irrelevant-tone effects, though Elliott and Cowan did.

However, the present study is the first one in which, despite any such measurement difficulties, a positive relation was observed between working memory and the ability to filter out irrelevant sounds. One of the main methodological differences in this study, as compared to previous work, was the level of difficulty of the task. This ISE task used a series of consonants as the to-be-remembered items, whereas previous studies have used the digits 1–9. Although the only keys that participants could type on the keyboard were those in the response set, the keys were not marked in any way and it appeared to affect the difficulty level of the task. Mean levels of performance were lower than reported data, such as Elliott and Cowan (2005). It is unlikely that participants were able to memorise the items in the response set and, as result, did not perform as well. This finding of lower performance with consonants as compared to digits was also shown by Hughes, Vachon, and Jones (2005), and they discussed the role of stimulus familiarity in the task. Future research should address this issue because increasing the level of difficulty of the task may be responsible for the correlations we obtained here.

Mixed results were obtained on the question of whether the process of filtering out irrelevant sounds is similar or different in serial recall and colour naming tasks. No relation was observed between working memory and the ability to filter our irrelevant stimuli in the Stroop procedure, but the work of Kane and Engle (2003) suggests that such a relation should be easier to observe when the proportion of trials with consistency between the relevant colour and the irrelevant colour word is made much higher, so that attending to the spoken word would yield the correct result on most trials. In the present study, because only 15.4% of all trials included a colour word consistent with the printed colour, note that these consistent-colour words were not truly helpful to the subjects. With a 0 ms SOA they resulted in reaction times faster than noncolour or inconsistent-colour words, but still slower than in the silent control condition. We predict that, in a procedure in which the majority of trials were consistent-colour trials (cf. Kane & Engle, 2003), silence would produce slower responding than the consistent-word condition, so that attending to the consistent word would become truly helpful on most trials. (That information cannot be obtained from Kane and Engle as they did not use a cross-modal Stroop-like procedure and did not include stimuli with no irrelevant verbal component.)

However, another alternative is that the ability to avoid distraction from irrelevant sounds is not a unitary construct. The lack of correlations between performance in the cross-modal Stroop task and the measures of working memory could have been driven by the lack of a memory component in the Stroop task. As mentioned above, without the goal maintenance required by a high level of congruent trials, the cross-modal Stroop task did not share in the task requirements of the three other tasks in this experiment. The cognitive mechanisms required when avoiding distraction in a memory-demanding situation may be different from the cognitive mechanisms required in a situation where quick response times are instead the priority.

Additionally, this experiment allowed a comparison of two measures of working memory: running span and operation span. The positive correlation between these two measures provides evidence that they are in fact, measuring the same construct. However, the correlations were $r = .31$ when using the Ospan score and $r = .34$ when using the Ospan proportion measure. It is known that both of these measures correlate well with aptitudes (Cowan et al., 2005), and this ability to predict aptitudes may be what is driving the relationship observed in the present data set. Differences among the two working memory tasks could be responsible for the differences in predictive ability with the irrelevant-sounds serial recall task. This is also consistent with the idea that the ability to avoid distraction may not be one single ability, but instead of combination of abilities dependent upon task demands.

Previous work by other investigators has shown that the ability to overcome proactive interference (PI) is very important in the relationship between performance measures and working memory scores (Lustig, May, & Hasher, 2001). In the study by Lustig et al., measures were taken to minimise the amount of PI present in a typical working memory task. When this was done, correlations between performance on the working memory task and performance in a prose recall task dropped to zero. This work illustrates that an important component of working memory capacity is the ability to overcome PI. In the current study, the two working memory tasks that we used may induce participants to counteract the negative effects of PI in different ways. In running span, participants can use the focus of attention to perform the task successfully, while in operation span participants will have to make connections with items that have moved out of the focus of attention and reactivate these items at the time of recall. Previous evidence has demonstrated that running span, and another typical measure of working memory known as reading span, account for different patterns of variance, while a task such as counting span accounted for similar variance to running span (Cowan et al., 2003). Running span may correlate with measures of working memory that tap into this ability to hold items in the focus of attention, thus explaining the correlations with measures of intelligence while explaining the lack of correlations with the ISE.

More research is needed for the development of a model of the ability to avoid distraction from irrelevant sounds, including the idea that this ability may not be a unitary construct. The present study provides several important pieces of information regarding the relationships among working memory and the ISE, as well as the relationship between the two irrelevant-sound tasks used here. The results from the tone condition of the serial recall task are especially noteworthy. Future research will examine the relationship between operation span and the irrelevant-tone condition more closely, as well as the level of difficulty of the serial recall task.

REFERENCES

Beaman, C. P. (2004). The irrelevant sound phenomenon revisited: What role for working memory capacity? *Journal of Experimental Psychology: Learning, Memory, and Cognition, 30*(5), 1106–1118.

Beaman, C. P., & Jones, D. M. (1997). Role of serial order in the irrelevant speech effect: Tests of the changing-state hypothesis. *Journal of Experimental Psychology: Learning, Memory, and Cognition, 23*, 459–471.

Beaman, C. P., & Jones, D. M. (1998). Irrelevant sound disrupts order information in free recall as in serial recall. *Quarterly Journal of Experimental Psychology, 51A*, 615–636.

Colle, H. A., & Welsh, A. (1976). Acoustic masking in primary memory. *Journal of Verbal Learning and Verbal Behavior, 15*, 17–31.

Conway, A. R. A., Cowan, N., & Bunting, M. F. (2001). The cocktail party phenomenon revisited: The importance of working memory capacity. *Psychonomic Bulletin and Review, 8*, 331–335.

Conway, A. R. A., & Engle, R.W. (1996). Individual differences in working memory capacity: More evidence for a general capacity theory. *Memory, 4*, 577–590.

Cowan, N. (1995). *Attention and memory: An integrated framework* (Oxford Psychology Series, No. 26). New York: Oxford University Press. (Paperback edition published 1997)

Cowan, N. (2001). The magical number 4 in short-term memory: A reconsideration of mental storage capacity. *Behavioral and Brain Sciences, 24*, 87–185.

Cowan, N., & Barron, A. (1987). Cross-modal, auditory–visual Stroop interference and possible implications for speech memory. *Perception and Psychophysics, 41*, 393–401.

Cowan, N., Elliott, E. M., & Saults, J. S. (2002). The search for what is fundamental in the development of working memory. In R. Kail & H. Reese (Eds.), *Advances in Child Development and Behavior* (Vol. 29, pp. 1–49). San Diego, CA: Academic Press.

Cowan, N., Elliott, E. M., Saults, J. S., Morey, C. C., Mattox, S., Hismjatullina, A., & Conway, A. R. A. (2005). On the capacity of attention: Its estimation and its role in working memory and cognitive aptitudes. *Cognitive Psychology, 51*, 42–100.

Cowan, N., Towse, J. N., Hamilton, Z., Saults, J. S., Elliott, E. M., Lacey, J. F., et al. (2003). Children's working memory processes: A response-timing analysis. *Journal of Experimental Psychology: General, 132*, 113–132.

Ellermeier, W., & Zimmer, K. (1997). Individual differences in susceptibility to the "irrelevant speech effect". *Journal of the Acoustical Society of America, 102*, 2191–2199.

Elliott, E. M. (2002). The irrelevant speech effect and children: Theoretical implications of developmental change. *Memory and Cognition, 30*, 478–487.

Elliott, E. M., & Cowan, N. (2001). Habituation to auditory distractors in a cross-modal, color–word interference task. *Journal of Experimental Psychology: Learning, Memory, and Cognition, 27*, 654–667.

Elliott, E. M., & Cowan, N. (2005). Individual differences in memory span and in the effects of irrelevant sounds on memory performance: The coherence of the irrelevant sound effect. *Memory and Cognition, 33*, 664–675.

Elliott, E. M., Cowan, N., & Valle-Inclan, F. (1998). The nature of cross-modal, color–word interference effects. *Perception and Psychophysics, 60*, 761–767.

Engle, R. W., Kane, M. J., & Tuholski, S. W. (1999). Individual differences in working memory capacity and what they tell us about controlled attention, general fluid intelligence, and functions of the prefrontal cortex. In A. Miyake & P. Shah (Eds.), *Models of working memory: Mechanisms of active maintenance and executive control* (pp. 102–134). New York: Cambridge University Press.

Hockey, R. (1973). Rate of presentation in running memory and direct manipulation of input-processing strategies. *Quarterly Journal of Experimental Psychology A, 25*, 104–111.

Hughes, R. W., Vachon, F., & Jones, D. M. (2005). Auditory attentional capture during serial recall: Violations at encoding of an algorithm-based neural model? *Journal of Experimental Psychology: Learning, Memory, and Cognition, 31*, 736–749.

Jones, D. M., & Macken, W. J. (1993). Irrelevant tones produce an irrelevant speech effect: Implications for phonological coding in working memory. Journal of Experimental Psychology: Learning, Memory, and Cognition, 19, 369–381.

Kane, M. J., Bleckley, M. K., Conway, A. R. A., & Engle, R. W. (2001). A controlled-attention view of working-memory capacity. *Journal of Experimental Psychology: General, 130*, 169–183.

Kane, M. J., & Engle, R. W. (2003). Working memory capacity and the control of attention: The contributions of goal neglect, response competition, and task set to Stroop interference. *Journal of Experimental Psychology: General, 132*, 47–70.

Kane, M. J., Hambrick, D. Z., Tuholski, S. W., Wilhelm, O., Payne, T. W., & Engle, R. W. (2004). The generality of working memory capacity: A latent-variable approach to verbal and visuospatial memory span and reasoning. *Journal of Experimental Psychology: General, 133*, 189–217.

LeCompte, D. C., Neely, C. B., & Wilson, J. R. (1997). Irrelevant speech and irrelevant tones: The relative importance of speech to the irrelevant sound effect. *Journal of Experimental Psychology: Learning, Memory, and Cognition, 23*, 472–483.

Lustig, C., May, C. P., & Hasher, L. (2001). Working memory span and the role of proactive interference. *Journal of Experimental Psychology: General, 130*, 199–207.

Moray, N. (1959). Attention in dichotic listening: Affective cues and the influence of instructions. *Quarterly Journal of Experimental Psychology, 11*, 56–60.

Mukunda, K. V., & Hall, V. C. (1992). Does performance on memory for order correlate with performance on standardized measures of ability? A meta-analysis. *Intelligence, 16*, 81–97.

Neath, I., Farley, L. A., & Surprenant, A. M. (2003). Directly assessing the relationship between irrelevant speech and articulatory suppression. *Quarterly Journal of Experimental Psychology, 56*(A), 1269–1278.

Pollack, I., Johnson, L. B., & Knaff, P. R. (1959). Running memory span. *Journal of Experimental Psychology, 57*, 137–146.

Salamé, P., & Baddeley, A. (1982). Disruption of short-term memory by unattended speech: Implications for the structure of working memory. *Journal of Verbal Learning and Verbal Behavior, 21*, 150–164.

Schneider, W., Eschman, A., & Zuccolotto, A. (2002). *E-Prime user's guide.* Pittsburgh, PA: Psychology Software Tools, Inc.

Stroop, J. R. (1935). Studies of interference in serial verbal reactions. *Journal of Experimental Psychology, 18*, 643–662.

Treisman, A. M. (1960). Contextual cues in selective listening. *Quarterly Journal of Experimental Psychology, 17*, 242–248.

Turner, M. L., & Engle, R. W. (1989). Is working memory capacity task dependent? *Journal of Memory and Language, 28*, 127–154.

Wood, N., & Cowan, N. (1995). The cocktail party phenomenon revisited: How frequent are attention shifts to one's name in an irrelevant auditory channel? *Journal of Experimental Psychology: Learning, Memory, and Cognition, 21*, 255–260.

EUROPEAN JOURNAL OF COGNITIVE PSYCHOLOGY
2006, 18 (1), 109–137

Relationships between working memory and intelligence from a developmental perspective: Convergent evidence from a neo-Piagetian and a psychometric approach

Anik de Ribaupierre and Thierry Lecerf

FPSE, University of Geneva, Switzerland

The objective of this paper, in line with the other papers of this special issue, is to show the potentialities of combining intelligence research and cognitive psychology. The development of intelligence is here addressed from two usually separate perspectives, a psychometric one, and a neo-Piagetian one. Two studies are presented. In Experiment 1, children aged 6, 7, 9, and 11 years ($N = 100$) were administered two working memory tasks and three Piagetian tasks. In Experiment 2, children aged 8–12 years ($N = 207$), young adults aged 20–35 ($N = 160$), and older adults aged 60–88 years ($N = 135$) were administered working memory and processing speed tasks, as well as the Raven Standard Matrices task. Regression and commonality analyses were run to analyse the age-related variance in the Piagetian tasks (Study 1), and in the Raven task (Study 2). In both experiments, working memory accounted for a large part of the age differences observed, but more so in Study 1 (Piagetian tasks) than in Study 2 (Raven task). It is concluded that working memory mediates the effect of age on fluid intelligence during childhood and during adulthood.

The objective of this paper, in line with the thematic covered by this special issue, is to provide further evidence of the relationship between the development of working memory (WM) and the development of intelligence, by relying on

Correspondence should be addressed to Anik de Ribaupierre, FPSE, University of Geneva, 40, Bd. du Pont d'Arve, 1205 Geneva, Switzerland. Email: Anik.DeRibaupierre@pse.unige.ch

The present studies were made possible by grants nos. 1127671.89, 1114052565.97, and 1213065020.01 of the Swiss National Research Fund. We want to thank all the present and past collaborators of the unit of differential psychology for their help in collecting and in analysing the original data, in alphabetical order: Nathalie Aguilar-Louche, Christine Bailleux, Erika Borella, Frédérique Bozon, Christophe Delaloye, Sylvain Dionnet, Barbara Joly-Pottuz, Céline Jouffray, Ineke Keizer, Joëlle Leutwyler, Catherine Ludwig, Francisco Pons, Ana Sancho, Anne Spira, Laurence Thomas, Florence Vallée. Our thanks go particularly to all the participants, children and adults, who agreed to participate in these two large studies.

two different lines of research. The first approach is neo-Piagetian; indeed, it is often forgotten that Piaget (e.g., 1947) explicitly stated that he was studying the development of intelligence. Moreover, although Piaget never referred to fluid intelligence and rarely, altogether, to intelligence in a psychometric sense, we consider that Piagetian tasks constitute very good measures of fluid intelligence. Neo-Piagetians, for instance Pascual-Leone (1987) or Case (1985), considered that the increase of WM capacity with age accounts for cognitive development as studied with Piagetian tasks. The second perspective is what is more usually, at least in the Anglophone tradition (e.g., Lautrey & de Ribaupierre, 2004), understood as the study of intelligence, that is, a psychometric perspective, concerned with individual differences. Most often, this perspective has focused on individual differences in young adults; extensions to a developmental approach can be made, however. Recent, cognitivist approaches such as Kyllonen's (e.g., Kyllonen & Christal, 1990), from a psychometric, factorialist perspective, or Engle's (e.g., Engle, Tuholski, Laughlin, & Conway, 1999b), from an experimentalist standpoint, suggest that WM overlaps very largely, if not fully, with fluid intelligence.

Two studies will be presented. In the first study, Piagetian tasks pertaining to several domains—the balance task, the islands task, and the lines folding task—were administered to children together with two neo-Piagetian measures of working capacity. In the second study, the Raven task—very representative of the psychometric approach to intelligence—was administered to children, young adults, and older adults together with two WM tasks, the reading span, and the matrices tasks. In both cases, it will be shown that most of the age-related variance in the intelligence tasks can be accounted for by the age differences in the WM tasks.

Although several definitions of WM have been offered, there is, nevertheless, a large consensus according to which WM serves to process and maintain temporary information to be used in other cognitive tasks. Its main function is to maintain memory representations (whether short- or long-term ones) when concurrent processing, distraction, and/or attentional shift also takes place (de Ribaupierre, 2000; Engle, Kane, & Tuholski, 1999a; Miyake & Shah, 1999; Richardson, 1996; see also Elliott, Barrilleaux, & Cowan, 2006 this issue). Moreover, it is also largely accepted that the capacity of WM is severely limited, to the extent that only a limited amount of information can be effortfully or attentionally activated (Cowan, 1995; Engle et al., 1999a, 1999b). Recently, Cowan (2001) suggested that, in adults, only four chunks can be activated at any one time, across different situations. This suggestion of an invariant capacity for processing information across situations is very similar to the neo-Piagetian position, initiated by Pascual-Leone (e.g., 1970) more than 30 years ago, according to which a general limit in processing resources sets constraints on the cognitive level that can be reached in any one task. In the adult cognitivist literature, there remains an important controversy as to whether WM is a specific system, and whether it consists of several components (e.g., a processing and a storage component). In the present paper, we will simply consider, in line with a number of developmentalists or of individual differences researchers (e.g., de Ribaupierre, 2000; Engle et al., 1999a) that WM serves essentially to hold and process attentionally information and is relatively domain free.

It is not the aim of this paper to summarise the results of decades of research on individual differences in intelligence, nor on the development of intelligence. We will just briefly summarise recent work that has centred on the relationship between WM capacity and general cognitive performance. Such evidence has steadily accumulated in the last two decades. For some authors, there is an almost total overlap between WM and fluid intelligence (e.g., Colom, Flores-Mendoza, & Rebollo, 2003; Colom, Rebollo, Palacios, Juan-Espinosa, & Kyllonen, 2004; Jensen, 1998). Relying on psychometric and factorial methods, Kyllonen and Christal (1990) suggested for instance that individual differences in intelligence are due to at least four sources—processing speed, working memory capacity, breadth of declarative knowledge, and breadth of procedural knowledge—and proposed such a framework as an alternative to the standard hierarchical abilities model (Burt, 1949; Carroll, 1993; Cattell, 1971). Remember that, in the Cattell's model, which has become a standard model in individual differences research, reasoning ability or general fluid intelligence (Gf) is considered to be the core of "intelligence". It refers to the ability to solve novel problems and adapt to new situations; it also refers to nonverbal material and is considered to be relatively culture free. Among the four sources of individual differences in intelligence, Kyllonen and Christal also suggested that WM capacity is the central factor.

Numerous studies, finding their origin in cognitive psychology rather than in psychometrics, have also now shown that WM capacity is related to general fluid intelligence (Conway, Cowan, Bunting, Therriault, & Minkoff, 2002; Fry & Hale, 1996; Salthouse, 1992a, 1992b; Salthouse, Babcock, Mitchell, Palmon, & Skovronek, 1990). For example, Engle et al. (1999b) using structural equation modelling showed that WM tasks (operation span test, reading span, counting span) were directly linked to Gf tasks (Raven and Cattell tests), and more so than short-term memory tasks. With reference to Baddeley and Hitch's (1974) model of WM, Engle et al. (1999b) suggested a particularly close relation between Gf and the central executive (see also de Ribaupierre, 2000; Pascual-Leone & Ijaz, 1989). In agreement with Kyllonen and Christal's (1990) conclusions, they proposed that WM is not modality specific, and predicts performance on a large number of cognitive tasks (see also Conway et al., 2002). For Engle et al. (1999a), controlled processing is the critical element common to the WM tasks and the Gf tasks or higher order tests. Engle and collaborators showed in several studies that high versus low span subjects (as defined on the basis of complex WM span tasks) differ in terms of controlled attention, but not in terms of automatic activation (e.g., Engle, Cantor, & Carullo, 1992).

A stronger relation of WM tasks with Gf than with other aspects of general intelligence, such as crystallised intelligence (Gc) or spatial abilities (Gv), could constitute an argument in favour of the domain generality of WM, rather than its domain specificity. Two studies were conducted to assess more precisely the relationships between WM and general intelligence or *g* (Ackerman, Beier, & Boyle, 2002; Süss, Oberauer, Wittman, Wilhelm, & Schulze, 2002). For example, Süss et al. (2002) administered the Berlin Intelligence Structure Model (BIS) and a number of WM tasks varying in terms of their content (verbal, numerical, etc.) and their functional facet (e.g., simultaneous storage and processing of information; see Oberauer, Süss, Schulze, & Wittman, 2000; Oberauer, Süss, Wilhem, & Wittman, 2003). As in Kyllonen and Christal's (1990) study, results showed that WM was strongly related with reasoning ability. Nevertheless, the fit of the structural equation models was improved when WM and intelligence measures were also related at the level of specific primary factors. Süss et al. therefore concluded that specific working memory resources, rather than general capacity, represent the limiting factor for their corresponding counterparts in the structure of mental abilities. In contrast, Kane et al. (2004) reported evidence, also using structural equations modelling, that a unitary WM construct was strongly correlated with general fluid intelligence. Nevertheless, they also recognised that domain-specific storage and rehearsal processes contribute to WM performance.

Recently, Ackerman, Beier, and Boyle (2005) argued against the view that WM and Gf are isomorphic, basing their argument on a meta-analysis of 86 samples who had been administered WM and measures of intellectual abilities. Because the median correlation between WM and intelligence (*g* factor) did not exceed .48, they concluded that WM and general intelligence are highly related, but are neither identical nor nearly identical constructs (see also Conway, Kane, & Engle, 2003). This important paper suggests that the relationship between WM and intelligence is complex, and that more experiments are required, in particular to better understand the relationships between WM, intelligence and processing speed. In their comment on this paper, Oberauer, Schulze, Wilhelm, and Süss (2005; see also Kane, Hambrick, & Conway, 2005) reanalysed the same set of data and found that the correlation between WM and intelligence was around .70. More importantly still for our view, Oberauer et al. (2005; see also Wilhelm & Oberauer, 2006 this issue) stressed the role of WM as a theoretical construct and rightly pointed to the fact that underscoring a high correlation between WM and intelligence does not mean that these two constructs should be considered identical; because the construct of WM originates in theories of cognition, in which the concept of a very limited processing capacity plays a central role, it can help understanding complex performance such as studied in fluid intelligence tasks. This is exactly what neo-Piagetians suggested, with respect to developmental aspects.

It should be remarked that the controversy relative to the generality vs. the specificity of WM might also be due in part to the composition of the sample. Indeed, Shah and Miyake (1996) or Süss et al. (2002) used university student samples, which are therefore relatively homogeneous on general ability. In contrast, Kane et al. (2004) used a more general population. Thus, when participants were relatively homogeneous on general ability, results tended to show a stronger influence of domain-specific abilities, as one could expect. While the debate about specificity or generality of WM is not yet fully overcome, it is sufficient to show, for our present purpose, that general intelligence performance is related with WM capacity. In other words, higher level processing is limited to some extent by the limitations of WM.

Some authors also further argue that the relationship observed between WM capacity and Gf abilities can be accounted for by processing speed (Fry & Hale, 1996; Jensen, 1998; Kail & Salthouse, 1994; Salthouse, 1992a; Wilhelm & Oberauer, 2006 this issue), particularly so when age effects are to be explained. Assigning a mediating role to processing speed has become almost standard as far as cognitive ageing is concerned (e.g., Salthouse, 1996; Salthouse & Meinz, 1995). A number of studies with young adults also reported evidence that the speed with which people perform simple cognitive tasks (elementary cognitive tasks, ECTs) are correlated with general cognitive ability (Deary, 1995, 2000). However, Conway et al.'s (2002) results were not consistent with this hypothesis: Only WM capacity, but not processing speed, was a predictor of Gf intelligence. They suggested that it is not speed *per se* that predicts Gf, but memory or attentional components (Juhel, 1991; Kranzler & Jensen, 1989). The important role of speed in older adults has been demonstrated many times, however. Such a divergence might be due to a difference in the type of processing speed tasks used. Whereas most tasks used with young adults are relatively simple, such as inspection time paradigms (e.g., Deary, 1995), those usually given to older adults are somewhat more complex and might call for more attentional or strategic processing. For instance, Salthouse (1992a) mentions that perceptivocognitive speed tasks are more age-related than motor speed tasks. A second point worth stressing is that the processes underlying individual differences might differ from those at the basis of age differences; therefore, processing speed tasks could perhaps account for a larger part of the variance in the case of age differences than in the case of individual differences. A developmental approach could contribute to clarifying the situation, all the more so as a lifespan approach is adopted. This is one of the objectives of the second study reported in the present paper.

Much of lifespan developmental psychology has stemmed from the psychometric perspective—while also drawing from developmental and social psychology—and sought to understand which general processes, probably at work throughout the life span, might account for both individual and age differences in intelligence (e.g., Baltes, Staudinger, & Lindenberger, 1999; Schaie

& Hertzog, 1986). Working memory is frequently advanced as representing one of those general mechanisms that account for age differences in intelligence tasks, as well as processing speed, inhibition, and control processes (see also Dempster, 1991). The present paper will focus essentially on the relation between WM and intelligence, while also considering the role of processing speed.

The other developmental perspective which we will consider in this paper is the neo-Piagetian approach to cognitive development. For many years, and following the pioneering work of Pascual-Leone (1970), neo-Piagetians have indeed suggested that the increase of WM, or of attentional capacity (e.g., Chapman, 1990), during childhood is one of the causal factors of general cognitive development such as was studied by Piaget for instance (Case, 1987, 1992b; de Ribaupierre & Bailleux, 1994, 2000; Pascual-Leone, 1970, 1987). Attentional capacity or WM capacity[1] at a given age imposes an upper limit on cognitive performance, and probably on Gf. In Pascual-Leone's (1970, 1987) model, for example, attentional capacity (M capacity) increases from one to seven units (or chunks) between age 3 and age 15, yielding stages of a 2 year duration. Using very elaborate task analyses, Pascual-Leone showed that a given performance in various tasks required a minimal level of M capacity, without which the child would perform below that level; reaching the required M level does not guarantee, however, that the task be passed, due in particular to the necessity for the child to master the content and develop strategies. Thus, M capacity is seen as a necessary but not sufficient condition to perform at a given level.[2] Although the growth of M capacity—essentially due to biological factors—is the most important mechanism from a developmental point of view, it should be stressed that Pascual-Leone (e.g., 1987) argues for the importance and interplay of several other mechanisms (operators I, F, L, etc.), including an inhibition mechanism and executive schemes. In particular, the model introduces a distinction between the "field of mental attention" and the "field of working memory or centration" (Pascual-Leone & Ijaz, 1989). The field of mental attention contains those schemes or mental representations that are activated by the M-operator, the I-operator, and executive schemes; it is very similar to Cowan's (1995) focus of attention. The field of working memory or

---

[1] Those terms have been used somewhat interchangeably. Most neo-Piagetians did not propose a very detailed account of WM, but consider that WM tasks provide good indices of the capacity in processing resources as far as attentional processing is concerned. This is because WM tasks do not draw on specific knowledge, and because they call for attentional processing.

[2] This hypothesis of an implicative relation explains why the correlations are not necessarily high: A high level in a cognitive task such as a Piagetian task has to be associated with a relatively high M capacity; however, high M capacity is not necessarily associated with a high cognitive level, hence correlations that may be only moderate.

centration also contains additional schemes or mental representations that are directly activated (i.e., effortlessly) by the stimulus.

Case's model (1985, 1992a), which also aims at integrating Piaget's theory with cognitive psychology, as well as with Pascual-Leone's model, suggests that cognitive development between 4 months and 19 years consists of four major stages (sensorimotor, interrelational, dimensional, and vectorial operations), each of which is divided in three substages (unifocal, bifocal, and elaborated). These substages differ by the number of elements represented, and the transition of one stage to another stage takes place by a process of hierarchical integration of executive structures. That is, during the dimensional stage, for instance, the child can activate and maintain from one to four schemes (or units), dealing with quantity; during the fourth substage, these schemes can be integrated within a single, higher order unit of representation (representing systems). The children's capability for hierarchical integration is determined by the size of what Case labelled the "short-term storage space" (number of schemes that can be stored or processes), the growth of which is due to an increase in operational efficiency.

The main purpose of both studies reported in this paper was to address the question of the relationship between WM capacity—as indexed by neo-Piagetian attentional or WM capacity tasks—on the one hand, and general intelligence ability—as assessed by conventional Piagetian tasks (Study 1) or by Gf tasks such as the Raven Matrices (Study 2)—on the other hand. While the first study was only conducted with children, the second one was performed with children, young adults, and older adults. More specifically, the objective of the first study was to determine whether age differences (in children) in Piagetian intelligence tasks (balance, islands, and lines folding) were accounted for by attentional capacity tasks (CSVI and peanut tasks). The second study aimed at determining how much of the age-related variance in the Raven's Matrices task in children, young adults, and older adults could be explained by WM. Because of the importance granted to processing speed in the field of cognitive ageing, processing speed tasks will also be considered, in the second study, as moderator variables of the effect of age on fluid intelligence. The extent to which WM capacity explained age-related variance in general intelligence tests was assessed by means of regression and commonality analyses (Cohen & Cohen, 1983; Pedhazur, 1997).

STUDY 1

This study was a part of a larger 5-year longitudinal project on the development of WM, during which a number of cognitive tasks were administered (e.g., de Ribaupierre & Bailleux, 1995). In the present paper, we will focus only on two working memory tasks: the CSVI (compound stimuli visual information; Pascual-Leone, 1970, 1987) task, and the peanut task (Case, 1985; de Ribaupierre, Neirynck, & Spira, 1989), and on three Piagetian tasks: the balance task (adapted from Inhelder & Piaget, 1955; see also Case, 1985; de Ribaupierre, 1975; Siegler, 1981), the island task (Piaget, Inhelder, & Szeminska, 1948), and the lines folding task (Piaget & Inhelder, 1966). For reasons of space and because the longitudinal approach of that study is not really relevant to the present paper, only the results of the second year of this large longitudinal study will be presented here.[3] It suffices to say that results turned out very similar on the other years of the study.

Method

Participants. For the second year of the longitudinal study, the sample consisted of 100 children (6, 7, 9, and 11 years old) with complete data on the tasks reported here.[4] It was representative of the Geneva primary school population, and comprised about 50% of girls and 50% of boys. The distribution by age group is indicated in Table 1.

Tasks and procedure. The balance task is a well-known Piagetian task (Inhelder & Piaget, 1955), and is considered to be an indicator of the formal stage of operations (Figure 1). Material consists of a balance beam, with 12 equidistant holes on each of the two arms. In this study, two types of items were administered: standardised items (A items) and semistandardised items (B items). In items A, two different weights were placed by the experimenter at various distances and the arms were locked; children had to decide whether the balance would be level when released. The balance was never unblocked, so that children never received feedback. Five items of different difficulty were administered. In items B, children had to place two different weights at the correct position for the balance to be level. Three different items B were administered. The balance, for items B, was unlocked for each item, so that children could reach the correct solution by trial and error, and, probably, learn from this feedback, from item to item. For both items A and B, justifications were requested for each item and taken into account for scoring. The order of administration was identical for all participants: Items A were administered first, followed by the administration of the items B, the latter providing some feed-back as to the accuracy of the response. Responses were scored into six ordered levels of performance, for each item, according to a scale based on theoretical

---

[3] We are grateful to one anonymous reviewer for this suggestion. The choice of the second year (rather than for instance the first year) is due to the fact that more Piagetian tasks were administered on that year than on the first one.

[4] At the onset of the study, the sample consisted of 30 children per age group. Attrition rate (essentially due to the children moving out of town) in this longitudinal study was approximately 5%; moreover, some children did not present complete data.

TABLE 1
Study 1: Mean level of performance by task and age group (standard deviations in parentheses)

Age	N	Peanut-purple	Peanut-colour	CSVI	Balance items A	Balance items B	Lines folding	Islands
6	22	9.7	7.3	12.0	1.9	1.2	2.5	1.3
		(2.7)	(2.1)	(6.9)	(0.3)	(0.7)	(0.9)	(0.5)
7	23	10.3	8.6	15.7	2.0	2.1	3.3	1.7
		(2.3)	(1.8)	(6.6)	(0.3)	(1.1)	(0.8)	(0.9)
9	27	16.8	12.6	31.2	3.0	4.1	5.1	2.9
		(3.4)	(3.0)	(10.1)	(0.9)	(0.5)	(1.0)	(1.3)
11	28	19.1	14.9	42.9	3.6	4.6	5.8	3.9
		(3.6)	(3.6)	(12.2)	(1.0)	(0.9)	(0.6)	(1.4)

CSVI: total number of correct trials (max. = 84). Peanut-purple and peanut-colour: total number of correct responses (max. = 25). Balance task items A, balance task items B, lines folding, and islands task: median level across items (max. = 6).

analyses in terms of dimensions of transformation (see Thomas, Pons, & de Ribaupierre, 1996, for a complete description). A median score was then calculated for each type of items.

The *island task* was adapted from Piaget (Piaget et al., 1948) and Rieben, de Ribaupierre, and Lautrey (1983). In this task, a compact wooden block was first presented. Children had to imagine that this block was a building (a "house") constructed on an island and had to reconstruct it with small wooden blocks. The new building had to contain the same volume as the model while built on islands

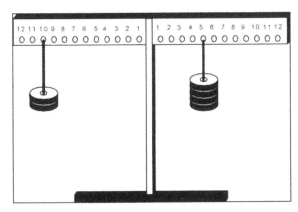

Figure 1. The balance task. An example of a proportional item: weight 2 at distance 10 = weight 4 at distance 5.

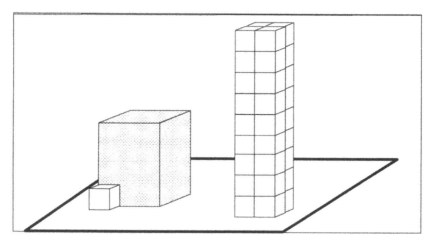

Figure 2.   Study 1: The islands task. Reconstruction of the model block (compact block) on the 2 ×
2 island.

of a different surface. The model corresponded to 36 wooden blocks (3 × 3 ×
4) and was placed on a 3 × 4 island. The surfaces (islands) on which the
children had to reproduce this volume were 1 × 3, and 2 × 2 (see Figure 2). For
each reconstruction, children had first to give a verbal response by anticipation
(i.e., announce how high their construction would be) and then to realise this
construction (which were respectively 12 and 9 floors high). As for the balance
task, children were systematically required to justify their response/action. Each
item was scored using a six ordered levels of performance scale. The levels of
performance were defined in terms of the dimensions of transformation proposed by Rieben et al. (1983; Rieben, de Ribaupierre, & Lautrey, 1990). A
median score was computed for the entire task.

The *lines folding task* was adapted from Piaget and Inhelder (1966) and
Rieben et al. (1983); it involves mental imagery. Children had to imagine the
bottom-up folding of a translucid sheet of paper on which coloured, geometrical
figures were drawn (Figure 3). Children's task was to draw the figure (with the
correct colours), which would be visible when the paper was folded by half.
Four items were administered. As for the other Piagetian tasks, children's
responses were scored using a six ordered levels of performance scale, based on
the dimensions of transformation proposed by Rieben et al. (1983, 1990). A
median score was computed across items for each child.

The *compound stimuli visual information task* (CSVI) was designed by
Pascual-Leone (1970) to assess M-capacity. In contrast with the task used by
Pascual-Leone, which called for motor responses, a computerised version was
administered, and children responded on a keyboard (Figure 4). First (learning

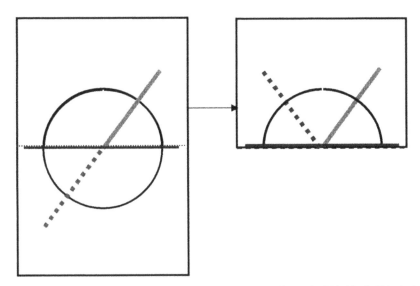

Figure 3. Study 1: The lines folding task. The translucid sheet has to be folded by half. Left: the full figure, as presented to the child. Right: the result of the folding.

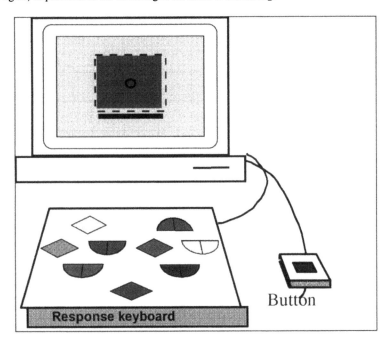

Figure 4. Study 1: The CSVI task. Example of a compound stimulus containing seven simple stimuli (large size, red colour, square shape, purple background, outline, underline, circle in the middle).

phase), children learned to associate a simple visual stimulus (e.g., square shape, large size, red colour, etc.) with one key of a keyboard; they had to learn the response to eight simple stimuli (six for the youngest age group). For instance, they learned to press a yellow diamond key each time a square shape was shown on the screen, or a yellow half-circle key each time a red shape was shown. Learning was continued until children made no error across different blocks. In the test phase, compound stimuli, composed of a number of the simple stimuli learned previously, were presented during 5 s. Compound stimuli contained from two to six simple stimuli, such as a red small square (two simple stimuli) or a large red square with a cross in the middle (four simple stimuli). Children had to respond, by pressing on the corresponding keys, to all the simple stimuli they detected; response was only allowed once the compound stimulus had disappeared from the screen. Twelve items were administered for each level of complexity. The score used in this paper was the number of entirely correct trials, i.e., items for which all the simple stimuli presented were correctly responded to.

The *peanut task* was adapted from Pascual-Leone (de Ribaupierre, Lecerf, & Bailleux, 2000; de Ribaupierre et al., 1989) and Case (1985) and measures WM. A clown figure (M. Peanut) was presented on a sheet of paper, with coloured spots on it (16 possible locations; Figure 5). This clown figure was then removed, and a second blank clown figure was immediately presented on a sheet of paper. The

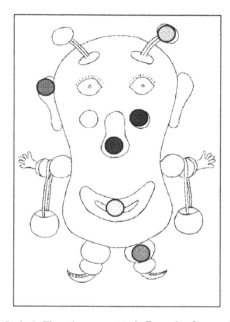

Figure 5.   Study 1: The colour-peanut task. Example of a complexity 6 item.

children's task was to recall the location of spots by placing coloured chips on this figure. Two versions were administered: a purple-peanut in which all spots were of the same colour and a colour-peanut in which spots were of different colours (seven possible colours). In the coloured version, children had to recall both the colour and the location. The number of locations or the number of colour—location associations to remember varied from two to five, with five items for each level of complexity. Trials of different complexity were randomly distributed throughout the task, with the same order for all children. Overall exposure time was 1 s per spot; thus, a clown figure with three spots was presented during 3 s. The score used here was the total number of correct trials.

Results and discussion

Table 1 presents descriptive statistics by age group and by task. As mentioned previously, the objective of the present study was to assess whether and to which extent WM capacity explained age-related variance in the Piagetian tasks. Therefore, regression and commonality analyses were used, designed to identify the proportion of variance in the dependent variable that may be attributed to each independent variable, and to their combination (see Pedhazur, 1997, for a complete description). Regression analyses were therefore conducted, using each of the Piagetian tasks as the dependent variable. In a first step, age was entered as a single predictor for each task; this procedure allowed to assess the amount of variance accounted for by age. Then, the three WM tasks (CSVI and the two versions of the peanut task) were entered together as predictors. Finally, the four variables (age and the three WM tasks) were used as predictors. Commonality analyses made it then possible to assess how much of the variance was unique to age, to WM, and shared by both predictors (Pedhazur, 1997; see also Salthouse, 1992a); likewise, it was possible to assess how much of the age-related variance was accounted for by WM. Table 2 presents the R^2 obtained for age, for age and WM, as well as the amount of age-related variance shared with the WM tasks, for each task.

The results showed that the effect of the two sets of predictors varied somewhat across the tasks, but explained an important part of the variance. Age

TABLE 2
Study 1: Results of the regression and commonality analyses

(N = 100)	Balance items A	Balance items B	Islands	Lines
R^2	.488	.704	.684	.482
R^2 age and WM	.587	.737	.704	.536
Proportion of age-related variance shared with WM (commonality analysis)	.922	.816	.834	.935

accounted for 48–70% of the total variance while age and WM together explained 54–74%. Most importantly, almost all of the age-related variance on any task was shared with the WM tasks. For example, 92.2% of the age-related variance in the balance items A was shared with the WM tasks. These findings are consistent with those reported by Salthouse (1992a) in older adults with different cognitive tasks, who systematically observed that most of the age differences on general cognitive tasks disappeared when WM or processing speed was controlled for.

These results are relatively novel findings. Within a neo-Piagetian perspective, WM tasks were generally used to predict whether children would be observed at a specific cognitive level, given their WM capacity (e.g., Case, 1985; de Ribaupierre & Pascual-Leone, 1979; Stewart & Pascual-Leone, 1992). Theoretical analyses were performed to predict the minimal WM level required by a particular task (or a particular item within a given task). Data were analysed with the objectives (a) to validate the theoretical task analyses and (b) to demonstrate, using for instance prediction analysis (e.g., Hildebrand, Laing, & Rosenthal, 1977), that (almost) no child was observed beyond the predicted level. This in turn showed the existence of upper limits in the possible performance on the Piagetian tasks, due to the constraints imposed by WM capacity. While theoretically very profound, such an approach has also been criticised for its high level of inferential uncertainty, linked to the necessity of detailed, and possibly controversial, task analyses. In contrast, the present analyses merely pursued a quantitative objective, and aimed at assessing the extent to which age (and individual) differences in WM tasks account for age (and individual) differences in the Piagetian tasks. In that sense, they represent a complement, and a further support to the theoretically based analyses of the neo-Piagetians, by showing that most of the age differences in the Piagetian tasks can be accounted for by the WM tasks, that is, by tasks in which strategies or previous knowledge are certainly less important than it can appear to be in Piagetian tasks.

STUDY 2

As mentioned in the introduction, the objective of this experiment was to estimate whether age differences in an intelligence task were essentially accounted for by WM tasks, as in Study 1 or in a number of studies by other researchers. The data presented here were part of a large 4-year project, during which diverse working memory, processing and inhibition tasks were administered to children, young adults, and older adults. In view of the objective of this paper and of this special issue, the focus will be placed on the relation between WM and fluid intelligence, as assessed by Raven's Matrices task. Nevertheless, given the importance granted to processing speed by cognitive ageing researchers, the processing speed tasks used in the project will also be included. This allowed assessment of whether the potential effect of WM on age differences in intelligence is essentially due to age differences in processing speed, as Salthouse (e.g., 1996) argued.

Method

Participants. A total of 207 children, 160 young adults, and 135 older adults participated in the study and presented complete data for the set of tasks reported here (Table 3). The mean age was 9.9 years (range: 8–12 years) for the children's sample, 22.4 (range: 22–35 years) for the young adults, and 69.9 (range: 60–88 years) for the older sample. The young adults sample was further subdivided into two equivalent groups to conduct statistical analyses with children, on the one hand, and with older adults, on the other hand; in some comparisons, older adults were also subdivided, into those aged 60–70 years and those older than 70 years of age. The children sample was representative of the Geneva primary school population. The younger adults were University students and participated as one of several options for obtaining partial credit in a Psychology course. The older adults were recruited from the community (in majority from the University for the Third Age of the University of Geneva) and were repaid their travelling costs to the laboratory.

Tasks. The participants were administered a very large battery of tasks, but the present study will report on the following six tasks: the Raven Standard Progressive Matrices task to assess fluid intelligence (Gf), the reading span and

TABLE 3
Study 2: Descriptive statistics, by age group and by task (standard deviation)

Age group	N	Mean age	Raven	Matrices	Reading span	D2	Pattern comparison	Letter comparison
8	28	8.00	28.36	1.07	1.84	14.55	188.57	292.39
			(8.85)	(0.53)	(0.47)	(3.30)	(59.82)	(96.09)
9	52	9.00	32.04	1.42	2.26	15.34	174.75	228.21
			(9.40)	(0.47)	(0.40)	(4.34)	(43.25)	(76.70)
10	52	10.00	34.44	1.64	2.41	17.93	153.29	201.12
			(7.93)	(0.41)	(0.41)	(3.93)	(30.77)	(54.58)
11	51	11.00	36.76	1.79	2.54	19.49	135.37	172.25
			(7.22)	(0.35)	(0.41)	(5.01)	(25.13)	(57.97)
12	24	12.00	40.42	1.96	2.64	21.85	120.42	150.96
			(8.40)	(0.41)	(0.33)	(3.88)	(18.98)	(36.34)
Total children	207	9.95	34.28	1.58	2.35	17.66	155.23	207.34
			(8.95)	(0.50)	(0.47)	(4.82)	(42.98)	(78.39)
Young adults	160	22.40	53.21	2.62	3.08	34.22	86.65	105.44
			(3.14)	(4.21)	(0.35)	(4.53)	(18.30)	(23.90)
Older adults	135	69.94	41.70	2.02	2.62	25.01	132.98	157.95
			(6.07)	(8.56)	(0.50)	(0.47)	(6.38)	(35.21)	(39.34)

the matrices tasks to assess working memory (WM), and the pattern comparison, the letter comparison, and the D2 tasks, to assess processing speed.

The computerised *reading span task* was adapted from Daneman and Carpenter's task (1980; de Ribaupierre, Pous, Morier, & Lecerf, 1994; Friedman, & Miyake, 2004), and measures working memory capacity. This test includes both processing (reading and judgement of sentence) and storage (remembering of the last word). Participants had to read aloud a small series of syntactically and semantically simple sentences (from two to five in each series), and to determine whether each sentence was semantically plausible, while keeping track of the last word of each sentence. Recall of the last words was asked for at the end of each series. Four items were administered for each level of complexity (four items with 2 sentences; four items with 3 sentences, etc.). Thus, 16 items were presented to each participant and randomly distributed across the tasks, with a fixed order for all participants. Response accuracy as well as latencies were recorded. The score used in the present study is an accuracy score and corresponds to the mean number of last words correctly recalled. The last words correctly recalled were averaged across the 16 items (and across the five levels of complexity: 2, 3, 4, and 5); maximal score was 3.5.

The computerised *matrices task* was originally proposed by Loisy and Roulin (1992), and is considered to measure WM capacity. A matrix consisting of 25 cells (5 × 5) was presented on the screen of a Dell computer. Mono- or bisyllabic words appeared simultaneously, each in a different cell of the matrix. Participants had to recall both the words and their positions. The exposure time was 1 s per word; thus, an item with four words was presented for 4 s. In the recall phase, administered immediately after the presentation, a blank 5 × 5 matrix was presented. Participants had to point to the correct location (cell) and to say aloud the word. Twelve items were administered to each participant, the complexity of which could vary from two to six. An adaptive procedure was used. Therefore the complexity of the items varied continuously during the test, depending on the subjects' last response: In case of success, an item containing one more word (and also position) to recall was administered; in case of failure, an easier item was presented. For all participants, the first item consisted of two words. The numbers of correctly recalled words across the 12 items, of correctly recalled positions, and of correct word–position associations were recorded. The score used in the present study is the mean number of correct word–position associations across the 12 items.

The *pattern comparison* task was adapted from Salthouse (1992a), and measures processing speed. Pairs of geometrical patterns were presented on an A4 sheet of paper, and participants had to judge whether the two patterns were identical. Responses were given by writing an O ("Oui" for same) or an N ("Non" for different patterns). The task comprised two parts, with 30 pairs within each part. Time to complete each part was recorded. The score used in the present study is the total time to complete the two pages.

The *letter comparison* task was also adapted from Salthouse (1992a), and measures processing speed. Two strings of six to eight letters were presented side by side on an A4 sheet of paper and participants had to judge whether the two strings were identical. Responses were given by writing an O ("Oui" for same) or an N ("Non" for different string of letters). The task comprised two parts, with 21 pairs in each part. Time to complete each part was recorded. The score used in the present study is the total time to complete the two pages.

The *D2* task was adapted from Brickenkamp's (1998) test, and consists of 10 test lines (instead of 14 lines in the original test) with 47 characters in each line, presented on an A4 sheet of paper. Each character consists of a letter, "d" or "p" marked with one, two, three, or four small dashes. Participants were required to scan each line during 20 s (after which time they were required to go to the next line) and cross out all occurrences of the letter "d" with two dashes while ignoring all other characters. The score used in the present analyses was the total number of characters correctly crossed out on each of the last nine lines.

The *Raven Standard Progressive Matrices* task was used as indicated in the manual (Raven, 1938/1956). In this experiment, the task was unspeeded (i.e., no time limit). The score used in the current paper was the total number of correct responses.

Procedure.   Participants were run individually. As mentioned previously, the tasks presented in this paper were part of a larger project, in which WM tasks, processing speed tasks, and inhibition tasks were also administered. These tasks were administered on three, sometimes four different sessions. The matrices and the pattern comparison tasks were administered during the first session; the D2 was given during the second session; the reading span, pattern comparison, and Raven tasks were administered during the third session. At the beginning of the first session, a set of background questions was asked to the older adults, focused on formal education, language, and health, as well as a short vision test. In each experimental task, there were also a few practice trials.

Results and discussion

Descriptive statistics.   Before conducting analyses, the reliability of the processing speed tasks was estimated, using a split-half method corrected with the Spearman-Brown procedure for the pattern comparison and the letter comparison tasks, and an alpha coefficient for the D2 task. The coefficients were high for all age groups and for all tasks. Within the children's sample, the coefficients were .924, .942, and .937, for the pattern comparison, the letter comparison, and the D2, respectively. Within the young adults' sample, the coefficients were .919, .920, and .918, respectively. Finally, for the older adults, the coefficients were .946, .902, and .961, respectively.

Table 3 presents the descriptive statistics for the different tasks and for the age groups. Figure 6 presents composite standardised scores for each group of tasks and each age group. To allow for an easier comparison of the performance of the different age groups and the different tasks, scores of each task were standardised, relatively to young adults, which allows for a comparison of age differences across tasks. Thus, for each task, the young adults sample presents a mean of 0 and a standard deviation of 1; the scores of the other age groups reflect their position with respect to the young adults. To summarise the data further, these standardised scores were then averaged for WM tasks (word–position associations in the matrices task, and mean number of correctly recalled words in the reading span task), on the one hand, and for processing speed tasks (pattern comparison, letter comparison, and D2), on the other hand. As can be seen in Figure 6, age differences were large for the three sets of tasks. Thus, as concerns WM tasks, 8-year-old children were, on average, located at −3.21 standard deviations from the young adults, 12-year-old children and older adults

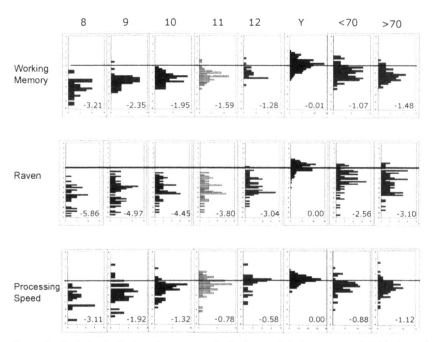

Figure 6. Study 2. Distribution of average standardised scores (relative to young adults) by type of task, and age group. The construction of the composite scores is described in the text. The numbers indicated on each distribution corresponds to the group mean.

were close to each other, and were respectively located at −1.28 and −1.48 standard deviations from young adults; all age groups differed from each other.

Commonality analyses. As in Study 1, regression and commonality ana-lyses were used to assess whether and to which extent WM capacity explained age differences in the Raven Progressive Matrices. They were run separately for children and young adults, on the one hand, and for young and older adults, on the other hand; this is one of the reasons why the young adults sample was divided in two subsamples. There were two reasons why analyses were run separately for children and young adults, on the one hand, and for young and older adults, on the other hand. First, age trends are not linear across the life span; similar performance was expected from the older participants and from the older children despite the difference in age, so that the relation between age and performance was not expected to be linear across the entire sample. Second, we were also interested in assessing whether the interplay of age, WM, and pro-cessing speed differs in these two periods of the life span. These analyses are somewhat more complex than in Study 1 as there were three sets of variables (age, WM, and processing speed) to account for part of the variance in the Raven task. Table 4 reports most of the results. In a first step, the performance in the Raven's task was regressed on the different variables, to assess the amount of variance accounted for by each variable and by their combination. That is, each variable was first entered as a single predictor: (a) age; (b) the two WM

TABLE 4
Study 2: Regression and commonality analyses

Predictor	Children and young adults	Young and older adults
Regression analyses: R^2 values		
Age	.513	.401
WM	.544	.504
Speed	.612	.387
Age + WM	.619	.573
Age + Speed	.625	.480
WM + Speed	.669	.558
Age + WM + Speed	.673	.592
Commonality analyses: Partitioning of the total variance		
Unique age	.004	.034
Unique WM	.048	.112
Unique speed	.054	.019
Age and WM	.009	.059
Age and speed	.071	.035
WM and speed	.058	.060
Age and WM and speed	.429	.273

scores simultaneously (i.e., the mean number of correctly recalled words in the reading span task and the mean number of correctly recalled word–position associations in the matrices tasks); (c) the three processing speed scores simultaneously (i.e., total time for the pattern comparison and for the letter comparison tasks, respectively, and the number of correctly crossed-out signs in the D2 task). In a second step, combinations of these predictors two by two were entered in the regression model. Finally, all the predictors were entered together. The procedure suggested by Pedhazur (1997; see also Salthouse, 1992b) was then applied, making it possible to partition the variance into its different components, to assess the contribution of each variable (unique variance of each predictor), as well as that of their various combinations.

Table 4 shows that the three variables together accounted for 67% and for 59% of the total variance in the Raven's task, for the children and young adults' sample, and for the young and older samples, respectively. The age-related variance was high in both subsamples: When age alone was entered as a predictor, it accounted for 51% of the variance in the children and young adults' sample, and for 40% of the variance in the young and older adults' sample. However, the unique contribution of age was small, as it was reduced to less than 5% in both samples once the contribution of the other predictors and of their combination was controlled for, in the commonality analysis. Thus, as Salthouse often likes to phrase it (e.g., Salthouse, 1996), the contribution of age was reduced by about 99% in the children and young adults' sample (from .513 to .004) and 91% in the young and older adults' sample (from .401 to .034), while processing speed and WM accounted for almost all of the age effects.

As concerns the age-related variance (Figure 7), commonality analyses showed that it was accounted for by a combination of WM and processing speed

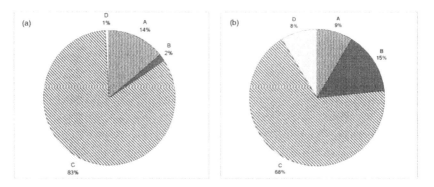

Figure 7. Study 2: Partitioning of the age-related variance in the Raven's Matrices task (commonality analyses) by subsample. Age-related variance for (a) children and young adults and (b) young and older adults. A: age variance shared with speed; B: age variance shared with working memory; C: age variance shared with speed and working memory; D: unexplained age variance.

which explained 83% and 68%, for the young and the adult samples, respectively. Processing speed alone accounted for a further part (14%) of the age differences in the young sample, whereas WM played a relatively more important role (15%) to account for age differences in the adult sample.

Similar analyses were run within each of the children's and the older adults' groups, respectively. Although the overall age-related variance was obviously lower than when young adults were included, results remained similar. Thus, for the children group only, the R^2 for age was equal to .15, of which 76% was accounted for by a combination of processing speed and WM, 17% by WM, and 6% by processing speed. Age differences within the older adults sample were small[5] (R^2 = .032); nevertheless, it was essentially accounted for by WM and processing speed together (50%) and by WM (38%).

In sum, most of the age-related variance in Raven's was accounted for by a combination of WM and processing speed, rather than by either predictor alone, for both groups but more particularly so in the children sample. Processing speed accounted for more of the age differences within the children and young adults' sample, whereas WM explained more of the adult age differences. It is noteworthy to remember that the Raven score used in the present analyses was the number of correct responses without any time constraint.

GENERAL DISCUSSION

The objective of this paper was to address the question of the relationship between general intelligence ability and WM capacity, both from a differentialist and from a developmental perspective. This relationship has been hypothesised and studied within two very different research traditions, as reflected here. The first one is the psychometric perspective, which is interested in individual differences in intelligence, usually in young adults and from a quantitative point of view. The second one is the neo-Piagetian perspective, aimed at identifying mechanisms responsible for the qualitative changes observed with age in Piagetian-type tasks. More recently, lifespan developmental approaches have suggested that age differences in intelligence tasks may be explained by age differences in WM, and/or in processing speed; yet they focused essentially on age differences during adulthood. These perspectives appear to present vast differences, both among themselves and from cognitive psychology: the type of tasks used (e.g., standardised vs. experimental), an emphasis placed on quantitative versus qualitative differences with age or between individuals, and the type of statistical analyses proposed. Yet, as has now been argued by a number of other authors as well, the objective of these

---

[5] This is a particularly small value, in comparison with age differences obtained in previous studies (e.g., de Ribaupierre, 2001). It is noteworthy that Salthouse (e.g., 1996) also reports large between-study variation in the age differences within older adult samples.

perspectives is very similar, that is, it consists in understanding individual differences and age differences in cognitive functioning. Moreover, an interest for the relationship between WM and intelligence has also been recently shown by cognitive psychologists, traditionally more interested in processes underlying cognitive functioning in young adults. Although individual differences should not be equated with developmental differences (see also Engle et al., 1999a, for such an argument; de Ribaupierre, 1993), these two types of difference should nevertheless complement each other and contribute to a better understanding of cognitive functioning in adults. By presenting a study representative of a neo-Piagetian perspective and a study inspired both by present lifespan developmental work and by cognitive psychology, our goal was thus to show that such traditions are, in fact, not as far apart as they might seem at first glance, and that both are also relatively close to adult cognitive psychology. With this objective in mind, four classical Piagetian tasks as well as two working memory tasks (CSVI and peanut) were administered to four groups of children, in Study 1. WM tasks were administered, together with the Raven's Matrices task and processing speed tasks to children, young adults, and older adults, in Study 2.

In both studies, a strong relationship was observed between WM, on the one hand, and both age and individual differences in cognitive performance, on the other hand. In fact, this relation was even stronger in Study 1. Thus, WM explained more than 80% of the age-related variance in all the Piagetian tasks used. This implies that, once age differences in WM were controlled for, there was almost no age difference left in these tasks. The rate of attenuation of age differences is close to what Salthouse observed in many studies conducted with young and older adults. However, it was often the case, in Salthouse's studies, that the age-related variance was not very high. In contrast, in Study 1, close to half of the total variance was due to age, even more in some tasks. Results were also in agreement with the neo-Piagetian models that have suggested for many years that the growth of attentional capacity or WM capacity is one of the causal factors of general cognitive development (Case, 1987, 1992a, 1992b; de Ribaupierre & Bailleux, 1994, 2000; Pascual-Leone, 1970, 1987). In these models, it is considered that WM capacity places constraints on and acts as a limit of the general cognitive functioning, hence on the cognitive level that can be reached in any one task; an increase in WM capacity accounts for the possibility to reach a higher cognitive level. In particular, Pascual-Leone and Case proposed, by relying on theoretical task analyses, that a given level of WM capacity was a prerequisite for functioning at a given level in a cognitive task. This is an implicative relation in the sense that a given cognitive level cannot be reached if WM capacity is not sufficient; however, a relatively high WM capacity does not guarantee that the corresponding cognitive level is reached. Empirical tests of this relation of implication were generally successful (e.g., Case, 1985; de Ribaupierre & Pascual-Leone, 1979; Stewart & Pascual-Leone, 1992; see also Thomas et al., 1996, who tested such an implicative relation of

WM capacity on general cognitive functioning with the data used in the present paper). The present study addressed this question from a quantitative point of view, showing that most of the age differences can be equated with age differences in WM capacity.

In the second study, as it could be expected on the basis of Study 1 and of a number of studies conducted in the field of cognitive ageing in the last two decades, WM also accounted for a large part of age and of individual differences in intelligence as assessed by the Raven task. This result was also consistent with those reported by individual differences researchers, who demonstrated that individual differences in intelligence aroused in part from working memory capacity (Kyllonen & Christal, 1990). The R^2 values associated with WM, when WM tasks were entered as single predictor of the total variance in the Raven's task, were high (.54 and .50 in the children's and the adults' samples, respectively). However, the partitioning of the variance made possible by the commonality analyses showed that the specific contribution of WM, once the other variables were controlled for, was much lower: It decreased to 5% and 11%, respectively, for the total variance. When considering only the age-related variance, the unique contribution of WM was 2% and 15%, respectively. It is noteworthy that similar results were obtained with respect to processing speed, sometime held for a better mediator of the effect of age on fluid intelligence than WM (e.g., Salthouse, 1996). When processing speed tasks were used as predictor (total variance), their R^2 value was .61 and .39 in the children's and the adults' samples, respectively; their unique contribution, once the other predictors controlled, decreased to about 5% and 2%, respectively. The unique contribution of speed to the age-related variance was 14% in the children's sample and 9% in the adults' sample. Similar results were obtained when age differences were considered within the children's sample and within the older adults' sample only, with no inclusion of the young adults.

These results, and the comparison of the two studies, allow to draw several conclusions. First, it appears more interesting to consider that WM and speed work in concert, rather than independently, to explain age differences in fluid intelligence. That is, neither WM nor speed alone are sufficient to account for individual differences or for age differences; they are not fully overlapping either[6] (see also Wilhelm & Oberauer, 2006 this issue). Rather it is their combination that appears to exert the largest influence on age differences.

It is interesting to remark that the age-related variance was larger in Study 1 than in Study 2, when considering only the children's sample in the latter study. The role of WM was also more important in Study 1, even though the age range

---

[6] Similar results were obtained in a previous study (de Ribaupierre, 2001), in which structural equations modelling showed that a model postulating two correlated latent variables rather than a single latent variable for processing speed and WM tasks provided a better fit.

was comparable (7–11 years of age vs. 8–12 years). Perhaps, and very speculatively, the Piagetian tasks are more pure indicators of fluid intelligence, and less influenced by individual differences in knowledge base and/or in strategies; as a result, age differences are larger. Probably Piaget would have liked such an interpretation as he was interested in developing tasks (and a method of examination) that went as close as possible to the "true" competence level of a child. Of course, an alternative and more trivial hypothesis to understand the different role played by WM in the two studies is linked to the tasks used; perhaps, in Study 1, the WM tasks carried most of the age-related variance because no other task was used. Processing speed would have explained as much, or more (although this would be difficult) of the age-related variance, had such tasks been used.

Second, age differences in the Raven task seem to rely on somewhat different processes depending on the period of the life span which is considered. The relative role of processing speed seems larger when comparing children and young adults, whereas the relative role of WM seems more important when young and older adults are compared. A similar result was obtained in a previous lifespan study (de Ribaupierre, 2001), in which the interplay of processing speed, WM, and inhibition was also slightly different for a sample composed of children and young adults and for a sample composed of young and adult samples. The relative influence of processing speed was more important to account for age differences between children and young adults, whereas that of inhibition was somewhat larger to explain age differences between young and older adults. It is difficult to compare these results with those described in the literature, because of the scarcity of studies using the same tasks across the life span (but see Borella, Carretti, & Mammarella, 2006 this issue, for further analysis of the relationships between WM, inhibition, and the Raven matrices in young and older adults). Moreover, and in contrast with the field of cognitive ageing, processing speed is rarely considered as a potential moderator of child developmental differences in cognition (Kail & Salthouse, 1994).

Finally, it is interesting to consider the present results in the context of the debate open by Ackerman et al. (2005). We agree with these authors when they conclude that WM is not isomorphic to g or to Gf. Indeed, in the present study and congruent with the results of their meta-analysis, WM tasks did not account for all of the variance in the Raven's task or in the Piagetian tasks; this was not even the case when WM was combined with processing speed. This implies that a significant part of individual variability was not captured by WM, suggesting that Gf tasks call for other processes, too. In contrast, WM and processing speed did account for almost all of the age-related variance, attesting that individual and developmental differences should be distinguished. However, we also agree with Oberauer et al. (2005), who argue that WM should be regarded as an explanatory construct for intellectual abilities; this does not mean that WM explains *all* of the individual differences in intelligence. Rightly, Oberauer et al.

consider that g is "conceptually opaque" as it only represents the common variance of a set of tasks that have been used for many years to measure intelligence but does not reflect any explicit theoretical concept. In contrast, WM is a theoretical construct and can help "bridging the gap between research on individual differences in abilities and cognitive science, including experimental cognitive psychology and formal modelling of cognitive processes" (Oberauer et al., 2005, p. 64). Our results thus show that WM is also a useful construct as far as developmental differences in fluid abilities are taken into consideration. Indeed, age is just as conceptually opaque as g, or even more. Extending Oberauer et al.'s argument to a developmental perspective leads to the conclusion that investigating further the role of WM, inasmuch as WM tasks measure limits in processing resources, will increase our understanding of age differences in intelligence. This is obviously in line with the neo-Piagetian postulate that the development of WM is a major ingredient of cognitive development in general.

REFERENCES

Ackerman, P. L., Beier, M. E., & Boyle, M. O. (2002). Individual differences in working memory within a nomological network of cognitive and perceptual speed abilities. *Journal of Experimental Psychology: General, 131*(4), 567–589.

Ackerman, P. L., Beier, M. E., & Boyle, M. O. (2005). Working memory and intelligence: The same or different constructs? *Psychological Bulletin, 131*(1), 30–60.

Baddeley, A. D., & Hitch, G. J. (1974). Working memory. In G. Bower (Ed.), *Recent advances in learning and motivation* (Vol. 8, pp. 47–89). New York: Academic Press.

Baltes, P. B., Staudinger, U. M., & Lindenberger, U. (1999). Lifespan psychology: Theory and application to intellectual functioning. *Annual Review of Psychology, 50*, 471–507.

Borella, E., Carretti, B., & Mammarella, I. C. (2006). Do working memory and susceptibility to interference predict individual differences in fluid intelligence? *European Journal of Cognitive Psychology, 18*(1), 51–69.

Brickenkamp, R. (1998). *Test d'attention concentrée.* Paris: Les Editions du Centre de Psychologie Appliquée.

Burt, C. (1949). The structure of the mind: A review of the results of factor analysis. *British Journal of Educational Psychology, 19*, 100–111, 176–199.

Carroll, J. B. (1993). *Human cognitive abilities: A survey of factor-analytic studies.* Cambridge, UK: Cambridge University Press.

Case, R. (1985). *Intellectual development: Birth to adulthood.* New York: Academic Press.

Case, R. (1987). Neo-Piagetian theory: Retrospect and prospect. *International Journal of Psychology, 22*, 773–791.

Case, R. (1992a). *The mind's staircase: Exploring the conceptual underpinnings of children's thought and knowledge.* Hillsdale, NJ: Lawrence Erlbaum Associates, Inc.

Case, R. (1992b). Neo-Piagetian theories of child development. In R. J. Sternberg & C. A. Berg (Eds.), *Intellectual development* (pp. 161–196). Cambridge, UK: Cambridge University Press.

Cattell, J. B. (1971). *Abilities: Their structure, growth, and action.* Boston: Houghton Mifflin.

Chapman, M. (1990). Cognitive development and the growth of capacity: Issues in neo-Piagetian theory. In J. T. Enns (Ed.), *The development of attention: Research and theory* (pp. 263–287). Amsterdam: Elsevier Science Publishers.

Cohen, J., & Cohen, P. (1983). *Applied multiple regression/correlation for the behavioral sciences* (2nd ed.). Hillsdale, NJ: Lawrence Erlbaum Associates Inc.

Colom, R., Flores-Mendoza, C., & Rebollo, I. (2003). Working memory and intelligence. *Personality and Individual Differences, 34*, 33–39.

Colom, R., Rebollo, I., Palacios, A., Juan-Espinosa, M., & Kyllonen, P. C. (2004). Working memory is (almost) perfectly predicted by *g*. *Intelligence, 32*, 277–296.

Conway, A. R. A., Cowan, N., Bunting, M. F., Therriault, D. J., & Minkoff, S. R. B. (2002). A latent variable analysis of working memory capacity, short-term memory capacity, processing speed, and general fluid intelligence. *Intelligence, 30*, 163–183.

Conway, A. R. A., Kane, M. J., & Engle, R. W. (2003). Working memory capacity and its relation to general intelligence. *Trends in Cognitive Sciences, 7*(12), 547–552.

Cowan, N. (1995). *Attention and memory: An integrated framework.* New York: Oxford University Press.

Cowan, N. (2001). The magical number 4 in shortterm memory: A reconsideration of mental storage capacity. *Behavioral and Brain Sciences, 24*, 87–187.

Daneman, M., & Carpenter, P. A. (1980). Individual differences in working memory and reading. *Journal of Verbal Learning and Verbal Behavior, 19*, 450–466.

Deary, I. J. (1995). Auditory inspection time and intelligence: What is the direction of causation? *Developmental Psychology, 31*(2), 237–250.

Deary, I. J. (2000). Simple information processing and intelligence. In R. J. Sternberg (Ed.), *Handbook of intelligence* (pp. 267–284). Cambridge, UK: Cambridge University Press.

Dempster, F. N. (1991). Inhibitory processes: A neglected dimension of intelligence. *Intelligence, 15*, 157–173.

De Ribaupierre, A. (1975). *Mental space and formal operations.* Unpublished PhD thesis, University of Toronto, Canada.

De Ribaupierre, A. (1993). Structural and individual differences: On the difficulty of dissociating developmental and differential processes. In R. Case & W. Edelstein (Eds.), *The new structuralism in cognitive development: Theory and research on individual pathways* (pp. 11–32). Basel, Switzerland: Karger.

De Ribaupierre, A. (2000). Working memory and attentional control. In W. Perrig & A. Grob (Eds.), *Control of human behavior, mental processes, and consciousness* (pp. 147–164). Mahwah, NJ: Lawrence Erlbaum Associates, Inc.

De Ribaupierre, A. (2001). Working memory and attentional processes across the lifespan. In P. Graf & N. Ohta (Eds.), *Lifespan development of human memory* (pp. 59–80). Cambridge, MA: MIT Press.

De Ribaupierre, A., & Bailleux, C. (1994). Developmental change in a spatial task of attentional capacity: An essay toward an integration of two working memory models. *International Journal of Behavioral Development, 17*(1), 5–35.

De Ribaupierre, A., & Bailleux, C. (1995). Development of attentional capacity in childhood: A longitudinal study. In F. E.Weinert & W. Schneider (Eds.), *Memory performance and competencies: Issues in growth and development* (pp. 45–70). Hillsdale, NJ Lawrence Erlbaum Associates, Inc.

De Ribaupierre, A., & Bailleux, C. (2000). The development of working memory: Further note on the comparability of two models of working memory. *Journal of Experimental Child Psychology, 77*, 11–127.

De Ribaupierre, A., Lecerf, T., & Bailleux, C. (2000). Is a nonverbal working memory task necessarily nonverbally encoded? *Cahiers de Psychologie Cognitive–Current Psychology of Cognition, 19*, 135–170.

De Ribaupierre, A., Neirynck, I., & Spira, A. (1989). Interactions between basic capacity and strategies in children's memory: Construction of a developmental paradigm. *Cahiers de Psychologie Cognitive, 9*, 471–504.

De Ribaupierre, A., & Pascual-Leone, J. (1979). Formal operations and M-Power: A neo-Piagetian investigation. In D. Kuhn (Ed.), *New directions in child development: Vol. 5. Intellectual development beyond childhood* (pp. 1–43). San Francisco: Jossey-Bass.

De Ribaupierre, A., Pous, O., Morier, S., & Lecerf, T. (1994, July). *Visual versus auditory presentation in a verbal working memory task.* Paper presented at the international conference on Working Memory, University of Cambridge, UK.

Elliott, E. M., Barrilleaux, K. M., & Cowan, N. (2006). Individual differences in the ability to avoid distracting sounds. *European Journal of Cognitive Psychology, 18*(1), 90–108.

Engle, R. W., Cantor, J., & Carullo, J. J. (1992). Individual differences in working memory and comprehension: A test of four hypotheses. *Journal of Experimental Psychology: Learning, Memory, and Cognition, 18*(5), 972–992.

Engle, R. W., Kane, M. J., & Tuholski, S. W. (1999a). Individual differences in working memory capacity and what they tell us about controlled attention, general fluid intelligence, and functions of the prefrontal cortex. In A. Miyake & P. Shah (Eds.), *Models of working memory: Mechanisms of active maintenance and executive control* (pp. 102–134). New York: Cambridge University Press.

Engle, R. W., Tuholski, S. W., Laughlin, J. E., & Conway, A. R. A. (1999b). Working memory, short-term memory, and general fluid intelligence: A latent-variable approach. *Journal of Experimental Psychology: General, 128*(3), 309–331.

Friedman, N. P., & Miyake, A. (2004). The reading span test and its predictive power for reading comprehension ability. *Journal of Memory and Language, 51*, 136–158.

Fry, A. F., & Hale, S. (1996). Processing speed, working memory, and fluid intelligence: Evidence for a developmental cascade. *Psychological Science, 7*, 237–241.

Hildebrand, D. K., Laing, J. D., & Rosenthal, H. (1977). *Analysis of ordinal data.* Thousand Oaks, CA: Sage Publications.

Inhelder, B., & Piaget, J. (1955). *De la logique de l'enfant à la logique de l'adolescence: essai sur la construction des structures opératoires formelles.* Paris: Presses Universitaires de France.

Jensen, A. R. (1998). *The g factor: The science of mental ability.* New York: Praeger.

Juhel, J. (1991). Relationship between psychometric intelligence and information-processing speed indexes. *Cahiers de Psychologie Cognitive, 11*, 73–105.

Kail, R., & Salthouse, T. (1994). Processing speed as a mental capacity. *Acta Psychologica, 86*, 199–225.

Kane, M. J., Hambrick, D. Z., & Conway, A. R. A. (2005). Working memory capacity and fluid intelligence are strongly related constructs: Comments on Ackerman, Beier, and Boyle (2005). *Psychological Bulletin, 131*(1), 66–71.

Kane, M. J., Hambrick, D. Z., Tuholski, S. W., Wilhelm, O., Payne, T. W., & Engle, R. W. (2004). The generality of working memory capacity: A latent-variable approach to verbal and visuo-spatial memory span and reasoning. *Journal of Experimental Psychology: General, 133*(2), 189–217.

Kranzler, J. H., & Jensen, A. R. (1989). Inspection time and intelligence: A meta-analysis. *Intelligence, 13*, 329–347.

Kyllonen, P., & Christal, R. E. (1990). Reasoning ability is (little more than) working-memory capacity? *Intelligence, 14*, 389–433.

Lautrey, J., & de Ribaupierre, A. (2004). Psychology of human intelligence in France and in French-speaking Switzerland. In R. J. Sternberg (Ed.), *International handbook of intelligence* (pp. 104–134). Cambridge, UK: Cambridge University Press.

Loisy, C., & Roulin, J.-L. (1992). *Multiple short-term storage in working memory: A new experimental approach.* Paper presented at the fifth conference of the European Society for Cognitive Psychology, Paris.

Miyake, A., & Shah, P. (1999). Toward unified theories of working memory: Emerging general consensus, unresolved theoretical issues, and future research directions. In A. Miyake & P. Shah (Eds.), *Models of working memory* (pp. 442–482). Cambridge, MA: Cambridge University Press.

Oberauer, K., Schulze, R., Wilhelm, O., & Süss, H.-M. (2005). Working memory and intelligence—their correlation and their relation: Comment on Ackerman, Beier, and Boyle (2005). *Psychological Bulletin, 131*(1), 61–65.

Oberauer, K., Süss, H.-M., Schulze, R., & Wittman, W. W. (2000). Working memory capacity—facets of a cognitive ability construct. *Personality and Individual Differences, 29*, 1017–1045.

Oberauer, K., Süss, H.-M., Wilhelm, O., & Wittman, W. W. (2003). The multiple faces of working memory: Storage, processing, supervision, and coordination. *Intelligence, 31*, 167–193.

Pascual-Leone, J. (1970). A mathematical model for the transition rule in Piaget's developmental stages. *Acta Psychologica, 32*, 301–345.

Pascual-Leone, J. (1987). Organismic processes for neo-Piagetian theories: A dialectical causal account of cognitive development. *International Journal of Psychology, 22*, 531–570.

Pascual-Leone, J., & Ijaz, H. (1989). Mental capacity testing as a form of intellectual-developmental assessment. In R. J. Samuda, S. L. Kong, J. Cummins, J. Pascual-Leone, & J. Lewis (Eds.), *Assessment and placement of minority students* (pp. 143–171). Toronto, Canada: Intercultural Social Sciences Publications.

Pedhazur, E. J. (1997). *Multiple regression in behavioural research: Explanation and prediction* (3rd ed.). Orlando, FL: Harcourt Brace College Publishers.

Piaget, J. (1947). *La psychologie de l'intelligence*. Paris: Armand Colin.

Piaget, J., & Inhelder, B. (1966). *L'image mentale chez l'enfant*. Paris: Presses Universitaires de France.

Piaget, J., Inhelder, B., & Szeminska, A. (1948). *La géométrie spontanée chez l'enfant*. Paris: Presses Universitaires de France.

Raven, J. C. (1956). *Standard Progressive Matrices*. Issy-les-Moulineaux, France: Editions Scientifiques et Psychotechniques. (Original work published 1938)

Richardson, J. T. E. (1996). Evolving issues in working memory. In J. T. E. Richardson, R. W. Engle, L. Hasher, R. H. Logie, E. R. Stoltzfus, & R. T. Zachs (Eds.), *Working memory and human cognition* (pp. 120–154). Oxford, UK: Oxford University Press.

Rieben, L., de Ribaupierre, A., & Lautrey, J. (1983). *Le développement opératoire de l'enfant entre 6 et 12 ans. Elaboration d'un instrument d'évaluation*. Paris: Editions du CNRS.

Rieben, L., de Ribaupierre, A., & Lautrey, J. (1990). Structural invariants and individual modes of processing: On the necessity of a minimally structuralist approach of development for education. *Archives de Psychologie, 58*, 29–53.

Salthouse, T. A. (1992a). *Mechanisms of age-cognition relations in adulthood*. Hillsdale, NJ: Lawrence Erlbaum Associates, Inc.

Salthouse, T. A. (1992b). Working-memory mediation of adult age differences in integrative reasoning. *Memory and Cognition, 20*(4), 413–423.

Salthouse, T. A. (1996). The processing-speed theory of adult age differences in cognition. *Psychological Review, 103*(3), 403–428.

Salthouse, T. A., Babcock, R. L., Mitchell, D. R. D., Palmon, R., & Skovronek, E. (1990). Sources of individual differences in spatial visualization ability. *Intelligence, 14*, 187–230.

Salthouse, T. A., & Meinz, E. J. (1995). Aging, inhibition, working memory, and speed. *Journals of Gerontology: Series B. Psychological Sciences and Social Sciences, 50b*(6), P297–P306.

Schaie, K. W., & Hertzog, C. (1986). Toward a comprehensive model of adult intellectual development: Contributions of the Seattle longitudinal study. In R. J. Sternberg (Ed.), *Advances in the psychology of human intelligence* (pp. 79–118). Hillsdale, NJ: Lawrence Erlbaum Associates, Inc.

Shah, P., & Miyake, A. (1996). The separability of working memory resources for spatial thinking and language processing: An individual approach. *Journal of Experimental Psychology: General, 125*(1), 4–27.

Siegler, R. S. (1981). Developmental sequences within and between sequences. *Monographs of the Society for Research in Child Development, 46*, 6.

Stewart, L., & Pascual-Leone, J. (1992). Mental capacity constraints and the development of moral reasoning. *Journal of Experimental Child Psychology, 54*, 251–287.

Süss, H.-M., Oberauer, K., Wittman, W. W., Wilhelm, O., & Schulze, R. (2002). Working-memory capacity explains reasoning ability—and a little bit more. *Intelligence, 30*, 261–288.

Thomas, L., Pons, F., & de Ribaupierre, A. (1996). Attentional capacity and cognitive level in the balance task. *Cahiers de Psychologie Cognitive, 15*, 137–172.

Wilhelm, O., & Oberauer, K. (2006). Why are reasoning ability and working memory capacity related to mental speed? An investigation of stimulus–response compatibility in choice reaction time tasks. *European Journal of Cognitive Psychology, 18*(1), 18–50.

EUROPEAN JOURNAL OF COGNITIVE PSYCHOLOGY
2006, 18 (1), 138–158

Intelligence and executive functioning in adult age: Effects of sibship size and birth order

Sara Holmgren and Bo Molander

Department of Psychology, Umeå University, Sweden

Lars-Göran Nilsson

Stockholm University, Sweden

Several studies have demonstrated that social influences from having been brought up in a family with few siblings and early in birth order result in higher scores on intelligence tests in childhood and adolescence as compared to having been brought up in large sibships. The present study examined whether influences of such social factors would have long-lasting effects on intelligence (block design and word comprehension) and executive functions (working memory and verbal fluency) in adulthood and old age, i.e., long after the individuals had moved out of the family structure they were born in. After having controlled for socioeconomic status and a variety of health conditions affecting cognition in adult life, a sibship size effect was demonstrated for executive functions but not for intelligence. The social influences of birth order affected only executive functions and working memory in particular; earlier born individuals performed better than later born individuals in tests assessing executive function but not in tests assessing intelligence. Implications for the relationship between executive functioning and intelligence, and implications for the Confluence and Resource Dilution Models (Blake, 1981; Downey, 1995, 2001; Zajonc, 1976) are discussed.

Most modern theories of cognitive development claim that social and environmental factors during childhood and adolescence are crucial for intellectual functioning later in life (e.g., Bussey & Bandura, 1999; Erikson, 1963; Fischer & Bidell, 1998; Gibson & Pick, 2000; Siegler, 1998; Vygotsky, 1986). Zajonc and colleauges (e.g., Zajonc, 1976;1986, 2001; Zajonc & Markus, 1975; Zajonc &

Correspondence should be addressed to Lars-Göran Nilsson, Department of Psychology, Stockholm University, SE-10691 Stockholm, Sweden. Email: lgn@psychology.su.se

The Betula Study is funded by the Bank of Sweden Tercentenary Foundation (1988-0082:17), Swedish Council for Planning and Coordination of Research (D1988-0092, D1989-0115, D1990-0074, D1991-0258, D1992-0143, D1997-0756, D1997-1841, D1999-0739, B1999-474), Swedish Council for Research in the Humanities and Social Sciences (F377/1988-2000), and the Swedish Council for Social Research (1988–1990: 88-0082, and 311/1991-2000).

Mullaly, 1997) have argued that sibship size and birth order are good examples of such social/environmental factors influencing intellectual functioning in childhood; as sibship size and birth order increase, intelligence declines. Empirical support for the effect of sibship size and birth order is plentiful for childhood and adolescence (e.g., Belmont & Marolla, 1973; Downey, 2001; Kuo & Hauser, 1997; Mercy & Steelman, 1982), but very scarce for adulthood and old age.

Two major theoretical accounts have been proposed to account for these effects. Zajonc (1976, 2001; Zajonc & Marcus, 1975) proposed the Confluence Model, saying that three major factors are responsible for these effects: (1) Parents provide relatively more attention to each child in a small sibling group than to each child in a larger group. The same holds true for children born early as compared to late. (2) First-born children and children in small sibling groups are exposed to more adult language than children born later and children in larger sibling groups. That is, the linguistic environment becomes less mature as more children enter the family. (3) The general intellectual environment also becomes less mature as more children enter the family. Furthermore, regarding birth order, the act of tutoring younger siblings helps the older children to process information cognitively, which in turn improves linguistic and general intellectual abilities.

The alternative account, the Resource Dilution Model, proposed by Blake (1981) and developed further by Downey (1995, 2001), states essentially two factors as responsible for the sibship size and birth order effects. This is that the finite parental resources are reduced as more siblings enter the family and that the relative richness of the family environment affects the cognitive development.

Although there are similarities among these two theoretical accounts, a theoretical consensus is still lacking in the scientific community regarding the proper mechanism for the sibship-size and birth-order effects. The obvious similarity between the confluence model and the resource dilution model is that the available parental resources, in a general sense, are larger in families with few children and for those children born early in a family. By parental resources "in a broad sense" Downey (1995, 2000) means resources that are basic for the child's survival (e.g., a place to live, food, clothes, protection, and supervision), the interests parents take in their children in daily routines (e.g., helping with homework, proving opportunities for sports and hobbies, taking interest in friends) and to make investments that enhance the child's opportunities in life (e.g., hiring a maths tutor, buying computers, and saving money for education).

The aim here is not to evaluate these two models of the effects of sibship size and birth order for intellectual ability. Rather, the aim is to examine whether the effects of these social variables hold more extensively than previously having been investigated. Building on the notion that these effects of sibship size and birth order are true and assuming that parental resources in a broad sense, material or intellectual, do have an effect on the intelligence of the child, it is of interest to know for cognitive psychology whether these effects remain to influence intelligence also in adulthood and old age. There is no data available showing whether the effects of sibship size and birth order on intellectual functioning extend throughout the life span. One purpose of the present study was, thus, to examine this issue.

As noted above, the measures used in previous research to assess the intellectual effects of sibship size and birth order were complete intelligence tests or subtests of such tests assessing various aspects of intelligence. We will follow this tradition in the present study by using standardised tests assessing visuospatial and verbal components of intelligence. The Block Design Test of Wechsler Adult Intelligence Scale (WAIS; Wechsler, 1981), reflecting visuospatial constructional ability, is strongly correlated with full-scale WAIS IQ, and is a good predictor of general intellectual ability (Groth-Marnat & Teal, 2000; Snow, Kyllonen, & Marshalek, 1984). The Block Design Test is thought to reflect fluid aspects of intelligence involving relatively unfamiliar materials and requiring fast and efficient solutions to novel problems. Another intelligence test used in the present study is the Word Comprehension Test used in many intelligence test batteries to assess verbal ability (e.g., WAIS: Kaufman, Reynolds, & McLean, 1989; Wechsler, 1981; the Army Alpha: Jones & Conrad, 1933; the Primary Mental Abilities Battery: Schaie, 1985; SRB: Dureman, Kebbon, & Österberg, 1974; Dureman & Sälde, 1959). Tests of word comprehension and vocabulary are thought of as reflecting crystallised intelligence; they assess world knowledge in a broad sense, draw on previous experience, and have relatively limited speed demands. In previous studies on sibship size and birth order there is generally a lack of data on comparisons of the individual tasks constituting the IQ measures. One exception, though, is Marjoribanks (1976a, 1976b), who, for sibship size and birth order, reported larger negative correlations for language/verbal tasks than for spatial/reasoning tasks in children 11–15 years of age. Such a result is in line with the importance Zajonc ascribes language in his Confluence Model (cf. Marschark, 2006 this issue). On the other hand, school education and professional education later in life is likely to compensate for some of the linguistic and verbal deficiencies that originated in the family environment. It is thus difficult to predict the level of performance in word comprehension as compared to block design in our adult groups. What could be said, however, and in line with Schaie (1994), is that a crystallised factor like word comprehension is less vulnerable to ageing compared to a fluent factor like block design (e.g., Baltes, Staudinger, & Lindenberger, 1999). Thus, an interaction between age and sibship size or birth order is more likely to appear for block design than for word comprehension (cf. Cornoldi, 2006 this issue).

Previous research on the effects of sibship size and birth order has, thus, primarily been based on intelligence tests. In addition to such tests, the present study also employed tests derived from recent developments in modern cognitive psychology covering several domains that, reasonably, are strongly involved in determining intellectual functioning. One cognitive domain that should be of interest in this regard is that of executive functions. Several definitions of executive functions have been proposed. Salthouse, Atkinson, and Berish (2003, p. 566) define executive functions as control "processes responsible for planning, assembling, coordinating sequencing, and monitoring cognitive operations". Rabbitt (1997) stated that executive functions are a group of cognitive actions dealing with novelty, planning, monitoring performance, and inhibiting task-irrelevant information. Generally, executive functions refer to a set of processes used to control and monitor behaviour in novel situations. Tasks that do not demand preexisting knowledge structures, but rather require processing in novel situations, are more sensitive to age-related decline. Fluid intelligence tests also involve relatively unfamiliar material and demand efficient solutions to novel problems. Tests assessing fluid aspects of intelligence show robust decline across the adult age span (Baltes et al., 1999).

There are primarily two reasons for including tests of executive functioning when examining the effects of sibship size and birth order throughout the adult life span. One reason was to extend knowledge about the effects of sibship size and birth order beyond mere intelligence. To the best of our knowledge, there is no such systematic extension made in previous research. Notably, the claim has been made that performance on executive functions reflect general intellectual ability (Obonsawin et al., 2002), but little is still known about similarities and differences between these two domains. Also, the concept of executive function itself and the tasks used for assessing executive functioning is under scrutiny (e.g., Bryan & Luszcz, 2001; Miyake, Emerson, & Friedman, 2000; Salthouse et al., 2003). The present study may contribute to further understanding of two of the tasks commonly considered as belonging to executive functioning domain.

One of the tests of executive function used here emanates from a series of tests developed by Baddeley, Lewis, Eldridge, and Thompson (1984) to assess working memory. In this task participants are presented with a list of words and are asked to free recall as many of these words as possible immediately after presentation. Concurrently with the encoding of these words, participants sort a deck of cards in one black and one red pile. It is interesting to include working memory in the present context, not least because of the current debate about the relationship between working memory and intelligence (e.g., Ackerman, Beier, & Boyle, 2005; Beier & Ackerman, 2005; Kane, Hambrick, & Conway, 2005; Oberauer, Schulze, Wilhelm, & Süß, 2005). According to these authors working memory and intelligence might be seen as different but much related concepts (cf. Borella, Carretti, & Mammarella, 2006 this issue; de Ribaupierre & Lecerf, 2006 this issue; Wilhelm & Oberauer, 2006 this issue). Another test of executive function used in the present study was that of verbal fluency. Participants were asked to generate as many words as possible with the initial letter A during a period of 1 min. In general, we assume that executive functioning should be less influenced by social factors like sibship size and birth order than overall intelligence and in particular in comparison to word comprehension. In summing up so far, a second aim of this study is to extend the scope of tasks used for examining the effects of sibship size and birth order to tasks beyond those assessing intelligence.

The data to be used for examining the effects of sibship size and birth order on intelligence and executive functions emanate from the Betula Study—a prospective cohort study of memory, health, and ageing (Nilsson et al., 1997, 2004). By using the database of Betula, there is ample opportunity to examine the effects of sibship size and birth order at various stages of adulthood and old age. Another demographic variable that also should be controlled for in any study examining the effects of some independent variables on intellectual ability is sex of the participants. As has been demonstrated in Betula (Herlitz, Nilsson, & Bäckman, 1997; Maitland, Herlitz, Nyberg, Bäckman, & Nilsson, 2004) and elsewhere (e.g., Halpern & LaMay, 2000; Voyer, Voyer, & Bryden, 1995), there is in general a female superiority in verbal tasks, whereas spatial tasks typically show a male advantage. Thus, there are reasons to include sex of the participants as a factor in this study. All in all, there are reasons to believe that third-order interactions between sibship size (or birth order), age, and sex may show up in the analyses.

Although main effects of age and sex on intelligence and executive functioning are of interest in the general context of cognitive psychology, of greater interest is to explore whether age and sex interact with sibship size and birth order, respectively. However, relatively few participants in the oldest cohorts make any three-way interaction pattern difficult to obtain and interpret. Given that the effects of sibship size and birth order are genuine in childhood and adolescence when persons are living in the family from which they receive parental resources and support, it might be argued, in line with what is claimed from a genetic approach, that these effects should decrease in importance as individuals move out of the original families. For example, general intelligence is said to be inherited and not affected permanently by siblings' rearing environment (e.g., Bouchard, 1998; Plomin & Petrill, 1997; Plomin, DeFries, McClearn, & McGuffin, 2001). Effects of the environment disappear with age, it is said, and in particular this should be true for shared family environment. Already in late adolescence, parents' education, income, and child-rearing practice is said to play little role for intelligence (Gottfredson, 2004). Thus, it might be argued that the effects of sibship size and birth order, if any effects at all, should be largest in young middle age and decline successively thereafter to be rather small in old age. This is not to say that the effects of social and environmental factors in general are small in old age. On the contrary, such factors are at least as strong and important as in young age. The influence of other social and environmental factors emerging at later stages of life may play a more important role in old age (e.g., major life crises, professional training, workplace conditions, travelling, the media, etc.). The case that can be made is simply that those social and environmental factors, whose influence is gained in childhood, may not maintain its potency for the rest of life.

In addition to the three aims of the study already mentioned (extension of the study population to the adult life span, controlling for possible interactions with the sex variable, and extension of the tasks employed beyond intelligence), a fourth aim of the study was to control for possible confounding variables affecting the effect of sibship size and birth order on intellectual functioning. Such confounding variables may be of, at least, two kinds: socioeconomic status and health. It is obvious that socioeconomic status may be a confounding variable to both sibship size and birth order, making it difficult to draw conclusions about the role of these two variables separately. As reported by several authors (e.g., Blake, 1981, 1989; Downey, 1995, 2001), a lower socioeconomic status is related to families with more children. In controlling for this variable, we have used number of years in formal education as a proxy to socioeconomic status. However, this issue is somewhat complicated since education also varies quite dramatically across age of the individual, both with respect to the number of years spent in school and the quality of the education provided. For example, 15 years of schooling for somebody 80 years of age does not mean the same as the same number of years of education for somebody who is, say, 30 years of age. For this reason, we have divided the participants into three different age groups (35–45, 50–60, and 65–85 years of age) and made the analyses separately for these three age ranges with control for socioeconomic status within these age ranges.

Health is another variable that might be confounded with sibship size and birth order, and in that it is related to lifestyle and socioeconomic status (e.g., Bäckman et al., 2004; Lee, Kawachi, Berkman, & Grodstein, 2003). Since considerable amounts of health data are available in the Betula Study, we have also controlled for this risk of confounding by excluding individuals who suffer from diseases known to affect cognitive performance. These diseases are dementia, heart attack, circulation disorders, stroke, hypertension, and diabetes. These diseases are known to affect cognitive performance negatively (e.g., Bäckman, Jones, Small, Agüero-Torres, & Fratiglioni, 2003; Nilsson & Söderlund, 2001; Stachran, Ewing, Deary, & Frier, 1997).

By these arrangements we claim to have a healthy sample with control for sex and socioeconomic factors on the basis of which we can assess the effects of sibship size and birth order on intelligence and executive functions among middle-age, young-old, and old-old participants. In summary, we predict that sibship size and birth order, as social influences, should affect word comprehension rather than block design and any of the executive-function measures. Moreover, we predict that these effects of sibship size and birth order, if any effects at all, should be found early in adulthood rather than late since it has been claimed that the effects of shared family environment on intellectual functioning should be reduced as chronological age increases (Bouchard, 1998; Gottfredson, 2004; Plomin et al., 2001). Finally, we expect to find a main effect of sex favouring men in the block design test and a main effect of sex favouring women in working memory and fluency.

METHOD

Participants

This study is based on data from the Betula Study (Nilsson et al., 1997). Three samples of participants were included. The design of the study is described in detail in Nilsson et al. (1997, 2004). Only those aspects of the design that are of relevance for the present study will be described here. Sample 1 (S1) consisted of 1000 participants in the ages of 35, 40, 45, 50, 55, 60, 65, 70, 75, and 80 years, with 100 participants in each age cohort; in sample 2 (S2) there were 998 participants in the same ages as in S1 with 100 participants in each age cohort, except the oldest cohort, which included 98 participants. The third sample (S3) included 956 participants; these participants were of the ages 40, 45, 50, 55, 60, 65, 70, 75, 80, and 85 years, with 100 participants for age cohorts 40–65. There were 99, 99, 98, and 70 participants in age cohorts 70, 75, 80, and 85 years, respectively. Participants in the three samples were randomly and independently drawn from the population registry in Umeå, a city of about 108,000 people in northern Sweden. It was judged necessary to include at least three samples from the Betula Study here to guarantee a large enough number of cases over the whole range of sibship sizes and birth order. After exclusion of participants with dementia, heart attack, circulation disorders, stroke, hypertension, and diabetes, there were 1510 participants divided into three age cohorts: one middle-age group (35–45 years of age) consisting of 627 participants, one young-old group (50–60 years) consisting of 496 participants, and one old-old group (65–85 years) consisting of 387 participants. The data to be reported here emanate from the first wave of data collection for each sample (S1: 1988–1990; S2 and S3: 1993–1995).

Sibship size varied from 1–16 and birth order varied from 1–15. In order to gain power in the statistical analyses, the participants were divided into three groups in each variable. For sibship size, the groups consisted of 1–2, 3–4, and 5–16 siblings, respectively, and the groups contained 418, 579, and 513 participants, respectively. Likewise, the three groups of birth order consisted of participants, who were born first, second and third, and fourth to fifteenth, with 535, 612, and 363 participants, respectively. Characteristics of the sibship size and birth order subgroups are shown in Table 1.

It can be seen in Table 1 that there are differences between the different sibship-size groups with respect to variables that might affect the performance in tests on intelligence and executive functions. Of particular interest in this context is the educational variable (number of years in formal education), which

TABLE 1
Characteristics of participants across age groups

	Sibship size								
	1–2			*3–4*			*5–16*		
Age group	35–45	50–60	65–85	35–45	50–60	65–85	35–45	50–60	65–85
N	233	113	72	258	199	122	136	184	193
% female	52.4	54.0	66.7	50.4	52.3	53.3	50.7	51.6	49.7
Age (years)									
M	40.3	53.9	70.4	40.3	54.3	70.8	40.7	55.2	72.8
SD	4.01	3.92	5.46	3.95	4.04	5.54	3.89	3.91	5.91
Education (years)									
M	10.9	8.5	13.3	11.2	8.3	12.6	9.5	7.8	13.9
SD	3.59	3.67	3.06	4.14	3.18	3.17	3.43	4.91	3.27

	Birth order								
	1			*2–3*			*4–15*		
Age group	35–45	50–60	65–85	35–45	50–60	65–85	35–45	50–60	65–85
N	244	175	116	269	201	142	107	121	135
% female	53.8	54.3	56.8	51.3	53.2	57.7	46.7	49.6	45.9
Age (years)									
M	40.4	54.6	71.8	40.5	53.9	71.2	40.0	55.4	72.3
SD	4.10	4.00	6.09	3.89	3.93	5.51	3.76	3.96	5.79
Education (years)									
M	13.8	10.9	8.2	13.0	10.7	8.6	13.2	9.5	7.5
SD	3.30	3.84	3.19	3.11	3.91	5.85	3.06	3.49	2.47

might be regarded as a proxy for socioeconomic status. This variable differs significantly between groups for both sibship size, $F(2, 1490) = 44.1$, $p < .001$, and birth order, $F(2, 1507) = 20.7$, $p < .001$. In the following analyses, we will thus use education as a covariate. Although, there is no reason to expect that sex should be a critical variable for intelligence, we include sex as an independent variable for the sake of known sex differences in the tasks assessing executive functions (e.g., Herlitz et al., 1997). Differences in frequencies of men and women among the subgroups were tested by chi-squared, and neither for sibship size nor birth order were there significant effects ($ps > .05$).

Test battery

A detailed description of the tasks included in the Betula test battery can be found in Nilsson et al. (1997). A short description of those tasks included in the composites of intelligence (word comprehension, block design) and executive functions (word fluency, working memory) is presented next.

Word comprehension. Participants were given a 30-item multiple-choice synonym test to be completed in 7 min. The participants were to choose the word that has the same meaning as the target word among five alternatives (Dureman et al., 1974; Dureman & Sälde, 1959). A 10 year test–retest correlation of this measure is .79 for the youngest age group.

Block design. Block design is a standardised test of visuospatial ability from the Wechsler Adult Intelligence Scale (Wechsler, 1981). This task involves putting sets of coloured blocks together to match patterns on cards. There are two demonstration cards, seven task cards, and nine blocks (cubes) with the colour red on two sides, white on two sides, and red and white on two sides. The participants were instructed to motorically form different designs with the blocks by copying nine designs bound into a booklet. The 10 year test–retest correlation of this measure is .79 for the youngest age cohort.

Verbal fluency. The participants were instructed to generate orally as many words as possible with the initial letter A in 1 min. The test leader wrote the words down on a paper during the test and the participants received score for each correct word. The 10 year test–retest correlation of this measure is .65 for the youngest age cohort.

Working memory. In this working memory task, developed by Baddeley et al. (1984), participants were presented auditorily with a word list of 12 items in one single trial. A card-sorting task was provided as distractor during the study of the words; the participants were told to motorically sort black and red cards at the same pace as the words were presented. A free recall test followed immediately after the presentation of the list. The retrieval time was set to 45 s. The 10 year test–retest correlation of this measure is .59 for the youngest age cohort.

Health assessment and social variables

In the Betula Study an extensive health examination is included together with a number of questionnaires and interviews concerning social and socioeconomic variables. The health examination was conducted by nurses and covers objective measures, such as measures based on blood samples and measures of blood pressure, as well as subjective health measures. Among the social variables are marital status, type of dwelling, education, profession, and childhood variables, including sibship size and birth order. A detailed description of the Betula health assessment and social variables is presented in Nilsson et al. (1997).

Statistical analysis

Tests of intelligence (block design, word comprehension) and executive function (working memory, word fluency) were transformed to z scores and aggregated. The data were analysed by the means of SPSS for Windows, version 11.

Differences between groups of participants were tested by analyses of variance (ANOVA) and analyses of covariance (ANCOVA). Post hoc analyses were performed by means of the Bonferroni test.

RESULTS

Analyses were performed on the whole sample of participants separately for sibship size and birth order. For each of these two factors, analyses of the intelligence measures are presented first followed by analyses of the executive functioning measures. Also, as pointed out in the introductory section, analyses were performed separately for each age group. In the latter case, education was entered as a covariate. However, there is still an age variation to account for in the middle-age (35–45 years), young-old (50–60 years), and old-old (65–85 years) groups that can be of importance in the age-sensitive tasks used here. Thus, sibship size, birth order, age (within age cohorts), and sex were the factors of the ANCOVAs, with education as a covariate.

Sibship size

A 3 (sibship size) × 3 (age) × 2 (sex) ANOVA for the aggregated intelligence measure of block design and word comprehension showed significant effects of sibship size, $F(2, 1492) = 5.53$, $p < .01$, $\eta^2 = .007$, age, $F(2, 1492) = 80.3$, $p < .001$, $\eta^2 = .14$, and sex, $F(1, 1492) = 4.07$, $p < .05$, $\eta^2 = .003$, A posteriori Bonferroni tests revealed significant differences between the largest and the two smaller sibship groups, between all three age groups, and men performed better than women ($ps < .05$).

A similar ANOVA was performed on each of the two components of the aggregated measure. For block design the analysis revealed only significant effects of age, $F(2, 1492) = 171$, $p < .001$, $\eta^2 = .19$, and sex, $F(1, 1492) = 25.0$, $p < .001$, $\eta^2 = .02$, the old-old group performing worse than the young-old group, and the latter group performing worse than the middle-age group ($ps < .05$). Men performed better than women in this task. The analysis on word comprehension showed significant effects of sibship size, $F(2, 1492) = 6.59$, $p < .005$, $\eta^2 = .01$, and age, $F(2, 1492) = 32.5$, $p < .001$, $\eta^2 = .04$. Participants in the sibship size "5–16" group performed worse than the other two groups. The old-old group performed worse than the other two age groups. The main effects of sibship size for the aggregated measure, as well as for each separate measure are presented in Figure 1.

The Sibship size × Age × Sex ANOVA conducted on the aggregated executive functioning measure yielded significant effects of sibship size, $F(2, 1484) = 6.15$, $p < .005$, $\eta^2 = .008$, age, $F(2, 1484) = 68.0$, $p < .001$, $\eta^2 = .08$, sex, $F(2, 1484) = 6.08$, $p < .05$, $\eta^2 = .004$, and Sibship size × Age × Sex, $F(4, 1484) = 4.61$, $p < .005$, $\eta^2 = .01$. Sibship size group "5–16" performed worse than the other two groups, and all three age groups differed significantly

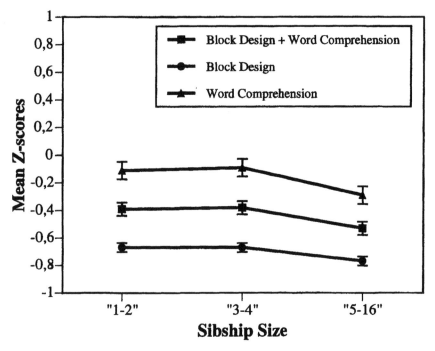

Figure 1.   Intelligence as a function of sibship size. The intelligence measure is based on performance in block design and word comprehension. Error bars are standard errors.

from each other. Women outperformed men in the two youngest age groups, but not in the oldest group ($ps < .05$).

The analysis performed separately on the working memory measure showed significant effects only for age, $F(2, 1484) = 59.1$, $p < .001$, $\eta^2 = .07$, a Sibship size × Age, $F(4, 1484) = 3.49$, $p < .01$, $\eta^2 = .01$, and a Sibship size × Age × Sex interaction, $F(4, 1484) = 2.48$, $p < .05$, $\eta^2 = .01$. This interaction indicates a stronger negative effect of sibship size in the oldest age group among men as compared to the two younger groups ($ps < .05$). For verbal fluency significant effects were obtained for sibship size, $F(2, 1492) = 5.95$, $p < .005$, $\eta^2 = .01$, sex, $F(1, 1492) = 10.0$, $p < .005$, $\eta^2 = .01$, age, $F(2, 1492) = 26.8$, $p < .001$, $\eta^2 = .04$, and Sibship size × Age × Sex, $F(4, 1492) = 2.42$, $p < .05$, $\eta^2 = .01$, showing higher performance for women and a more marked decline among those men belonging to the largest sipship group ($ps < .05$). The main effects of sibship size for the aggregated executive function measure, as well as for the separate measures, are illustrated in Figure 2.

The separate analyses of age groups with education as a covariate were performed next. In these analyses we present only significant effects related to sibship size, as main effects of age and sex are of less importance here. For the

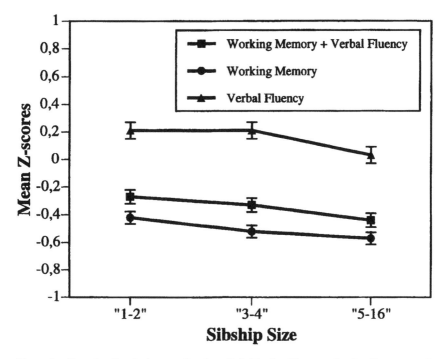

Figure 2. Executive functioning as a function of sibship size. The executive-function measure is based on performance in word fluency and working memory. Error bars are standard errors.

aggregated intelligence measure, sibship size did not reach significance as a main effect or in interactions in any of the three age groups. A similar analysis on block design alone did not show any significant effects of sibship size in any of the three age groups. For word comprehension, there was a significant Sibship size $\times$ Age $\times$ Sex interaction in the old-old group, $F(8, 354) = 2.17, p < .05, \eta^2 = .05$. As shown in Figure 3, the decrease in performance was most pronounced in the old-old age group, especially for men. For women, performance showed an unexpected inverted U-shape form, such that the smallest sibship performed at just about the same level as the largest sibship and lower than the middle-size group.

The analyses of the aggregated executive functioning measure with control for education showed a significant Sibship size $\times$ Age interaction for the young-old group, $F(4, 472) = 2.58, p < .05, \eta^2 = .02$, and a Sibship size $\times$ Sex interaction in the old-old group, $F(2, 349) = 3.93, p < .05, \eta^2 = .01$. The Sibship size $\times$ Age interaction in the young-old group indicates a larger age deficit in the smallest sibship group. The Sibship size $\times$ Sex interaction in the old-old group shows a larger decline in performance as a function of the size of the sibship for men than for women.

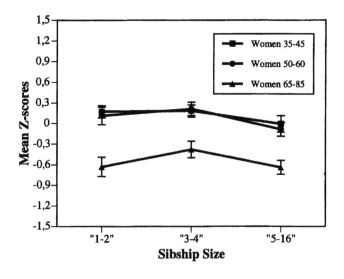

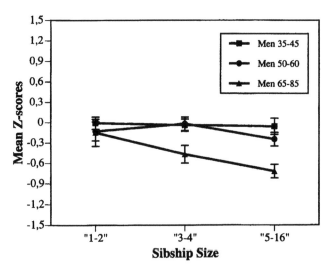

Figure 3. Word comprehension as a function of sibship size, age, and sex. Top panel: women. Bottom panel: men. Error bars are standard errors.

The analyses on working memory showed a significant main effect of sibship size in the oldest group, $F(2, 349) = 3.80$, $p < .05$, $\eta^2 = .02$, showing worse performance in the "5–16" sibship size group as compared to the "1–2" and "3–4" groups ($ps < .05$). The overall data pattern for working memory is very much the same as that demonstrated in Figure 3 for word comprehension.

Interestingly, in examining the sex difference in the oldest group, it was found that the low performance for women in the smallest sibship (1–2 siblings) can be attributed to sibships with one child only ($p < .05$). Lower performance for families with one child as compared with families with two children has previously also been obtained by Zajonc and others (e.g., Breland, 1974; Zajonc, 2001). The analyses on verbal fluency did not show any significant effects for sibship size.

Birth order

The overall 3 (birth order) × 3 (age) × 2 (sex) ANOVAs performed on composite intelligence and executive functioning measures did not reach significance with respect to birth order. Only the working memory subcomponent of executive functioning reached statistical significance, $F(2, 1501) = 3.66$, $p < .05$, $\eta^2 = .01$. The Bonferroni test showed the group with first-born individuals to perform better than the group of those individuals born second or third, $ps < .05$ (see Figure 4).

The analyses performed on each of the three age groups, controlling for education, showed a significant Birth order × Age interaction for block design

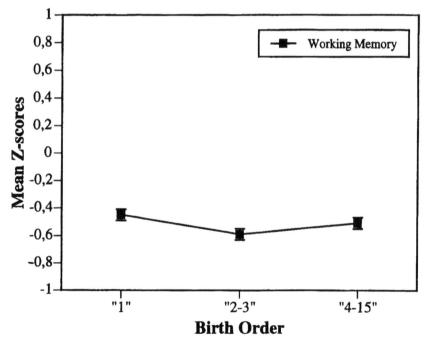

Figure 4. Working memory as a function of birth order. Error bars are standard errors.

in the middle-age group, $F(4, 600) = 2.77, p < .05, \eta^2 = .02$, indicating a larger age deficit for participants in the highest birth order group. For the word fluency measure of executive functioning, there was also a significant Birth order × Age interaction in the middle-age group, $F(4, 600) = 2.45, p < .05, \eta^2 = .02$.

In order to reduce the risk of a possible confounding of family size and birth order, we also performed separate analyses of family size with five or more children, dividing this group in birth order positions as done in previous analyses, that is, "1", "2–3", and "4–15". Due to the limited number of cases in some of the age groups for the family size "5–16" category, data were collapsed across the age variable. The overall 3 (birth order) × 2 (sex) ANOVAs conducted on the composite intelligence measure and the subcomponents revealed no main effects of birth order or any interactions with the sex variable. For the composite measure of executive function, the ANOVA revealed a significant main effect of birth order, $F(2, 498) = 9.56, p < .005, \eta^2 = .02$, showing that first-born children performed better than both the other two groups. The ANOVA for working memory also showed a significant superiority for first-born participants, $F(2, 498) = 4.95, p < .01, \eta^2 = .02$. It was not possible to analyse each age cohort separately and control for education because of small number of participants in several cells.

DISCUSSION

In line with predictions, the present study demonstrates that healthy individuals in adulthood and old age show a decreasing performance in tests assessing intelligence and executive functions as sibship size increases. When analysing the data at the level of individual tasks, the same data pattern was found for working memory, but not for block design. We predicted that sibship size would have a rather limited effect on executive functioning, perhaps at the level of its effect on block design, and definitively at a lower level than the effect on word comprehension. However, the effect of sibship size was significant for executive functions, and as strong as that for word comprehension. For both working memory and fluency, men in the oldest age cohort were those most affected by sibship size. We interpret this finding as showing that the effect of sibship size on executive function may not be strong, but the effect can be seen for those participants whose prerequisites for managing working memory and fluency tasks are known to be poor (e.g., Herlitz et al., 1997).

When controlling for socioeconomic status within each age cohort, sibship size did not affect the aggregated intelligence measure or either of the two subcomponents, block design and word comprehension. As shown in Figure 3, there was, however, a three-way interaction again involving sibship size, age, and sex. The sibship size effect was negative and linear for men in the oldest age cohort. This result again suggests that the effect of sibship size is not strong in adulthood and old age, but can, apparently, be demonstrated for those participants, whose capabilities in cognitive tasks also are strongly affected by the age and sex variables (see Herlitz et al., 1997). Somewhat speculatively, the low performance for women in the smallest sibship group in the oldest age cohort might be due to the fact that first-born women during the first years of the twentieth century were not offered education beyond basic schooling because they were expected to help their families with household and other duties (cf. Reis, Petersson, Castro-Caldas, & Ingvar, 2001). Caution is justified here, however, as the three-way interactions involving the oldest groups are based on fewer cases than the younger groups, and are thus more vulnerable to errors.

Several significant effects were found for executive functions when controlling for socioeconomic status. There was one significant interaction between sibship size and sex in the young-old cohort and one interaction between sibship size and age for the oldest age cohort. The latter interaction showed the same data pattern as was shown in the overall analysis when socioeconomic status was not controlled for. That is, there was a linearly decreasing performance as sibship increased in size. For working memory, there was again a significant main effect of sibship size in the oldest age cohort. For fluency, however, this effect did not reach significance. All in all, the effect of sibship size is reliable in the expected direction for executive function, and in particular for working memory, even after controlling for socioeconomic status. Thus, the data pattern obtained in old age is similar to that found in many previous studies for children and adolescence (e.g., Berbaum & Moreland, 1985; Davis, Cahan, & Bashi, 1977; Mercy & Steelman, 1982; Rodgers, 1984; Smith, 1984; Zajonc & Markus, 1975). However, a word of caution should be mentioned regarding the generalisability of the present results to intelligence and executive functions in general, since the data are based on a relatively limited set of tasks.

Birth order did not show any reliable effects at the aggregate level for intelligence or for executive functions. Only the working memory subcomponent of executive function showed that first-born individuals performed better than those born later. When controlling for socioeconomic status, an interaction between birth order and age was found for block design, and a similar interaction was found for fluency. These interactions indicated a successive decrease in performance from first-born individuals in the middle-age group, which, thus, is in line with the Confluence Model (Zajonc, 1986).

These results are interesting in that they suggest family structure during childhood to be more related to adult cognitive functioning than previously thought. The data stand in sharp contrast to several proposals in previous research. For example, it has been claimed that general intelligence is inherited and not affected permanently by siblings' rearing environment (e.g., Bouchard, 1998; Plomin et al., 2001). The observed interaction in the present study between sibship size and age, showing a larger sibship-size effect with increasing age does not seem to be on par with the claims by Bouchard (1998), Gottfredson (2004), and Plomin et al. (2001) that g is highly heritable and not permanently affected by the rearing circumstances that siblings share.

The present results instead indicate that social and environmental factors during childhood do have a positive effect on intelligence in adulthood and old age. These data are in line with predictions that may be made from the Confluence Model (Zajonc, 1976, 2001) and the Resource Dilution Model (Blake, 1981; Downey, 2001), although these models do not make any specific predictions about effects for later parts of the life span. Downey (2001), a proponent of the dilution theory, said about the many studies demonstrating sibship size effects that "few patterns in the social and behavioural sciences reach this level of consistency" (p. 497). That this pattern extends to adulthood and old age is just another evidence of this consistency.

Predictions from the dilution model are mainly in line with the present results. However, it should be noted that the effects of sibship size in the present data are generally stronger than the effects of birth order, which is not predicted by the Resource Dilution Model (Downey, 2001). Another problem for this model is the clear monotonic negative trend from few to many siblings obtained in many studies including the present one. It is likely that in many western countries, as for example in Sweden, economic resources are not that important for providing children with proper education, as most of the education is paid by the State, and welfare has increased steadily during the last 60 years. In a Scandinavian study on welfare trends (Hansen, Ringen, Uusitalo, & Erikson, 1993) it was concluded that class inequalities have decreased, as have income differences. In general, the Hansen et al. study shows decreasing associations among origin, education, and destination, a finding suggesting that education, in the Scandinavian countries at least, may not be as good proxy for socioeconomic status as commonly believed. Thus, it is not crucial whether a family has two or three children. Also, school reforms have created better possibilities and higher likelihood for higher education for children born later. Effects of sibship size are less marked for the younger groups than for the older groups in the present study, which is a result that very well might be due to a higher standard of living on the part of the parents of the younger groups. It should be of interest in future studies to examine whether effects of sibship size and birth order can be obtained in young families today, when fewer children are born, and day-care with other children is available for a child, but when families to a greater extent than before change in structure through parents' divorces and remarriages, or have both parents working.

It is evident from the present data that level of education is associated with the effects of sibship size and birth order. When education is controlled for, the effect of birth order disappears and the effect of sibship size is reduced. However, the correlation between education and the g factor, is quite high, around .70 (e.g., Jencks et al., 1972), and one possibility is of course to consider intelligence as more important for determining the level of education than education is for determining the level of intelligence. Furthermore, level of intelligence may be of importance for avoiding diseases (Gottfredson, 2004). If this is the case the effects of sibship size and birth order will be underestimated by controlling for education and diseases.

Performance on the intelligence measure and the executive-functioning measure showed some interesting differences. When controlling for the risk of a confounding between sibship size and birth order, the effects of these two variables remained for executive functioning but not for intelligence. The present findings suggest that the components of executive functioning are more dissimilar than the components of the intelligence measures with respect to effects on sibship size and birth order. In general, the working memory measure showed a pattern different from the other three components. Whereas block design, word comprehension, and verbal fluency do not differentiate much between the two first levels of sibship size, working memory is acting in a more linear pattern. Working memory also seems to be a more efficient measure to reveal significant differences in both the sibship size and birth order variables. Thus, it is questionable whether verbal fluency is a measure suitable enough for assessing executive functioning. That the working memory measure differs from the block design and word comprehension measures may be seen as support for the contention that working memory and intelligence are different constructs (e.g., Ackerman et al., 2005). Although it is still under discussion which components should constitute an executive function and how to measure it (e.g., Salthouse et al., 2003) such a measure is definitely one of many cognitive measures needed to pinpoint effects of sibship size and birth order.

It should be noted that this study was performed as a cross-sectional study. Some criticisms have been directed to such studies in examining sibship size and birth order effects. In particular, the birth order effect is said to be obtained in cross-sectional designs only (Rodgers, 2001; Rodgers et al., 2000), although arguments in favour of such designs are not lacking (Zajonc, 2001). Rodgers (2001) said that "the critical difficulty in using such data is that very little true within-family variability is actually contained in such data sources" (p. 507). Obviously, the birth order effects obtained here are rather limited, as compared to the effects of sibship size, despite the fact that a cross-sectional design was used. Systematic comparisons between data from cross-sectional and longitudinal designs should be made in order to settle this matter. Longitudinal data are emerging in the Betula Study and future examinations of the effects of sibship size and birth order will be made on the basis of both types of design.

REFERENCES

Ackerman, P. L., Beier, M. E., & Boyle, M. O. (2005). Working memory and intelligence: The same or different constructs? *Psychological Bulletin, 131*, 30–60.

Baddeley, A. D., Lewis, V., Eldridge, M., & Thompson, N. (1984). Attention and retrieval from long-term memory. *Journal of Experimental Psychology: General, 113*, 518–540.

Bäckman, L., Jones, S., Small, B. J., Agüero-Torres, H., & Fratiglioni, L. (2003). Rate of cognitive decline in preclinical Alzheimer's disease: The role of comorbidity. *Journal of Gerontology: Psychological Sciences, 58B*, 228–236.

Bäckman, L., Wahlin, Å., Small, B. J., Herlitz, A., Winblad, B., & Fratiglioni, L. (2004). Cognitive functioning in aging and dementia: The Kungsholmen Project. *Aging, Neuropsychology, and Cognition, 11*, 212–244.

Baltes, P. B., Staudinger, U. M., & Lindberger, U. (1999). Lifespan psychology: Theory and application to intellectual functioning. *Annual Review of Psychology, 50*, 471–507.

Beier, M. E., & Ackerman, P. L. (2005). Working memory and intelligence: Different constructs. Reply to Oberauer et al. (2005) and Kane et al. (2005). *Psychological Bulletin, 131*, 72–75.

Belmont, L., & Marolla, F. A. (1973). Birth order, family size and intelligence. *Science, 182*, 1096–1101.

Berbaum, M. L., & Moreland, R. L. (1985). Intellectual development within transracial adoptive families: Retesting the confluence model. *Child Development, 56*, 207–216.

Blake, J. (1981). Family size and quality of children. *Demography, 18*, 421–442.

Blake, J. (1989). *Family size and achievement.* Los Angeles: University of California Press.

Borella, E., Carretti, B., & Mammarella, I. C. (2006). Do working memory and susceptibility to interference predict individual differences in fluid intelligence? *European Journal of Cognitive Psychology, 18*(1), 51–69.

Bouchard, T. J., Jr. (1998). Genetic and environmental influences on adult intelligence and special mental abilities. *Human Biology, 70*, 257–279.

Breland, H. M. (1974). Birth order, family configuration, and verbal achievement. *Child Development, 45*, 1011–1019.

Bryan, J., & Luszcz, M. A. (2001). Adult age differences in self-ordered pointing task performance: Contributions from working memory, executive function and speed of information processing. *Journal of Clinical and Experimental Neuropsychology, 23*, 608–619.

Bussey, K., & Bandura, A. (1999). Social cognitive theory of gender development and differentiation. *Psychological Review, 106*, 676–713.

Cornoldi, C. (2006). The contribution of cognitive psychology to the study of human intelligence *European Journal of Cognitive Psychology, 18*(1), 1–17.

Davis, D., Cahan, S., & Bashi, J. (1977). Birth order and intellectual development: The confluence model in the light of cross-cultural evidence. *Science, 196*, 1470–1472.

De Ribaupierre, A., & Lecerf, T. (2006). Relationships between working memory and intelligence from a developmental perspective: Convergent evidence from a neo-Piagetian and a psychometric approach. *European Journal of Cognitive Psychology, 18*(1), 109–137.

Downey, D. B. (1995). When bigger is not better: Family size, parental resources, and children's educational performance. *American Sociological Review, 60*, 747–761.

Downey, D. B. (2001). Number of siblings and intellectual development: The resource dilution explanation. *The American Psychologist, 56*, 497–504.

Dureman, I., Kebbon, L., & Österberg, E. (1974). *Manual till DS-batteriet* [Manual for the DS-battery]. Stockholm: Psykologförlaget AB.

Dureman, I., & Sälde, H. (1959). *Psykometriska och experimentalpsykologiska metoder för klinisk tillämpning* [Psychometric and experimental methods for the clinical evaluation of mental functioning]. Stockholm: Almqvist & Wiksell.

Erikson, E. H. (1963). *Childhood and society* (2nd ed.). New York: Norton.

Fischer, K., & Bidell, T. R. (1998). Dynamic development of psychological structure in action and thought. In W. Damon (Series Ed.) & R. M. Lerner (Vol. Ed.), *Handbook of child psychology: Vol. 1. Theoretical models of human development* (5th ed., pp. 467–561). New York: Wiley.

Gibson, E. J., & Pick, A. D. (2000). *An ecological approach to perceptual learning and development.* New York: Oxford University Press.

Gottfredson, L. (2004). Intelligence: Is it the epidemiologists' elusive "fundamental cause" of social class inequalities in health? *Journal of Personality and Social Psychology, 86*, 174–199.

Groth-Marnat, G., & Teal, M. (2000). Block design as a measure of everyday spatial ability: A study of ecological validity. *Perceptual and Motor Skills, 90*, 522–526.

Halpern, D. F., & LaMay, M. L. (2000). The smarter sex: A critical review of sex differences in intelligence. *Educational Psychology Review, 12*, 229–246.

Hansen, E. J., Ringen, S., Uusitalo, H., & Erikson, R. (Eds.). (1993). *Welfare trends in the Scandinavian countries*. London: M. E. Sharpe.

Herlitz, A., Nilsson, L.-G., & Bäckman, L. (1997). Gender differences in episodic memory. *Memory and Cognition, 25*, 801–811.

Jencks, C., Smith, M., Acland, H., Bane, M. J., Cohen, D., Gintis, H., et al. (1972). *Inequality: A reassessment of the effect of family and schooling in America*. New York: Basic Books.

Jones, H. E., & Conrad, H. (1933). The growth and decline of intelligence: A study of a homogenous group between the ages ten and sixty. *Genetic Psychology Monographs, 13*, 223–298.

Kane, M. J., Hambrick, D. Z., & Conway, A. R. A. (2005). Working memory capacity and fluid intelligence are strongly related constructs: Comment on Ackerman, Beier, and Boyle (2005). *Psychological Bulletin, 131*, 66–71.

Kaufman, A. S., Reynolds, C. R., & McLean, J. E. (1989). Age and WAIS-R intelligence in a national sample of adults in the 20- to 74-year range: A cross-sectional analysis with education level controlled. *Intelligence, 13*, 335–253.

Kuo, H.-H. D., & Hauser, R. M. (1997). How does size of sibship matter? Family configuration and family effects on educational attainment. *Social Science Research, 26*, 69–94.

Lee, S., Kawachi, I., Berkman, L. F., & Grodstein, F. (2003). Education, other socioeconomic indicators, and cognitive function. *American Journal of Epidemiology, 157*, 712–720.

Maitland, S. B., Herlitz, A., Nyberg, L., Bäckman, L., & Nilsson, L.-G. (2004). Selective sex differences in declarative memory. *Memory and Cognition, 32*, 1160–1169.

Marjoribanks, K. (1976a). Birth order, family environment, and mental abilities: A regression surface analysis. *Psychological Reports, 39*, 759–765.

Marjoribanks, K. (1976b). Sibship size, family environment, cognitive performance and affective characteristics. *Journal of Psychology, 94*, 195–204.

Marschark, M. (2006). Intellectual functioning of deaf adults and children: Answers and questions. *European Journal of Cognitive Psychology, 18*(1), 70–89.

Mercy, J. A., & Steelman, L. C. (1982). Familial influence on the intellectual attainment of children. *American Sociological Review, 47*, 532–542.

Miyake, A., Emerson, M. J., & Friedman, N. P. (2000). Assessment of executive functions in clinical settings: Problems and recommendations. *Seminars in Speech and Language, 21*, 169–183.

Nilsson, L.-G., Adolfsson, R., Bäckman, L., de Frias, C., Molander, B., & Nyberg, L. (2004). Betula: A prospective cohort study on memory, health, and aging. *Aging, Neuropsychology, and Cognition, 11*, 134–148.

Nilsson, L.-G., Bäckman, L., Erngrund, K., Nyberg, L., Adolfsson, R., Buch, G., et al. (1997). The Betula prospective cohort study: Memory, health, and aging. *Aging, Neuropsychology, and Cognition, 4*, 1–32.

Nilsson, L.-G., & Söderlund, H. (2001). Aging, cognition, and health. In M. Moscovitch, M. Naveh-Benjamin, & H. L. Roediger, III. (Eds.), *Perspectives on human memory and cognitive aging: Essays in honor of Fergus Craik* (pp. 253–264). Hove, UK: Psychology Press.

Oberauer, K., Schulze, R., Wilhelm, O., & Süß, H.-M. (2005). Working memory and intelligence—their correlation and their relation: Comment on Ackerman, Beier, and Boyle (2005). *Psychological Bulletin, 131*, 61–65.

Obonsawin, M. C., Crawford, J. R., Page, J., Chalmers, P., Cochrane, R., & Low, G. (2002). Performance on tests of frontal lobe function reflect general intellectual ability. *Neuropsychologia, 40*, 970–977.

Plomin, R., DeFries, J. C., McClearn, G. E., & McGuffin, P. (2001). *Behavior genetics* (4th ed.). New York: Worth.

Plomin, R., & Petrill, S. A. (1997). Genetics and intelligence: What's new? *Intelligence, 24,* 53–77.

Rabbitt, P. (1997). Introduction: Methodologies and models in the study of executive function. In P. Rabbitt (Ed.), Methodology of frontal and executive function (pp. 1–38). Hove, UK: Psychology Press.

Reis, A., Petersson, K. M., Castro-Caldas, A., & Ingvar, M. (2001). Formal schooling influences two- but not three-dimensional naming skills. *Brain and Cognition, 47,* 397–411.

Rodgers, J. L. (1984). Confluence effects: Not here, not now! *Developmental Psychology, 20,* 321–331.

Rodgers, J. L. (2001). What causes birth-order-intelligence patterns? The Admixture hypothesis, revived. *The American Psychologist, 56,* 505–510.

Rodgers, J. L., Cleveland, H. H., van den Oord, E., & Rowe, D. C. (2000). Resolving the debate over birth order, family size, and intelligence. *American Psychologist, 55,* 599–612.

Salthouse, T. A., Atkinson, T. M., & Berish, D. E. (2003). Executive functioning as a potential mediator of age-related cognitive decline in normal adults. *Journal of Experimental Psychology: General, 132,* 566–594.

Schaie, K. W. (1985). *Manual for the Schaie-Thurstone Adult Mental Abilities Test (STAMAT).* Palo Alto, CA: Consulting Psychologists Press.

Schaie, K. W. (1994). The course of adult intellectual development. *American Psychologist, 49,* 304–313.

Siegler, R. S. (1998). *Children's thinking* (3rd ed.). Upper Saddle River, NJ: Prentice Hall.

Smith, T. E. (1984). Sex and sibling structure: Interaction effects upon the accuracy of adolescent perceptions of parental orientations. *Journal of Marriage and the Family, 46,* 901–908.

Snow, R. E., Kyllonen, C. P., & Marshalek, B. (1984). The topography of ability and learning correlations. In R. J. Sternberg (Ed.), *Advances in the psychology of human intelligence* (pp. 47–103). Hillsdale, NJ: Lawrence Erlbaum Associates, Inc.

Strachan, M. W. J., Ewing, F. M. E., Deary, I. J., & Frier, B. M. (1997). Is Type II diabetes associated with an increased risk of cognitive dysfunction? *Diabetes Care, 20,* 438–445.

Voyer, D., Voyer, S., & Bryden, M. P. (1995). Magnitude of sex differences in spatial abilities: A meta analysis and consideration of critical variables. *Psychological Bulletin, 117,* 250–270.

Vygotsky, L. S. (1986). *Thought and language.* Cambridge, MA: MIT Press.

Wechsler, D. (1981). *WAIS-R: Wechsler Adult Intelligence Scale–revised.* New York: Harcourt, Brace, Jovanovich.

Wilhelm, O., & Oberauer, K. (2006). Why are reasoning ability and working memory capacity related to mental speed? An investigation of stimulus–response compatibility in choice reaction time tasks. *European Journal of Cognitive Psychology, 18*(1), 18–50.

Zajonc, R. B. (1976). Family configuration and intelligence. *Science, 192,* 227–236.

Zajonc, R. B. (1986). The decline and rise of scholastic aptitude scores: A prediction from the Confluence Model. *The American Psychologist, 41,* 862–867.

Zajonc, R. B. (2001). The family dynamics of intellectual development. *The American Psychologist, 56,* 490–496.

Zajonc, R. B., & Markus, G. B. (1975). Birth order and intellectual development. *Psychological Review, 82,* 74–88.

Zajonc, R. B., & Mullaly, P. R. (1997). Birth order: Reconciling conflicting effects. *The American Psychologist, 52,* 685–699.

EUROPEAN JOURNAL OF COGNITIVE PSYCHOLOGY
2006, 18 (1), 159–160

Subject index

Age
  impact 3, 6, 7, 109
  intelligence development 109–137,
    138–158
  irrelevant information control 51–69
  speed of processing 19–20, 111, 112,
    113–114, 115, 122–133
Attention
  control 8, 11, 21, 52, 90–94, 103–104,
    111
  resources 14, 44, 51–52, 54, 114–115
Auditory disorders 70–84
Auditory distractions 90–108
Automatic processes 4, 5, 111

Birth order effect 138–158

Colour naming 90, 92–94, 96–101, 103,
  105
Complexity hypothesis 46–47
Conceptual knowledge 78–79
Crystallised intelligence
  general (Gc) 5–6, 37–38, 112
  speed of processing 24, 28, 37–41, 45,
    47

Deafness 70–84
Development
  deaf children 73–74, 76
  family influences 138–158
  intelligence 3, 6–7, 9, 12, 109–137
  processing speed 19, 109, 122–133
Distractions 8, 11, 21, 51–69, 90–108

Economic factors 143, 146, 152–154
Education 144–146, 149, 154–155
Executive functions 7–8, 10–11, 12, 14,
  54–55, 111, 138–155

Face processing 82–83
Family size/structure 138–158
Fluid intelligence
  general (Gf) 5–6, 37–38, 111–112,
    115, 123, 132
  working memory
    age impact 109, 110, 113, 141
    capacity/speed 13–14, 18–20, 23,
      37–47, 113, 131–133
    interference susceptibility 51–69

'g' factor 4, 5, 7, 10, 12, 18, 112, 133,
  153–154
Gc see Crystallised intelligence, general
Gender 142, 143–155
Gf see Fluid intelligence, general

Health 143, 146, 152, 155
Hierarchical intelligence 4, 5–6, 10–11
Hierarchical theories 6–8, 12, 13, 115

Individual differences
  distracting sounds 90–108
  fluid intelligence 51–69, 111
  intelligence 1–5, 129–130
  reasoning ability 19
Inhibitory mechanisms 52–53, 55, 114,
  132, 141
Intellectual functioning
  deaf individuals 70–84
  family influence 138–144
Intelligence
  see also Crystallized intelligence;
    Fluid intelligence
  concept 1–3, 4
  development 109–137
  family influences 138–158
  neuroscience contribution 8–11

nonverbal 70, 74–75, 81–83, 116–122
psychometric theories 4–6
types 4–5
working memory role 12–14, 18–50
Intrusion errors 51, 53–54, 57, 59–60, 63, 64–66
IQ measurement 6–8, 74–75, 140
Irrelevant information 11, 21, 51–69

Language 4, 70–84, 90–106, 139, 140, 143–155
Learning 10, 55, 76, 79–84, 141

Memory
    deaf individuals 76–81
    short-term 6, 14, 20, 81
Mental representations, relational 22–23, 43, 46
Mental retardation 3, 10, 13, 52
Multiple intelligence theory 4, 5
Myelinisation process 8–9, 19, 21

Neo-Piagetian approach 109, 110, 112, 114–122, 130–132
Neural efficiency hypothesis 9–11, 19, 21
Neuroscience, theories 8–11
Nonverbal intelligence 70, 74, 75, 81–83, 116–122

Occipital lobes 11

Parietal lobes 11
Personality characteristics 10
Prefrontal brain areas 7–8, 10–11
Problem solving
    concept of intelligence 2, 10
    deaf individuals 76, 80
    intelligence development 111
    intelligence measurement 7, 55
Psychometric theories 4–6, 111
Psychometric tools
    deaf individuals 74–76, 81

intelligence measurement 3–4, 7, 14
Raven's Progressive Matrices 51, 55, 109, 122–133

Reaction time 18–50
Reasoning 2, 5, 7, 18–50, 76, 112
Relational processing 22–23, 43, 46, 79–81

Serial recall 56–64, 90–106
Sibship effects 138–158
Signed language 70–84
Social influences 138–158
Spatial abilities 4–5, 70, 81–84, 112, 117–118, 140, 142
Speed of processing
    intelligence role 6–7, 8, 9, 14
    working memory capacity 18–50, 111–115, 122–133
Stimulus-response compatibility 18, 21–47
Structural models 22, 32, 39, 40–45, 111, 112
Synaptic connections 8, 9, 19, 21

Triarchical theory 7
Two-factor theory 5–6

Unitary models 4, 5, 112

Visuospatial abilities 70, 81–84, 140

Working memory capacity
    family influence 138, 155
    intelligence development 109–137
    intelligence role 7, 8, 11, 12–14, 111
    interference susceptibility 51–69, 90–108
    load 20–21
    operation span 90, 92–98, 101, 103, 105, 111
    and reaction time 18–50
    running memory span 90, 93–95, 98, 101, 103, 105–106